PÁNIC
RISING

True-Life
Survivor
Tales
from the
Great
Outdoors

D0094357

Brett
Nunn

SASQUATCH BOOKS
SEATTLE

Printed in the United States of America
Published by Sasquatch Books
Distributed by Publishers Group West
10 09 08 07 06 05 04 03   6 5 4 3 2 1

Book design: Stewart A. Williams
Interior maps: Gray Mouse Graphics
Production editor: Cassandra Mitchell
Copy editor: Don Graydon
Proofreader: Sherri Schultz
Author photo: Frank Ross

Library of Congress Cataloging in Publication Data

Nunn, Brett.
    Panic rising / by Brett Nunn.
        p. cm.
    ISBN 1-57061-350-8
    1. Adventure and adventurers—Northwest, Pacific. 2. Survival after airplane
accidents, shipwrecks, etc. I. Title.

G525.N76 2003
979.5—dc21   2003045664

Sasquatch Books
119 South Main Street, Suite 400
Seattle, WA 98104
(206) 467-4300
www.sasquatchbooks.com
books@sasquatchbooks.com

To my wife Becky: When I met you my dreams came true.

CONTENTS

ACKNOWLEDGMENTS

I am forever indebted to my wife, Becky, for her unfailing patience, support, and appreciation of the simple life. I am equally indebted to my parents, James and Susan Nunn, for their generosity, sacrifice, and love.

I thank Gary Luke of Sasquatch Books for trusting me with this marvelous project, along with his colleagues Novella Carpenter, Kate Rogers, Suzanne De Galan, and Cassandra Mitchell for their patience and enthusiasm.

Thanks to my agent Mark Ryan for stepping into the breach and handling the fine print.

None of this could have happened without the University of Washington and their ability to recruit and support teachers of incredible talent and dedication including Jessica Maxwell, Robert J. Ray, Jack Remick, Stewart Stern, Geof Miller, and Randy Sue Coburn.

Recreational Equipment Inc. of Seattle deserves thanks for their flexible schedule and financial support.

No writer survives without friends and colleagues, and I thank them all for feeding, housing, employing, encouraging, and humoring me through this effort.

For their help in gathering information and detail, I cannot thank enough the rangers and staff of Olympic, Mount Rainier, Crater Lake, and Glacier National Parks, Craters of the Moon National Monument, Hells Canyon National Recreation Area, and the River of No Return Wilderness; the U.S. Navy and U.S. Air Force; the Alaska State Patrol; the Pierce County Sheriff's Search and Rescue Office; the research librarians of Klamath Falls, Medford, and Kalispell libraries; and the Carnegie Hero Fund Commission.

Last but not least, I wholeheartedly thank all the people in this book and elsewhere who have generously shared their time and their stories with me.

INTRODUCTION

A venturesome minority will always be eager to get off on their own, and no obstacles should be placed in their path; let them take risks, for Godsake, let them get lost, sunburnt, stranded, drowned, eaten by bears, buried alive under avalanches—that is the right and privilege of any free American.

—EDWARD ABBEY

Ever since the first Native Americans hunted a whale off the Pacific Coast, paddled the untamed Columbia River, experienced an early blizzard crossing the Bitterroots, or met a grizzly bear on a game trail in the Rockies, there have been tales told of outdoor survival in the region now called the Pacific Northwest.

The contemporary stories in this book are a continuation of that tradition. They have been retrieved from all corners of Washington, Oregon, Idaho, Western Montana, Southeast Alaska, and British Columbia. They come from memories old and new, from tales told over campfires, from dusty archives, from yesterday's headlines, and at their most astonishing, direct from the source.

They are all true, but they are not my stories. I have merely assumed the role of caretaker, rescuing them from obscurity to be passed on as they were related to me. Each account has been crafted through hours of interviews obtained from many perspectives, including principal characters and their rescuers.

These are stories of defying death, of incredible luck, of incredible coincidence—of all the elements that come together over a single instance in time to mean the difference between tragedy and triumph. Some are mysteries offering more questions than answers. Others are studies in how a series of seemingly insignificant choices can lead to serious trouble. There are lessons to be learned in all of them, not the least of which is the incredible resiliency of the human spirit.

No one in this book is a professional adventurer risking life and limb on some far-off escapade. They are mainly people like you or me, a group of friends out for a day hike, a hunter walking through the woods, a skier looking for the easy way down, a family on a leisurely rafting trip, seasonal forest employees working a fire line to pay the bills. None of them ventured into the outdoors thinking that today, with no warning, they would suddenly be fighting for their lives.

If you have never been through a survival situation, it is all too easy to sum up someone else's desperate crisis as the result of pure stupidity. This is far from the truth. It can happen to anyone. Those who are comfortable in their chosen outdoor pursuit may be the most susceptible.

The difference between lost and found, between danger and safety, is a thin line that everyone walks sooner or later. Once crossed it is hard to get back, often easier to keep moving forward, and always too late when the seriousness of the situation becomes apparent.

We rarely ever learn what really happened out there. What went so wrong that people in the midst of everyday life suddenly found themselves in a battle with death? The accounts in this book may provide a few of those elusive answers, for these are the people who came back from the other side of that line. Their stories were chosen because they beat the odds.

There are many elements of a story that can be lost in the telling and many particulars that are best left unspoken. My hope is that I have done justice to what were often life-changing events for these survivors. I owe an immense debt to all the individuals who graciously shared their experiences with me. My main focus will always be to find the truth and reveal it accurately. Any oversights or omissions in the portrayals are purely mine.

The wilderness remains much as it has always been: beautiful, awe-inspiring, yet ultimately dangerous and unforgiving. The people portrayed in these pages discovered this reality the hard way. Their hope is that others may learn from their experiences and that lives might be spared in the process.

Chaos and confusion, white blocks falling,
rotating, roaring down into the pit.
Everything is suddenly still.

CHAPTER 1

AN ALMOST PERFECT DAY

Clouds lie heavy over the lowlands of Western Oregon on a morning in early June. After a couple of weeks of promising weather, the warm days of summer have been put on hold. Once again the people of greater Portland look to the sky and question their reasons for living in the Pacific Northwest.

Not far away, up in the western foothills of the Cascade Mountains, Dale is having a hard time waking up. Maybe it's the cloud cover or maybe it's thoughts of yesterday's failed summit bid on Mount Hood, cut short by a sudden snowstorm. Whatever the reason, he finally finds the energy to roll out of bed and shuffle, bleary-eyed, around his house.

Working as a bartender in the town of Government Camp leaves Dale free to ski and climb during the day. Today, though, the weather is overcast, gray, uninspiring. Yet he can't think of anything better to do. Might as well call and check on the conditions up at the ski area.

Clear skies above five thousand feet! A foot of fresh powder snow from yesterday's storm!

He's wide-awake now, rushing to gather ski gear, find his car keys, and get out the door.

Dale lives for these rare days. He's been skiing and climbing this mountain for years; started working at Timberline Lodge when he was sixteen. By the time he was twenty-one he was director of the ski patrol. Skiing off the top of 11,239-foot Mount Hood has become second nature, irresistible when the conditions are ideal.

A little after 10 A.M. Dale is pulling gear out of his car up at Timberline Ski Area. Just downslope at the tree line, clouds are lapping against the mountain like a rising tide. Above him Mount Hood is majestic, frosted in fresh snow and rising into a clear Oregon sky so blue it makes your heart ache.

The mountain air is vibrant with possibilities. Dale envisions his first tracks off the summit, a sinuous line down 2,700 vertical feet of untouched, sun-splashed powder. There is also the element of guilty pleasure. After all, only an hour away the denizens of Portland are hunkering down under gray clouds, wondering if the sun will ever return.

He hurriedly checks his pack to make sure all his backcountry equipment is in place and then heads for the lift. Now he wishes he had been up earlier. The prime skiing time would have been at dawn, before the mountain began warming in the sun. Even though he is running late, the day is too beautiful to pass up. Besides, the best skiing is always found up high where the cool temperatures keep the snow pristine.

The Palmer chairlift takes him up to 8,500 feet. He checks in with the ski patrol at the top of the lift. It has been a few years since his patrol days, but he still has friends here. They talk about the great snow as he straps his skis to his pack for the trek to the summit. Dale promises to taunt them with a full report of what is sure to be an incredible run off the top, and then he starts out for the south-side route to the summit. Time is on his mind. As the day heats up, the new snow will become more and more unstable.

The clouds play tag with him as he ascends, swirling up from below to catch him, then allowing him to climb out into the sun again.

Over eighteen years of climbing and hundreds of ascents in the Cascades, Dale has rarely seen a day this perfect. The snow, still light and powdery, sparkles in the high alpine air. The weather is warm and calm.

Absolutely perfect, he thinks to himself. *Just going to have to be careful traveling solo, avoid the avalanche slopes on the way down, play it safe.*

2

As he turns to look back down the mountain, a smile forms on his face. The Palmer lift has been enveloped in clouds. Except for three climbers high above, he appears to be the only person on the mountain. It's as if the snow gods have made this day just for him.

. . . — — — . . .

Two hours of climbing bring Dale to what climbers call the hogs-back, a narrow snow-covered ridge at 10,500 feet that rises above a hanging basin called Devils Kitchen and skirts the east flank of Crater Rock. The going has been difficult. Soft snow has slowed him down, even with the trail stomped down by the three climbers in front of him.

Thoughts of time and temperature still nag at Dale. He's gambling with an increasingly unstable snowpack as the day heats up. Normally at this altitude he would stop and put on crampons for the final seven hundred feet to the summit, but in the soft snow they are more of a hindrance. He adds the minutes saved into his calculations of risk and decides to continue upward.

The hogsback leads to the only real obstacle on the south route. At the base of the final stretch to the summit is a bergschrund, a crevasse-like moat that forms as the field of snow and ice pulls away from the mountain. This time of year it is visible only as a slight roll in the slope because a winter's worth of snow has bridged the void. Dale crosses the bergschrund and begins to ascend the steepest section of the climb. His years on the mountain tell him to be careful, cautious. The south-facing slope is warming up fast.

Snow begins clumping up on his boots. He pauses to skim a few snowballs down the slope. The balls pick up snow and form big pinwheels, then break up to form more. Probing with his poles, he can tell the snow is about twelve inches deep over ice. The snow is turning heavy and slide-prone in the heat of afternoon. He rules out climbing the rest of the way to the summit today—too risky in these conditions.

Dale kicks out a platform so he can put his gear on for the run down. Experience gives him confidence, but he also takes some comfort in what amounts to three thousand dollars of top-of-the-line equipment purchased for moments like these. He puts on ski pants, jacket, gloves. He skips the wrist straps for his ski poles, just in case he needs to get rid of the poles quickly in a slide. He slings his pack on his back, tightens the straps down, and then steps into his downhill bindings. Preparing for the worst and expecting the best has always been his practice.

Gazing down the first steep line, he knows the new snow won't hold. He edges off the platform and pushes a pile of snow ahead of him to clear a route down and over the bergschrund. The upper layer slabs away downhill, exposing a path too icy for turns. He descends, sideslipping, occasionally hopping to keep the unstable snow moving. Just a little insurance against avalanche.

As he follows the cleared path down across the bridged bergschrund, he hears a familiar sound from his ski patrol days. A loud boom rolls across the mountain. It sounds like the blasts used to set off avalanches so they won't threaten skiers. He can't tell exactly from which direction.

Too late for avalanche control, he thinks. *Too early for stump removal.*

His heart leaps in his chest. An avalanche! He whips his eyes around on the mountain. No avalanche in sight.

What the hell was that, a sonic boom?

He searches the sky overhead. He can't see any aircraft.

Dale looks back down at the snow under his feet just as fracture lines shoot off in front and behind.

In a surreal millisecond, the slope begins to break up around him like a shattered windowpane. Slowly at first, then faster, collapsing downward into an abyss.

His mind struggles to comprehend. *This is okay, I will just drop down on top of this stuff and climb back out.*

Hope is suddenly smothered by fear as he falls into darkness. He screams a quick prayer and squeezes his eyes shut as immense blocks of ice and snow break up and collapse in upon him.

Chaos and confusion, white blocks falling, rotating, roaring down into the pit. The front halves of his skis are pinned as a block the size of a pool table falls upon them and then smacks him hard in the face. A second block slams him from behind, pushing him down into a sitting position, stopping only when it wedges against the block in front of him.

Everything is suddenly still.

4

He seems to be alive.

Giddy, laughing to himself, Dale can't believe he is alive. But he can't move. He can breathe, though. There is light from somewhere, and air. He can see blood on the snow directly in front of his face. In the silence he listens for the sound of the avalanche that will roar down from the slopes above and finish the job, filling the air pockets and smothering him. But all is quiet.

He does a quick assessment. He can flex his toes and fingers. His back popped a bit when the block hit him from behind. His nose is bleeding from the first impact.

Everything feels fine, except that he is wedged deep in the bergschrund, under tons of snow and ice. The most he can do is move his hands and rotate his head from side to side. His feet, still in boots that remain snapped into bindings and skis, are locked solidly in place.

Twisting his head to the right, Dale can see a triangular passageway, about twelve inches high and ten inches wide, drawing white light from somewhere.

No way to get out through that, it's only about half the width of my body.

He struggles to keep panic at bay in his icy tomb. The first task is to scratch out breathing room in front of his face. Eventually he hollows out enough space to twist an arm around and reach into the underarm pocket of his pack.

A little more than a month ago Dale went shopping for a citizens band radio. Through all his years with the ski patrol he had carried a radio. Ever since leaving the patrol, he felt he was taking a big risk going into the backcountry without some form of communications. The salesmen at Radio Shack steered him toward the latest gadget.

"These cellular phones are going to be the new thing," they told him.

So Dale did his research and put off some of his bills to pay five hundred dollars for the Motorola Ultra Classic. At about the size of a large flashlight, it was the most compact model available.

He didn't hesitate at the expense. "Hey, if it's my life that matters, five hundred dollars is just a drop in the bucket."

Right now he wants out fast. The phone is his ticket. His ski-patrol friends on duty below can get up here quicker than anyone.

He slips the phone out and maneuvers it up to his face so he can see to dial. Years of working at the ski area have ingrained the number in his mind. He punches the buttons and holds his breath. The connection is rough, static, interference, and then he can clearly hear the receptionist answer the call.

He tells her what has happened.

"Please, please connect me with the ski patrol at Palmer lift."

The receptionist pauses. Dale knows that ski area policy doesn't allow phone calls through to the chairlifts. Can she really be hesitating for that reason?

"I really don't think I can do that," she says, "but let me put you on hold."

Before he can reply, a recorded men's chorus is broadcasting over the line. Cheery voices harmonize heartwarming lyrics into his ear. Dale is just about to lose it when the receptionist comes back.

"I can't do that."

"Like hell you can't! Let me talk to somebody else!" he screams into the phone.

The men's chorus comes back on.

Then another voice answers the phone. In the midst of spilling his story, he hears the line disconnect.

Trying to stay calm, he hits the redial button and gets the front desk on the line again.

The fear in his voice is too real. They put him through.

Brad picks up the phone at the Palmer lift. He knows Dale well and is shocked at the desperation in his voice. Dale is talking a mile a minute, telling him what happened.

"Look at it, man, the bergschrund is wide open. It wasn't there half an hour ago."

Brad turns to look up at the mountain.

"God, I can see it."

"It broke big, it broke all the way across, it's completely open and I'm buried in the bottom of it."

"Unreal. What do you want me to do?"

"Don't send any helicopters up here. They might set off an avalanche. Just get up here as fast as you can."

Brad tells him he is on his way. He alerts the other patrollers, arranges for a snow cat to bring up a back board and other rescue gear, and then heads up the mountain.

· · · ▬ ▬ ▬ · · ·

At best guess Dale estimates that Brad is at least two hours away. He can't afford to give up and wait.

Trapped in the icefall, the slightest slump of snow can finish him off. If he can dig his boots out, there may be enough room to rotate out of his bindings and free his feet.

He discovers a small hole alongside his left boot. His first pile of snow scrapings filtered down this hole and away somewhere, so there may be room for more.

He gets back to digging in the cramped space, twisting his wrists and neck, forcing his joints into painful angles, scratching with his fingers. The excess snow is funneled down into the hole.

The process is agonizing and exhausting in the tight space. Claustrophobic panic is always lurking right on the edge of his thoughts.

With a little more room, his knees can finally move. He pushes and pulls, massaging his legs when they begin to cramp. He just can't get the bindings to pop.

Dale's boots remain completely immobilized as he works at the snow packed around them. A little more scratching and shifting and he can shove his bare hands down alongside the plastic shells of the boots. Pushing at the snow for space, he finally snaps the buckles open.

The boots no longer hold his ankles tight, but there isn't enough room to pull his feet up and out.

Dale looks down the triangular shaft. If he can dig enough space for his body, he might be able to squeeze through and pull his feet out sideways.

Digging, scraping, sometimes biting at the snow. Pounding, pulling his gloves off to scratch at the ice, he slowly enlarges his space.

A ski patrol friend calls every so often via the cell phone to keep him calm and let him know help is on the way, yet Dale can think of nothing but escape.

He tries to squeeze into the shaft, but he can't bend his head over or twist his neck enough to go in headfirst. Carving a groove for his nose, he finally contorts and forces his body into the shaft.

Now there is no room to move his arms. He backs out and digs more.

Over the next half hour the physical effort of contorting in and out of the shaft saps his strength. His neck and side are cramping up in the tight space, but he refuses to give up. Five or six times he is in and out of the hole, hammering, scraping, clawing toward the light.

One last time he flops over into the space and stretches out as far as he can, straining to escape. His feet finally slip free of the boots.

The escape route is too tight to bring anything but his cell phone. Leaving his backpack behind, he worms out through the shaft.

Reaching the white light, Dale pops his head out of the hole to find a tumbled maze of massive blocks. Passageways three to four feet wide weave through the collapsed ice. He works his way up through the jumble, always headed for more light.

He squeezes, crawls, pulls, and eventually hoists himself out of the debris pile. Scrambling up to balance precariously on one large block, Dale finds himself in the middle of a trench that is twenty feet deep, fifty feet wide, and one hundred feet long where it runs across the slope.

The open air has never seemed sweeter. He fills his lungs with a deep breath. With the cell phone gripped in one hand, it is all Dale can do to find traction with just socks on his feet. Big gaps between the blocks around him drop into blue darkness. He gingerly works his way from block to block, bridging over gaps, praying not to fall through again. Near the edge he climbs one last hump of ice and pulls himself up to the downslope lip of the bergschrund.

· · · — — — · · ·

With his heart still pounding, Dale calls down to the ski patrol.

"I'm out of the icefall. I'm going to try and walk down. If you don't hear from me again, double-time it up here because I don't know, I might pass out, my back might seize up, but I think I can get down under my own power."

Now he sits at the top of a 45-degree slope at the 10,500-foot level, with nothing but socks on his feet. Between him and the relative safety of the climbers' trail lies an expanse of bare ice created when he broke the snow loose to clear a ski route down.

The slope has a gentle run-out about a hundred yards below, in Devils Kitchen. It looks safe enough to sit and glissade down the icy slope. Gathering the last of his nerve, still alert for avalanches, he pushes off, kicking the loose snow down in front of him.

Wheeling arms and legs, Dale struggles to keep from flipping head downhill as he gains speed. Sprawled for balance, one hand claws the passing snow. The other grips the cell phone. A small bump sends him flying through the air. Somehow he lands without a tumble, and his body slows to a stop as the slope levels out.

He picks himself up and climbs out of Devils Kitchen, back up to the hogsback. Just as he finds the trail, the three climbers who preceded him up the mountain earlier in the day are walking by, headed down.

They stare at him with mystified looks.

A man, in his socks, this high on Mount Hood?

While Dale tells them his story, they pull dry socks, food, and a pair of sunglasses from their packs for him. As a finishing touch, they fish out two plastic grocery sacks as their best offer for a waterproof layer to protect his feet from the snow. With his new footwear swishing at each step, they lead him down the mountain.

At Lower Crater Rock, Brad is climbing up at full speed when he comes across the three climbers descending with Dale.

A quick medical assessment reveals that Dale, other than being wet and a little beat-up, seems to have made it through with only minor injuries. Dale and Brad walk together down to Triangle Moraine, where a snow cat picks them up for the ride down to Timberline Lodge.

Reflecting on that day, Dale is clear that he was lucky. He admits that he could have avoided this accident. In the previous seventeen days he had made eleven ascents of Mount Hood in perfect ski mountaineering conditions. This may have left him a little less cautious about avalanche danger. Twelve inches of fresh snow on a crystal-clear day was just too seductive.

As far as climbing and skiing alone, he shudders to think what would have happened if he had been on the mountain with a partner.

"On that day there just was not enough luck for two people."

When Chris turns back toward the river, he
sees the fear in his father's eyes.

CHAPTER 2

SWEPT AWAY

F or Louis and Pat Barten, it would be a rare opportunity to
vacation with their adult children, son Chris and daughter
Alyssa. The trip down the Snake River would also include Alyssa's
husband, Marko. Chris had been the main instigator, making the
arrangements months ahead for the seven-day trip on the Snake as
it carves the border between Oregon and Idaho through Hells
Canyon. This tour met all their vacation requirements: a leisurely
voyage where the days would be hot, they could swim and relax,
and evenings would be spent around a campfire under the stars.

It's a Saturday on a blazing hot Fourth of July weekend in
Cambridge, Idaho, when the Barten party boards the rafting company shuttle with eighteen other excited vacationers. Introductions are made all around as the bus winds its way down off a high
plateau into the southern entrance of the canyon. Off to the west,
grass-covered foothills turning gold in the heat of the summer
climb toward the peaks of Oregon's Eagle Cap Wilderness. To the
north, the Seven Devils Mountains stand watch on the western
border of Idaho.

The summits slowly recede as the bus descends, winding
down and down toward the river hidden below. After many miles
of serpentine road, the asphalt comes to a dead end at Hells
Canyon Dam. Stepping off the bus, the passengers crane their
necks up, blinking into the brightness. Above them, on either side

of the river, layer upon layer of ragged basalt cliffs climb like giant stair steps for more than a mile into the blue sky.

Below them the Snake River whirls and swirls, limbering up powerful currents in preparation to make the roaring, foaming run for the next sixty miles through the deepest gorge in North America.

The guides marshal their clients down to the riverbank for a safety briefing. This is a powerful river, they say. Always wear your life vest. Always be cautious. Always do what your guides tell you to do. This is how you paddle; this is what you should do if you fall out of the boat.

For an hour they are taught how to handle themselves and the inflatable rafts they will be riding down the river. Then, with a few practice strokes, the party of four guided boats enters the main current and the adventure begins.

· · · — — — · · ·

Excitement ripples through the group as they raft through the first mild whitewater. The river winds between rock walls, gravel bars, and sand beaches. Green vegetation hugs the shoreline, oasis-like, in the bottom of this deep, dry canyon.

The guides point out historical sites and call out each rapid as they approach, coaching the paddlers on how each one will be run. A fast-action class-4 rapid gets the Barten family whooping and yelling; frothing water splashes over them, welcome relief as temperatures rise above 90 degrees Fahrenheit.

Around three o'clock they arrive at their first camp. The rafts are maneuvered into an eddy at a bend in the river, pulled up on shore, tied down, and secured for the night. The guides get to work setting up tents and the open-air kitchen. Half the group departs on a guided nature hike. The rest of the party lounges around the site, idling in the heat of the afternoon.

The air temperature is approaching 100 degrees. Just below the campsite, the eddy forms an inviting pool sheltered from the main current of the river. The idea is tossed around that wading at the river's edge would be a good way to cool off.

Donning their life jackets, the Bartens and a few of the other rafters stroll down to a small beach on the edge of the pool. The guides continue about their work, keeping a cautious eye on the group.

Chris Barten—in his early twenties, confident, a former high school swimmer—sits in the shallow water near the riverbank. He quickly discovers that if he lifts his legs off the bottom, the eddy is strong enough to pull him upstream at a good clip. Chris tests the current, cautiously at first. The swirling water carries him upstream a few yards, out a short distance from shore, back down-river for a few yards, then whips him right back into the shallows again. Pretty soon he is riding the eddy in easy circles, floating lazily along in his life jacket.

Eventually the others take notice. A few fun-seekers join him, including his father, Louis. Before long there are a handful of peo-ple whirling around in the eddy, laughing at the power of the cur-rent as they are whipped around in a circle that always brings them back into the shallows.

As the minutes pass, Chris is the first to become chilled in the cold water. It's time to get out and lie in the sun. He turns to swim toward shore. After several strokes the riverbank doesn't seem to be getting any closer.

He strokes harder.

Still no closer.

His years of swimming come back to him with the adrenaline pumping into his bloodstream. He fights for shore with everything he has as the eddy current disappears before his eyes, merging with the main current. Pulling at the water with powerful strokes, Chris slowly begins to make progress. By the time he thrashes into the shallows, it is all he can do to drag himself to dry land.

Of the handful of other people fighting to get back to shore, Louis is the farthest out. When Chris turns back toward the river, he sees the fear in his father's eyes. Chris's lungs are burning from his own struggle to shore. He can barely lift his arms. There is nothing he can do.

A figure sprints by Chris as Louis and two young girls are being swept downstream toward the biggest drop in the river, the class-4 Granite Creek Rapids. He turns to see one of the guides scrambling down the rocky shoreline with a throw bag containing a rope. At the last possible second the guide tosses the rope, and the girls are pulled to safety.

Louis knows he is in trouble. His rescuers, running along the riverbank, can't keep up as he accelerates with the main current. They yell at him to swim harder and he does, but the river has him now. Any chance of rescue fades as the people on shore fall farther and farther behind.

Okay, Louis tells himself, trying to stay calm, *this isn't any big problem. This is what we went through the training exercises for, right?*

Rolling onto his back, he assumes the feet-downstream position that the guides told the vacationers to take if they fell out of the raft and were carried through a rapid.

The current is rushing now. In front of him the water drops out of sight. He can hear the roar and see mist rising into the air from whatever is below. He aims for a gap between two large boulders in midriver. The current seems to mound up between the two rocks and hesitate.

In a flash Louis is sucked over the drop and down a jade-green water slide. Waiting below is the foaming face of a monstrous standing wave, tumbling over upon itself in the middle of the river. Air bubbles roar in his ears as he is shot through the wave and below the surface like a human torpedo. The river rushes by his face, up his nose. In the watery confusion, memories of swimming in ocean surf come to him. He concentrates on the images to fight against panic.

If I just hold my breath and relax, I'll come to the surface.

Subsurface currents pull him along, keeping him down. Moments pass that seem like hours. All he can see are blurred bubbles and green-tinted darkness. Cold water wraps him like a frigid blanket.

In the back of his mind a voice begins making demands: "I have to take a breath."

Rationality answers back: "You can't breathe underwater."

"I can't hold my breath any longer!"

"No, you are underwater."

"I've got to take a breath."

Held tightly in the grip of the Snake River, Louis opens his mouth for air. His world goes black.

• • • — — — • • •

Chris loses sight of his father as he is carried by the current, down and around a bend in the river. His mother scrambles down the riverbank, chasing after the guide who is trying to keep Louis in view.

The rafts have been anchored down. At a time when seconds can mean life or death, it will take minutes to launch a chase boat.

In the pandemonium, one of the guides grabs binoculars and sprints up on a small rise, focusing in on Louis as he is swept through the rapids. The guide begins a grim play-by-play for the group.

"He's going, he's going, all right he is going through, he is down, he's under, he's not up, he's not up, where is he?"

Silence falls over the group.

"I don't see hi. . . ."

A chill sweeps through Chris's body.

"Oh, he's up, he's up, he's up, I see him, he's there, he's there. . . ."

With the pause they all look up to the guide.

"There's a jet boat. There's a jet boat! Where did that jet boat come from?"

• • • — — — • • •

Stephen and Kenneth are brothers, both retired cardiologists. One has traveled up from Texas to visit the other in his hometown of Boise, Idaho, over the Fourth of July weekend. They have always talked about visiting Hells Canyon, and they aren't getting any younger. Even though the river trips are usually booked solid this time of year, they decide to take a chance and try for seats on the one-day tour: raft down, jet-boat up, be back in town before 10 P.M. Together with their wives they drive north to Cambridge, Idaho, in the early hours of what promises to be a beautiful summer day.

When they arrive at the tour offices, their gamble pays off. There is room for the four of them, and two spare seats as well.

As the day heats up they are left waiting at the put-in just below Hells Canyon Dam. The tour is an hour late getting started.

Despite their delayed departure, the two brothers and their wives have a wonderful day in the canyon. The wild river and rugged scenery live up to their dreams. At the end of the afternoon, as they wait for the jet-boat ride back, they recount the day's events with excitement. Once again the boat is late, only twenty minutes this time, but they are left wondering how much longer they will be down in the canyon.

What took them hours on a raft flashes by quickly on the jet boat as they return upriver, easily powering through the roughest water.

Halfway back the captain throttles down in the calm water below Granite Creek Rapids. A life vest floating down the river has caught his eye. Somebody lost some equipment. The least he can do is scoop it out of the river and return it to them.

Angling the boat in closer, he can see it is more than just a life vest. A human body floats face down in the river, arms outstretched, unmoving. The passengers can see it now. As the boat pulls alongside, somebody grabs a strap on the life vest. It takes four men to drag the waterlogged figure up over the gunwale and into the boat.

Many of them have never seen a drowning victim before. It is an older man. His skin is blue from lack of oxygen. He is unresponsive, no breathing, no pulse.

The two brothers step forward for a better look. The captain of the jet boat hesitates when they offer help. Then he hears someone say to let them through. They know what to do.

With the help of the captain, the two retired cardiologists quickly strap Louis to a back board, secure him in the boat, and begin CPR.

· · · — — — · · ·

Pat Barten and the river guide are running a losing race with the river currents. Louis is swept away from them and out of sight as they scramble along the rough, rocky shoreline, picking their way through the scrub and brush. They arrive at the base of the rapids to find the passengers on the jet boat pulling Louis from the water.

The captain spots them, yelling and waving from shore. He pulls over and picks them up. The two brothers ask Pat and the guide a rapid-fire series of questions about the injured man, as the captain spins the boat around to head up through Granite Rapids.

"Who was he with?"

"Was he drinking?"

"Does he have any heart problems?"

• • • — — — • • •

Back at camp a sigh of relief ripples through the group when they hear that Louis has been pulled from the water. Chris can't wait to give his father hell for going down the rapids before anyone else got to ride them.

The boat roars up the river to their campsite.

The words they hear are paralyzing.

"We need the medic bag! We need the medic bag! Where's the medic bag?"

The rafting medic comes running with the kit. He changes places with the rafting guide on the jet boat

Chris, Alyssa, and Marko run down to the shore. They can see Louis's motionless body laid out on a back board. The doctors are pumping away at his chest and breathing into his mouth.

The captain holds them back.

"You can't get on! There is no room. You can't get on!"

With the rafting medic and Pat, the boat is at full capacity. Any more people and there will not be enough power to make it through the rapids upriver.

"He's not breathing, there is no pulse" are the last words they hear as the jet boat roars upriver and out of sight.

The three of them stand there, unbelieving, in the sudden silence.

• • • — — — • • •

Hours pass at the campsite down along the river. Chris, Alyssa, and Marko have no appetite. They leave the dining area and sit together at their tents in the twilight, trying to figure out how everything went so wrong so fast.

They have no communications with the outside world. They have no radios; cell phones don't work down here. Nobody runs the river at night. They can't walk out. Nobody can tell them when they will be able to get any news in or out. The guides have told them they will try to get word to a jet boat tomorrow, and maybe the three of them can be picked up in the morning.

The words keep repeating in Chris's head: "He's not breathing, there is no pulse."

He doesn't know what to think. Images of a funeral play across his mind.

Darkness falls in camp. Most everyone has retired for the night, but sleep evades Chris as he sits in his tent thinking about his father and the river. Footsteps approach. One of the guides asks if he is awake. A river ranger has arrived in camp with news. He wants to talk to Chris and his sister.

How did a ranger get here? he wonders as he scrambles down to the fire with his sister and Marko. The three of them are introduced to a man named Roy, the chief river ranger.

A few hours earlier the ranger received a phone call. It was the owner of the rafting company, with news of Louis. She knew Roy was the only one who might be able to get word to the group. With darkness falling, Roy took a chance and ran his jet boat up the river to the base of Granite Creek Rapids. He walked the remaining distance in darkness along the riverbank.

"Two doctors on the jet boat revived your father. I was told he was awake and doing okay by the time they got to the dam. A helicopter took him to the hospital in McCall, Idaho. The doctors were concerned he might have water in his lungs. As far as I know he is okay and under observation at the hospital."

They have a thousand questions for Roy, but the ranger doesn't know any more.

"You probably want to come out with me tonight. I'll run you downriver to the landing at Pittsburg and we'll get to the hospital from there."

All three of them shake their heads.

"No, we know our dad; if he's alive and well he is going to want to come right back here."

Roy can't quite believe this, but they are adamant. If their father is okay, he and their mom will be back on the river as soon as possible.

"Okay," Roy says, still not convinced. "If they want to come back, they can get ahold of me and I will bring them up."

Either way, Roy has to get back to his boat tonight. Before he heads out, they come up with a plan. Whatever happens, Roy will find them on the river tomorrow night and bring news of Louis. If he is doing well and decides to rejoin the trip, Chris, Alyssa, and Marco will stay with the group and rendezvous with Louis and Pat farther downriver. If their father decides not to come back, then he isn't doing well. The three of them will then ride out with Roy and get to the hospital as quickly as possible.

· · · — — — · · ·

In the morning the rafting vacationers are somber from the shock of the previous day. The guides are in a funk as well. This is no way to start a seven-day tour. A few members of the group try to console Chris and his sister. For the most part everyone is quiet. Parents watch their children like hawks whenever they get near the river.

The group remains at the campsite past normal departure time. The medic guide has yet to return from the jet-boat trip upriver. With only three certified guides left in the party, equipment is shifted to three boats. The remaining raft will be left tied up on shore for the medic guide to pick up on his way downriver to rejoin the party.

As far as Chris can tell, everyone is just going through the motions. He rides in the back of the cargo raft as they pass through the big drop in Granite Rapids. The thrill of whitewater is gone.

When they pull up for lunch, Chris, Alyssa, and Marko gather away from the group. They have all come to the same conclusion. It is ridiculous for them to continue. They need to get off the river and be with their mother and father. When Roy comes back in the evening they will catch a ride out on his jet boat.

Lunch wraps up and the rafters are getting back in the boats when the Forest Service jet boat is spotted at a distance, coming upriver.

Chris's heart sinks. There was a clear plan last night. The ranger was going to meet them at camp tonight. It can be nothing but bad news for Roy to be back so soon.

As the jet boat approaches, Chris can see that Roy is not alone.

The boat pulls up to shore. Louis and Pat Barten stand up and greet the crowd gathered at river's edge.

Chris is stunned. "Oh my God. You were dead yesterday. What are you doing here?"

His parents climb out of the boat. They are ready to come back to the river.

The gloom over the trip is gone in a flash. The group is whole again and it is celebration time.

Pat and Louis, away for less than twenty-four hours, have rejoined the trip only four and a half miles below the previous night's camp.

· · · — — — · · ·

The next day Louis is ready to try one of the inflatable kayaks brought along for the trip.

Everyone in the party is hesitant: "Uhhh, okay."

He rides through a small riffle, all eyes glued to him.

The kayak flips halfway through. Suddenly two dozen voices are screaming, "He's out of the boat, he's out of the boat."

Every watercraft in the group converges as fast as everyone can paddle. Many hands reach out for him, and Louis is flung out of the water into the nearest raft.

There is an immediate and unspoken understanding among all members of the trip. Whether he likes it or not, that's enough kayaking for Louis Barten. He is not getting away from them again.

· · · — — — · · ·

Louis had no heartbeat or pulse for seven minutes from the time the two cardiologists began working on him in the back of the jet boat.

He doesn't remember much from the initial hour after his near-death. It was as if he was waking from a deep sleep in a hotel room in some unfamiliar city.

Am I just dreaming? Am I on a business trip?

He can hear people talking but he can't get his bearings. The confusion clears a bit and he realizes that people are asking him questions, but he can't make any sense of what they are saying.

20

The last thing I remember is that I was on the Snake River in Idaho.

He wants to talk. Suddenly he can understand the questions and he wants to talk, but he can't form any words. He can't utter a sound. His throat is so dry, drier than he can ever remember.

If I just had a little water in my mouth to moisten my throat, I could talk to these people.

He opens his eyes. He is on a boat going upriver. People are around him.

"Lay down, keep calm," they tell him.

He drifts in and out of consciousness.

By the time the boat arrives at the dam he is conscious enough to drink a little water.

They haul him out of the boat on the back board and put him in the back of a pickup truck. He is still extremely thirsty. They won't let him get up.

He is driven to a landing pad near the dam to await a helicopter. He still feels confused. He vomits water.

The doctors are concerned that there may be water in his lungs. He needs to get to a hospital for a thorough examination.

By the time the helicopter arrives, Louis is able to climb in under his own power. He is awake and alert during the flight to McCall.

Arriving at the hospital, he shows no physical signs of the near-death by drowning he experienced only hours before. The doctors find only a minuscule amount of the Snake River in his lungs.

Hypothermia, a sharp lowering of his body core temperature, is the only explanation doctors can give him for his miraculous recovery. Swimming in the cold water must have been enough to slow his body down. The icy temperatures in the bottom of the river shut his respiratory system down before his lungs could fill with water. The two cardiologists were able to restart his breathing and circulation before the lack of oxygen to his brain could cause damage.

Louis walks out of the hospital a celebrity. The doctors don't see many river accident victims come back to life.

His son Chris puts the whole experience in perspective.

"The rules had been told to us. Less than twelve hours earlier we all acknowledged how powerful the river was and how fast it could take someone's life. We acknowledged that at 10 A.M. that morning before we set foot in the river. We were pushing that limit and it got us.

"It is amazing in Hells Canyon how fast the river can get you, how fast you can go from fun to horror."

These five men know each other too well to place blame or get angry. They all followed the leader off the edge. Nobody forced them to come down here.

CHAPTER 3

JUST ONE LAST RUN

I t's a late November day that would hook even the most jaded snowmobiler. A foot of fresh powder blankets the rolling alpine terrain. The scent of ponderosa pine hangs in the crisp air. The Sisters, Broken Top, and Mount Bachelor are putting on a show, sparkling white in new cloaks of snow. They stand out tall and proud against a cloudless, crystal-blue sky. The view seems to stretch all the way to Idaho as seven snowmobiles come buzzing down the trail off the high country west of Bend, Oregon. The riders pull into the Dutchman Flat snow park just down the road from the ski lodge at Mount Bachelor.

As their machines cool down from a morning of hard riding, Joe, Kip, Kent, Kenny, John, Rick, and Chuck take their backpacks full of survival gear and toss them in the back of their vehicles. They peel off insulated winter clothing and sit down for a late lunch, lounging in the warmth of the afternoon sun.

It's not long before the food is gone. Some of the more restless members of the group check their watches. The time is 2:30 P.M. Nobody is eager to pack up and begin the long drive home. Besides, it's still early. The weather and snow are perfect. Why not take one last, quick run? They can be back with plenty of time to load the snowmobiles and get on the road before dark.

"Why the heck not?" is the general consensus. They all get ready to head out again. It's just going to be a quick trip, and the day has warmed up, so they leave their bulky packs and heavy clothes in their vehicles. They zip up their light jackets and coveralls, put on gloves and helmets, fire up their snow machines, and head back out for more fun.

Their route winds up through the forest to a high plateau. To the west are Broken Top Mountain and the Three Sisters Wilderness; to the southeast the low, rounded peak of Tumalo Mountain. To the north the plateau drops off quickly, breaking up into the many ravines leading down into the Bend watershed. The trail they are following loops east around Tumalo Mountain and will eventually lead them right back to their vehicles.

But trail riding is merely a way for this group to access the backcountry. They soon peel off the main drag to search for untracked snow along the ragged northern boundary of the plateau. Following a high ridge, they play catch-as-catch-can, chasing each other off the edge to ride down the steep side slopes. Powder snow flies, and then they roar back up on top to do it again. It's an irresistible game of tag that carries them farther and farther from the trail.

At some point Rick and Chuck become separated from the group in the maze of snowmobile tracks running back and forth across the forested ridge. When the time comes to head back, they circle around looking to meet up with their friends. When they stop to listen and call for the other five men, the forest offers only silence.

With evening approaching, they begin to wonder if the guys passed them in the woods somehow. Maybe they are waiting back at the snow park. They turn their sleds around and head down the winding trail. At Dutchman Flat, the trucks and trailers sit empty. They load their snow machines and wait.

Hours pass, darkness falls, and still there is no sign of the other five snowmobilers. Something serious has to have happened for none of the five to make it back out. With stars appearing in the sky, Rick and Chuck pull out a cell phone and call for help.

· · · — — — · · ·

When the Deschutes County Sheriff's office receives the call at 6:30 on Saturday evening, the people there know they need to move fast. Five men, ill equipped for a night out in subfreezing temperatures, are missing in the high country. On top of that, high winds and heavy snow are forecast to arrive sometime in the night. Three hasty teams of two snowmobilers each are immediately dispatched to begin searching in the darkness.

Within hours the wind picks up and clouds start streaming in from the west. With the clouds comes snow, pelting down through the darkness to be caught in the wind and whipped horizontally through the trees.

Throughout the night, searchers ride the vast network of trails that radiate out from the Dutchman Flat snow park. At times visibility drops to zero, their headlights illuminating only a blizzard of driving snow, everything else around them pitch-black. As morning approaches they have found no sign of the five missing men.

On Sunday morning a fresh group of snowmobile searchers arrives to spell the night crew. Other volunteers are passing out fliers describing the lost snowmobilers to anyone leaving the Dutchman Flat snow park. Joe's father has driven down to help in the effort. He tries to tell the searchers that they may be looking in the wrong places. The five missing men are cross-country riders. If they are lost, it is off trail somewhere.

With daytime visibility in the wind-driven snow down to one hundred yards, at best the search is an exercise in frustration. There is a huge expanse of country to traverse, crisscrossed with trails and now covered in fresh snow. The searchers are in just as much danger of getting lost as the men they are searching for.

· · · — — — · · ·

Tom Hartman, his sons Randy and Tracy, Les Robbins, and his son Ron have spent Sunday morning avoiding the heavy snow up high by riding the network of trails in the low country around the base of Mount Bachelor. When they stop for lunch at Elk Lake, a woman approaches with a question.

"Are you the five guys that are lost?"

They chuckle to themselves.

"No," Tracy replies. "I think we know where we are."

She tells them that five snowmobilers took off yesterday afternoon for a short ride up above Dutchman Flat. They carried next to nothing in the way of survival gear, and they haven't been seen since.

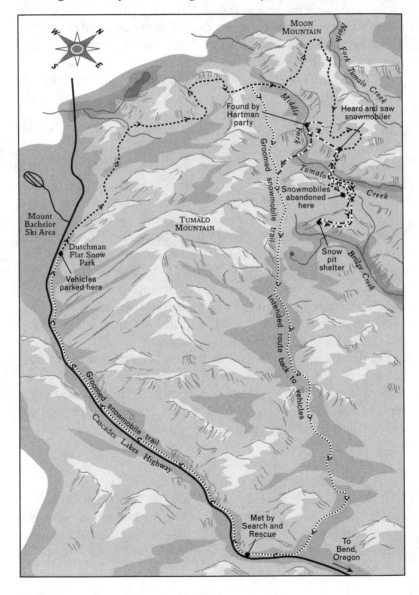

The Hartmans have been riding here for years. When people get lost up high, it means they are either stuck down in the watershed or way up in the Sisters Wilderness. With the current blizzard conditions up there, it would be real easy to get in trouble.

More than a little curious, the five-member Hartman party decides to take a loop through the high country before heading back to their cars. The trails down low are in terrible shape. Maybe with the fresh snow up top, they can at least salvage the day with a good run.

* * * ▬ ▬ ▬ * * *

When the Hartman party arrives above Dutchman Flat, conditions are at blizzard stage. Gusting winds buffet their snowmobiles. Blowing snow and dense fog obscure the landscape.

At this point late on Sunday afternoon, the search has been scaled back. Volunteers are stationed at key snowmobile trail intersections. As soon as conditions improve to the point that riders can see to search, snowmobile patrols will head back out. No one can say when this will be.

As the five Hartman snowmobilers make the last run of the day, they have the high country to themselves. Anyone less familiar with the landscape or less experienced with the weather has packed up and headed home.

As far as the Hartman party of veteran snowmobilers is concerned, they are at home as they spread out five abreast, riding across the wide-open plateau. Their machines sink up to their hoods in deep powder snow. Sky and snow blend together in the flat light. Depth perception and visibility are close to nonexistent. They know to just keep the throttle back and follow the hazy gray tree line that funnels down into the main trail to the east.

As the snowfield narrows, Tracy swerves back and forth, in and out of the forest. In the shelter of the trees, visibility improves slightly. On one weave something catches his eye, a splash of color off in the distance. Squinting his eyes to peer through the blowing snow, he can just barely make out a figure emerging from the trees in the distance.

· · · — — — · · ·

Joe, Kip, Kent, Kenny, and John leave Rick and Chuck behind as they chase each other through the trees. The five men exchange leads back and forth across the ridgeline. Each loop takes them farther east along the ridge in search of untracked snow, steeper slopes, and bigger thrills. Down toward the end of the ridge, they drop off the crest, one after another, following the leader down a slope steeper and longer than any before.

As they descend, the snow becomes deeper and deeper. When they finally find a place level enough to maneuver, it's as if the snow is bottomless. Their snowmobiles sink deeper below the surface as the men rev engines in the struggle to turn around. A few of their machines have long tracks that float better in the light snow. These take the lead trying to climb back up. When the lead long-track machine bogs down, a second sled leapfrogs around to break trail higher.

The slope is too steep to build any momentum. The machines bog down again and again. They men ride back and forth, trying different routes in the narrow canyon. They roar up, only to bury their snowmobiles, stall out, dig out, and then retreat back down the slope to try again.

As the afternoon hours pass, a sinking feeling spreads among the men.

Joe has always been the de facto leader of this group. He consults the map. It looks as though the terrain levels out down-canyon. Maybe by descending, they can work their way around into another creek drainage and back up to the main trail by a different route.

Pointing their snowmobiles downslope, they descend farther. The snow depth only increases. Way down-canyon they emerge from the trees on the bank of a creek. Cliffs drop down to the water on their right and left.

The five men get to work. With tree limbs and snow they build a bridge over the water. They buzz across to find more deep snow, and not far off a second creek. This time they build a ramp and jump across to a small plateau.

Down in this confusion of creeks and canyons they search back and forth for a return route up and out.

In one direction a third creek has cut a forty-foot-wide moat through the forest, with twelve-foot-high snowbanks for walls. In the other direction a ridge cuts down into the drainage. The near-vertical slopes are too steep for riding. Every time the group is forced to turn around, their machines sink deep below the snow surface.

With few daylight hours left, some in the group have become resigned to spending the night outdoors.

These five men, most of them friends since childhood, know each other too well to place blame or get angry. They all followed the leader off the edge. Nobody forced them to come down here.

One of them brings up a good point. Sooner or later Rick and Chuck are going to figure out that they are stuck out here. Someone will come looking.

They could stay right here and light a tree on fire—or light a snowmobile on fire—if that's what they have to do to stay warm or to signal for help.

Whoa now, most of them don't feel the situation is that desperate. Several of the snowmobiles are new, the ink barely dry on the titles. The idea of torching one of the brand-new, multithousand-dollar toys seems a little extreme.

Besides, one man says, the chance of anyone finding them way down here, far from the groomed trails, is slim.

Joe pulls out the map to show it to the group. The main snowmobile trail looks to be within easy walking distance uphill to the south. If they can get up near that main trail, they will have a far better chance of being found. At the very worst, they can probably walk out on their own late tonight.

The storm forecast for this evening weighs heavily on their minds as well. The five of them debate back and forth. Sleep in the snow or walk out? It doesn't seem that far, but wouldn't it be better to stay with the machines?

Finally it comes to a vote. Stay or go?

With more hands raised for go, the snowmobiles are parked in what looks to be a safe spot. A few landmarks are noted so the location can be found whenever they make it back—could be a week, could be springtime.

They check the sky and their watches before leaving. Given the hour of daylight remaining, an hour or so of dusk, plus a little luck, they should make it to the main trail before real darkness sets in.

· · · — — — · · ·

Three hours pass as the five men push, fight, and plow their way on foot up out of the canyons through chest-deep snow, sometimes stepping in drifts over their heads, stumbling and flailing to keep their balance. They are exhausted, soaked in sweat, and can go no farther.

The sun is long gone. If Joe is reading the map correctly, the main trail is still a good distance away over the next ridge. As the men shiver in the darkness, the situation is almost laughable. Just hours before they were riding in full winter gear, had backpacks full of survival gear, cell phones in their pockets. It's like a bad dream, except for the fact that the cold air feels very real through their light layers of clothing.

They're not getting out tonight. The only thing they can do now is find some way to get out of the weather. They will have to huddle together and try to keep from freezing.

The moon is shining just enough so that they can see around the small snow-filled clearing they stand in. They pick three trees growing close together and start digging down between them. Three and a half feet down, the snow turns to ice. With only their hands for tools, they can dig no farther.

One of them salvaged a folding saw from the snowmobiles. Limbs are trimmed off some of the surrounding trees. They knock the snow and ice off as best they can. The pit is lined with these boughs to provide insulation from the snow. As they work, a wind begins rattling the tops of the trees.

A length of climbing rope was also salvaged, and now they string it back and forth between the trees. More limbs are cut, then draped over the ropes to form a makeshift roof.

One of the men fishes a pack of matches out of his pocket. A fire is built directly in front of the shelter. All the wood is encrusted with snow and ice, and even with constant tending and blowing, the fire just smolders. The five men crowd around, trying to warm numb fingers and toes.

Standing by the fire, Joe watches as clouds stream in to obscure the moon and stars. With the temperature dropping well below freezing, the cold seems to siphon the warmth from their bodies. The wet wood puts off more smoke than flame. Stamping their feet, shivering, shuffling around, they just can't warm up. Desperate for heat, they begin burning anything they have that will catch flame. Money, credit cards, wallets, titles to the snowmobiles, everything is thrown into the fire in an attempt to stay warm.

As the clouds continue to build, the wind blows even harder. When snow begins to stream in horizontally through the trees, the men crowd into the snow hole.

The shelter seemed big when they built it. Now, wedging shoulders and knees into the cramped space, only four of them can get inside. Joe is last, and try as they might they can't make any more room.

Joe takes the first shift outside, sheltering behind one of the trees and as close to the fire as possible. The snow whips in under the visor of his snowmobile helmet, peppering the side of his face.

Joe is exhausted. Even with the wind and snow he begins to nod off. To keep from falling into the smoldering flames, he hooks his helmet visor over a branch. Every time his body relaxes into sleep the helmet catches on the branch, snaps his neck, and startles him out of drowsiness. With each helmet snap he calls out the names of his friends inside the shelter. He doesn't want anyone falling asleep and freezing to death on his watch.

Inside the shelter, the men might as well be inside a blast freezer. The wind builds to a point that it feels like a huge industrial fan roaring through the tree-limb walls. Their bodies are wracked with violent chills. Their hands and feet go numb. Joe can see the roof of the shelter vibrate from their shivering as he stands outside, teeth chattering, body shaking. Huddled close together, they shove each other and yell at each other to avoid the seductive sleep that precedes hypothermic death.

Throughout the night the five men rotate between the shelter and standing watch in the lee of the tree. The shelter shrinks because the only thing that burns reliably is the rope. Chunks are cut off and thrown in whenever the flames die down. Sooty smoke fills the space. They lean in close. The flames singe boots and gloves, yet they feel little heat in the subzero temperatures.

Even with patience severely tested by cold, thirst, and hunger, throughout the night they are able to joke about their situation, laughing between shivers, trying to keep up the humor that is really all they have left.

· · · — — — · · ·

Joe is taking a second shift outside when the landscape slowly transitions from black to gray. Clouds and fog obscure the sky. The wind is still carrying a full load of snow, but they have made it through the night. Eventually the men climb out of the shelter and gather around.

"Guys," Joe says, "I know a few of you aren't very religious, but we are going to stand right here, we are going to hold hands, and we are going to say a prayer because there is only one reason we made it through last night."

When they finish the prayer it is time to make a decision. All through the night they had hoped for clear weather. With open skies Joe's father would find a plane or a helicopter and be out looking for them.

Standing there in the driving snow with visibility at maybe one hundred yards, all hopes of a quick rescue are blown away in the bone-chilling wind.

The general consensus is that yesterday's fiasco took them too far off the beaten path for any ground searchers to find them easily. If they want to get out today, it is going to be up to them.

Joe pulls out the map and shows how close they are to the main trail. He estimates it is about a half mile away. If they just climb over the next ridge, they will come to it.

The rest of the group is hesitant. They don't really know what they will run into hiking cross-country. They can't even be sure they are going in the right direction. What happens if they head out like yesterday and get stranded somewhere?

Once again a vote breaks the debate. The decision is to follow their tracks back to the snowmobiles. If the conditions haven't changed, and they still can't get out on the machines, then this time they will light a tree or a snowmobile on fire, or do whatever else is necessary to survive.

In the gray light of dawn, with the wind howling and the snow pelting them, they lift their weary legs and follow yesterday's trail, barely discernible under a covering of fresh snow. They stumble into deep drifts, clothing stiff with ice, hands bunched into fists inside frozen gloves.

· · · — — — · · ·

Three hours pass as they plow a path downhill, back through the forest. They find their machines, now just lumps under the fresh blanket of snow. Nothing has changed since yesterday, except that the snow is even deeper and more difficult for the snowmobiles.

They gather around and Joe lays it out for them.

"Okay guys, here is the situation. Stay here, hope this storm blows over, hope there is a plane that comes out here looking for us. Or, we have about six hours of daylight; if we can get back up near the main trail, at least we have a chance of somebody seeing us."

The wind has not let up. The snow is coming down harder than ever. As tired as they are, no one likes the idea of staying here to spend another night out in the cold. The only sure route out in all of their minds is to follow the trail left in the snow from yesterday's ride down.

A quick vote is cast. They all agree to keep moving. The group turns wearily to follow the day-old snowmobile track, now just a faint depression weaving back across the landscape.

At first they trade off on trailbreaking duty, but as the incline increases, it becomes exhausting work. Steep, steep slopes and deep powder. They struggle to find footing, pulling each other out of holes. A few of them just don't have the energy to keep pace. Kip and John take the lead. Joe brings up the rear, pushing the group on from behind, as he tracks their progress on the map.

The small bottle of water Kip had is long gone. The rotten apple that Kenny pulled out of the depths of his backpack this morning proves too rotten for even starving men to stomach. Occasionally they scoop a little snow with their hands and suck out the moisture to slake their thirst.

They struggle on, one stumbling step at a time, legs leaden from exhaustion, up through a landscape cloaked in fog and blowing snow. Except for the sound of wind, all they hear is their own heavy breathing, their hearts pounding in their chests, and the crunch of snow under their boots.

Joe keeps pushing, not letting up. No one will be left behind.

Hours pass as they march into the blowing snow with heads down. Late in the afternoon one of the group pauses to look up through the fog. On the ridge above them he can see a shelter.

No one else can make anything out through the driving snow.

"It's right there up on the ridge, can't you see it?" he says.

They all stare through the falling snow until, maybe, they do see something. They weave off their route for a closer look.

The five men struggle up toward the ridge, hope rising out of the gloom. Maybe they can get out of the weather and warm up. Maybe they will find people to rescue them.

When they arrive on top, all they find is a pile of rocks. The detour was a bad idea—poor reasoning brought on by growing despair and exhaustion. It could mark the beginning signs of hypothermia, or dehydration.

A look passes among the five men. Some of them are starting to lose it, and they still have a long way to travel.

They retrace their footsteps and get back on the route. Kip stays in the lead with John. He is not going to die out here and leave his wife and kids. There is just no way.

Joe stays in the rear, pushing the stragglers along. Whenever someone hesitates, exhausted, claiming he can't go any farther, Joe makes him keep moving. At this point it is too late to wait for rescue. If they stop they die.

Occasionally they yell for help. In this wind someone would have to be only steps away to hear, but they have to try.

Finally, up on the high ridge, they walk into terrain they recognize from the day before. As they stand there getting their bearings, a sound filters in on the wind. About 150 yards down the ridge through the blowing snow, they see a snowmobile headlight coming right for them. They start jumping and yelling, waving their arms wildly. But a hundred yards off, the machine veers into the trees and is gone.

A huge disappointment—but there is one snowmobile, so there may be more.

They continue walking, heads down, wind howling, the snow falling now in thick flakes, slapping against their clothing. Joe stumbles. His feet aren't working right. It's as if he is drunk from exhaustion.

Half an hour passes. They stop for a break.

Kip and John have just started off again when Joe hears noises. At first he figures his mind is playing tricks. The sound becomes clearer, like the whine of a snowmobile, or maybe two. As he listens closely he tracks the sound moving left to right, beyond a tree line in the distance.

If they miss this chance they will be out another night. They may not make it another night. Kip and John are a hundred yards ahead, close to the tree line. He yells at them to run through the trees.

Nobody is in a good mood at this point and Kip is pissed.

"What are you yelling at me for?"

Joe yells one more time, "Snowmobile!"

Then Kip hears it too and takes off running, with John not far behind.

· · · — — — · · ·

From a distance Joe watches the race, trying to follow Kip's progress in the blowing snow while listening to the sound of the snowmobile, hoping to God that they meet.

Kip breaks through the tree line and begins waving his arms. Joe can see a snowmobile pull up, and then Kip's voice comes from across the distance to where Joe stands in disbelief.

"We are going to live!"

A second snowmobile pulls up, and then a third as Joe and the rest of the stragglers shuffle through the snow as fast as they can.

When they arrive, there are five snowmobiles—bear hugs and high fives all around. Everybody is laughing, crying, talking about the long walk, about burning everything in their wallets, freezing in the night, not knowing if they were going to make it.

Candy bars and water are passed around to the lost men. From Tom Hartman's point of view they are on their last legs, tired, wet, shivering. Their faces are black from huddling around the smoldering fire. He gives one of them his extra sweatshirt.

Once the group settles down, five weary men climb behind the five snowmobilers and the ride out begins. The trail is rough. The men are so tired, and their hands so cold, they can barely hang on. Several of them fall asleep on the way out.

The distance out by foot would have taken a day and a half. On the snowmobiles the ride passes in an hour.

* * * — — — * * *

Rescue crews meet the group out on the main highway and transport the five men to the Mount Bachelor Lodge, where they are treated for exposure and exhaustion. John's socks are frozen to his feet. Kent has breathing problems from inhaling fire smoke.

They are all warmed up, stabilized, and released to their relieved families, only a few hours after arriving at the lodge. They all agree that beyond the sheer luck of stumbling across the Hartman party, their key to survival was the bond of friendship that kept them together in the worst of conditions.

Looking back, Joe offers additional hard-won advice.

"Very few riders in the Northwest stay on the trail the whole time. Everyone has to go off and play in a meadow somewhere. If you think you have the slightest chance of going off the trail, take everything, *ev-ree-thing!* I would overprepare every time I go out.

"Yes, it is a pain to carry a backpack with all that stuff, but believe me, it is better than the alternative."

Jim slips into a full body harness.
There is one last check. Still not a whisper
of a breeze. Conditions are perfect.

CHAPTER 4

THE PRICE OF PROHIBITED
AIR DELIVERY

Around noon on a Wednesday in late September, two rangers are patrolling the Cracker Lake Basin backcountry in the Many Glaciers District of Glacier National Park. The morning is as calm as the scene on a picture postcard. Not far from Cracker Lake the rangers come across a man, his back to them, planting a flag in the middle of a meadow. The large orange pennant hangs limply from a ten-foot pole. The man has a handheld radio as well.

As they approach and call out, he seems to have been caught off guard.

"Hello. What's the flag for?"

"Oh . . . it's . . . my expedition flag."

"What expedition?"

"Uh . . . my expedition to Cracker Lake."

Rangers often struggle to understand the behavior of some park visitors and, as the conversation continues, this man volunteers very little information. As far as they can tell he presents no danger to himself or to the public, so they bid him good-bye and continue on their way.

· · · — — — · · ·

A mile to the south as the crow flies and 4000 feet above, three men gaze down from the top of the second-highest rock wall in the park. The north face of 10,074-foot Mount Siyeh drops straight down for a thousand feet, then tumbles another three thousand feet down shattered shale slopes and high angle cliffs into Cracker Lake Basin. Stand on this edge and the world drops away like an elevator with its cable cut.

Over the next hour and a half the three men, Jim, Ken, and Kevin, scout back and forth along the escarpment, looking over the edge, dropping small rocks, timing their descent, and watching to make sure they fall clean for the first thousand feet.

By 1:30 P.M. a decision has been made. Jim slips into a full body harness with a small pack attached to the back. He pulls the webbing belts tight in their buckles. Ken helps him double- and triple-check that the fit is secure.

Jim slips on a helmet.

Ken and Kevin take positions to the east and west along the high, rocky summit.

There is one last check. Still not a whisper of a breeze. Conditions are perfect.

Jim takes a few steps back, all that the narrow summit allows, then strides forward and leaps off the edge into open air.

His rock tests told him he has twelve seconds before impact—plenty of time to fit in the three-second count necessary to carry him away from the cliff so his parachute can open unhindered. The critical factor is body positioning: head up, chest out. With the mountain taking up half the sky, the chute has to be released on a forward heading to pull him clear and away from the cliff face.

He counts to three:

One. Position is good, his body pointed forward, head and chest high, as he falls the first hundred feet.

Two. Plunging through two hundred feet, his body starts to pivot head downward; he twists with hips and shoulders, trying to get back into position.

Three. With the rocky slopes coming up fast, he pitches his pilot chute to open the main.

As the main thunders open, inflating in a flash, his left shoulder drops. The ram air parachute pulls left, slamming him into the cliff. He bounces free, falling now with a half-inflated canopy.

The chute pulls left again, and he slams hard a second time, bashing his right leg on a jagged outcrop. In near free fall he swings out away from the rock face. His chute collapses, fluttering, as he plummets toward his death.

At the last moment, Jim's chute catches a little air. He is whipped around and hammered into the cliff a third and final time. A corner of the chute snags on a small horn of rock. The straps of his harness jerk him to a stop.

Loose cords and parachute fabric fall around him as he scrambles for a hold on the sheer face. One foot finds an inch-wide, crumbling ledge. His second foot can only rest on top of the first.

His hands move across the rock in jittery panic, feeling for a flake, a pocket, anything. A finger on his right hand finds a horizontal crack and he jams it in. His left forearm comes to rest on a hairline shelf. His left hand grips a small nubbin of rock.

"Fuuuuck!"

His heart is pounding. Beads of sweat pop out on his forehead. His hands are slick with perspiration.

Three taut parachute cords are all that hold him to the cliff. They lead up and out of sight. He can't see how the chute is snagged, but to judge by all the loose fabric and cords hanging around him, it can't be by much.

The base of the cliff is seven hundred feet of sheer, featureless rock below. It looks like six thousand as he balances on the tiny ledge.

"Fuuuuck!"

Three hundred feet above, his companions are calling to him.

"Jim, Jim, are you okay?"

"I've got one foot on a small ledge, almost nothing for handholds. I can feel blood running into my boot. I think my leg is broken."

"Try to stay calm, we're going to call Fred down below and tell him to go for help. You have to hang on."

With his left arm wedged on the shelf, Jim's wristwatch is right in front of his face. The hands are ticking slowly around. It's a few minutes to 2 P.M.

Down at Cracker Lake, Fred receives the call for help over his handheld radio. He packs up the orange pennant and heads out in search of the rangers he spoke with only a few hours before.

· · · — — — · · ·

On the mountain summit, the two men are helpless to do anything but yell down to Jim and tell him he's going to be okay, help is on the way.

In between yelling, they talk quietly. It's going to take Fred at least an hour, more like two, to hike the five miles out to the Many Glaciers Ranger Station. They spent more than six hours climbing up the mountain this morning. It's going to be hours before anyone can get up here.

When the three men first arrived at the summit and established contact with Fred on their short-range radios, they heard a third voice. Someone was talking about a lunch break. Ken and Fred quickly changed channels, not wanting to give away their plans.

Ken now switches back to the original frequency and starts broadcasting a distress call. Perhaps through an atmospheric fluke, or maybe because they are so high on the continental divide, the signal is picked up fifty miles southeast of the park in Browning, Montana, by a maintenance crew working on power lines.

A voice comes back over the radio in response to Ken's call.

"What's going on?"

Ken describes where they are and what happened. "We need help right now."

They are in luck. The man has a cell phone with him.

The man calls 911, and 911 dispatch puts him in contact with the Glacier County Sheriff's office, which calls Glacier National Park dispatch.

Within minutes, the power line maintenance man is talking over the radio with Ken and Kevin on the summit of Mount Siyeh, and then transferring the message via cell phone directly to the dispatcher at Glacier National Park. The search and rescue machinery begins to roll.

· · · — — — · · ·

Half an hour passes. Three hundred feet below, the hands of Jim's watch seem to have slowed to a crawl. His arms and shoulders are tiring from his grip on the rock. He yells upward in desperation.

"I don't know how much longer I can hang on."

Those three taut cords have been playing heavily on his mind. If he takes too much weight off the cords, the parachute could slide off. If he puts too much weight on the cords, the fabric might tear or the rock could flake off.

"How does the parachute look?" Jim asks. "How is it wrapped around the rock? Do you think it will hold my weight if I let go and hang from my harness?"

From far above neither Ken nor Kevin can see how the chute is attached. There will be only one chance to see if it will hold. They tell him not to try it.

"You're going to be okay," Kevin yells down. "We got through to the Park Service. They are going to get a chopper and get you out of here."

"How long is it going to be?"

Kevin turns to Ken, who is working the radio. "How long is it going to be?"

Ken radios out to the maintenance man in Browning, "How long is it going to be?"

The man in Browning puts the radio down, picks up his cell phone, and dials direct to the park. "How long is it going to be?"

The Park Service dispatcher tells him they are still mobilizing. At this point they can't commit to any arrival time.

The guy in Browning comes back on the radio. "They can't commit."

Ken turns to Kevin. "They can't commit."

Kevin yells down to Jim. "They are going to be here real soon, Jim. Just hang in there."

· · · — — — · · ·

Just after 3 P.M., with the distress calls from the mountain increasing in urgency, a helicopter is finally procured and a rescue team

41

consisting of two park rangers, Charlie and Kim, is in the air and on the way. Their job is to land near the summit, rappel down, and secure the parachutist before he falls the remaining 3,700 feet down the mountain.

As they circle Mount Siyeh from a distance, the cliff face looks absolutely featureless. To Charlie it appears as if the parachutist is pasted to the cliff, the parachute caught on only the most minuscule flake of rock.

Both pilot and rangers are looking out and down as they fly back and forth just above the craggy summit. Below them the two men are waving for help. The helicopter makes several passes before the pilot finds the only place to land, a small ledge just wide enough for one helicopter skid. The helicopter eases into a hover and the pilot brings the chopper down between two outcrops, the blade tips mere feet from the rocks: one skid on the mountain, the other hanging over the drop. The rangers hop out, unload bags of climbing gear, and head out for a second load of rescuers.

Pure luck has placed the landing site right above where Jim is caught. As the rangers set up anchors for a rope belay station, they question Ken and Kevin about Jim's harness, his parachute, and other technical details that will help them untangle his equipment and get him back up safely.

From the air Charlie mapped out a rappel route that looked to angle down and over toward Jim. The rock on the summit is crumbly shale. His approach has to be from the side to prevent any loose rock from cascading down on the trapped man.

When all is ready, Kim takes up his position at the belay station. Charlie ties into two ropes, backs up to the edge, puts his weight on the rappel rope, leans out over that long, long drop, and disappears over the side.

With extra-long rope lengths custom cut for the big walls in Glacier National Park, Charlie rappels almost three hundred feet down the shadowy face before stopping alongside the parachute to see just how well it is snagged. The chute looks relatively stable. A good twelve inches of fabric is wrapped tightly on a rock point. Surveying Jim's precarious position, and the tangle of fabric and parachute cords, he decides to stay put on the cliff face above.

Charlie talks calmly with Jim, coaching him on what will happen next. Now is not a time to panic. A sudden move by Jim could cut the parachute lines on the sharp rock, or cause the ledge he is standing on to crumble.

Charlie lowers the end of a rope to Jim, with a carabiner tied into it. Gingerly shifting his weight, Jim eases his right fingers out of the crack and reaches for the carabiner as it swings toward him. The small metal oval, with its securely locking gate, feels cool in his grip.

With a sweaty, shaking hand, he pushes the carabiner across his chest, searching for one of the D-rings on his harness.

There is the sound of metal on metal, a slight pressure as the gate opens, and a reassuring click when the carabiner locks shut.

Jim can breathe again. He's not in the clear yet, but he is now securely attached to the main rescue line.

Charlie sends down a short nylon sling with a carabiner at each end. Jim snaps into a second harness D-ring and then clips the other carabiner into the rescue rope. Now he is connected to the rope from two points of his harness.

Charlie is now able to put tension on the rope and give some relief to Jim's arms and legs. From his position above, it looks as if Jim's leg has stopped bleeding. He performs a medical evaluation from a distance, asking Jim if he can move his foot or put weight on the injured leg. There is some mobility. The leg may not be fractured.

For an hour and a half the two men dangle on the north face of Siyeh. Over this time the rescue crew, consisting of six more rangers with additional equipment, is shuttled by helicopter up to the mountaintop. The belay setup is reanchored and rerigged into a "pig" system. Like a block and tackle, it provides a mechanical advantage for rescue retrievals. The system will be used to haul Charlie and Jim back up to the summit.

By 5:30 the system is ready and Jim is raised up to Charlie's level. Charlie takes a closer look at the injured leg; he dresses the wound and splints it. He gathers the parachute, pulling it from the rock, then rerigs the ropes so that both he and Jim can be raised simultaneously.

An hour and a half later, Charlie and Jim are back on the summit. Jim is loaded in the helicopter and flown to West Glacier to be transferred to a second helicopter for the flight to Kalispell Regional Medical Center.

The rescue system is taken down and all the men, including Jim's partners, Ken and Kevin, are shuttled by helicopter off the top of Mount Siyeh. The last load of rangers and equipment lands in the glow of Park Service vehicle headlights brought out to illuminate the landing pad at Many Glaciers Ranger Station.

The rangers are always happy when they can bring one back alive.

. . . ⸺ ⸺ ⸺ . . .

Jim walked out of the hospital that night, extremely thankful for Park Service rangers and extremely thankful for his life. He was badly bruised and scraped up from the fall, but his leg was not broken.

Six months after the rescue, in an effort to send a message to anyone considering Glacier National Park as a good place for BASE jumping (parachuting from a Building, Antennae, Span, or Earth), Jim faced a federal charge of being involved in a prohibited air delivery. This law refers to an outdated practice of resupplying backcountry camps using parachute drops from cargo planes.

Jim's attempt at flight fell into a gray area in a spectrum of Park Service regulations that allowed paragliding (flying from point to point with a parachute-like wing) yet didn't specifically ban BASE jumping.

The Park Service's position was that BASE jumping has inherent risks that make it inappropriate in a setting such as Glacier National Park. A statement released by park officials said that not only did Jim's "illegal parachuting place himself at great risk but also the lives of those rangers charged with rescuing him."

In return for a plea of "no contest" to the main charge, the prosecutor agreed to drop an additional charge of prohibited use of an aircraft. Jim's parachute was returned to him, but he was ordered to pay the almost nine thousand dollars in rescue costs.

A flood of snow is cascading toward him.
There is only one chance for escape.

CHAPTER 5

HAVE I GOT A RUN FOR YOU

When the winter sports crowd in the Pacific Northwest dreams of paradise, hut skiing in British Columbia is often the subject. Escape from civilization to a remote base camp surrounded by high mountain snow bowls. Powder-filled ski runs stretch as far as the eye can see, and there is a week to ski them all. Nights are spent in the warmth of a cabin with gourmet meals for refueling and a sauna to steam the stiffness out of tired bodies.

In search of this nirvana, a group of Canadians and Americans travel to southeastern British Columbia. They helicopter in to a hut in the Flint Lakes region just north of Kokanee Glacier Provincial Park on a Saturday in February. The weather is clear. The sun forms a glaze on the snow slopes despite the frigid winter temperatures.

Jeff, Rob, Bob, husband and wife Warner and Elaine, and her son Dean are ski buddies, friends, colleagues. They all have strong backcountry skiing credentials, years on ski patrol, avalanche training, first-aid experience. They have hired a guide for half of the week to show them the area. The remainder of the time they are planning to explore on their own.

Two days are spent with the guide before a storm blows in late Tuesday. Snow falls heavily all day Wednesday. On Thursday the storm continues. Aware of the avalanche danger created by nearly two feet of fresh snow over the sun-melted crust from last Saturday, the six skiers venture out on their own to evaluate the snowpack.

Above the cabin they dig a snow pit and conduct a field shear test for avalanche potential. They identify a definite weak layer between the old and new snow, but the slope angle in the vicinity of the cabin isn't enough to be of concern. They spend the day skiing close by, taking care to stay in the trees and away from open slopes. Occasionally the hissing rumble of snow sloughing off the surrounding peaks filters through the forest.

On Friday the group is eager to get out and do some serious skiing on their last full day in the mountains. The weather cooperates as the sun comes out on a clear but very cold morning.

They have the guide for the day. He gives the green light on the snow conditions and leads them on an hour and a half climb, ascending a ridge to the north of the hut.

Breaking trail up through the fresh snow, they talk among themselves and agree to spread out with ten yards between each person, just a precaution to give room to maneuver in case someone starts a small snowslide.

At about 7,000 feet of elevation, they reach a narrow plateau on top of the ridge and stop for a rest. When everyone has caught their breath, the guide gets their attention.

"Hey, have I got a run for you."

· · · — — — · · ·

Off the south flank of the ridge, The Snag is a broad, inviting, open slope lined on either side with a thick growth of mature trees. A handful of routes weave downward between small groves of stunted, gnarled, bent-over trees and silvery snags, some with broken-off tops. The curve of the slope obscures the finish way below in the valley.

Hoping to build his clients' skiing appetite, the guide tantalizes them with the details.

"Fourteen hundred feet of vertical with an average slope of 38 degrees," he tells them.

The skiers fall into the pattern set earlier in the week. The guide will go first, leading the way. They will follow, one at a time, with about fifty yards between each skier. Everyone will gather halfway down.

The guide skis about twenty feet across the top and kicks at the slope in a few places to check for instability. He comes back to the group, gives the thumbs-up, and drops off the edge.

Karen, the guide's girlfriend, is next. Then, one after another at even intervals, Elaine, Warner, and Dean ski off the top. Jeff and Bob follow, and finally, hanging back for a few seconds longer, Rob points his skis over the edge and starts carving down the slope.

Rob is a few yards off the top when the small trees he can see down the slope start fluttering, as if something is shaking their trunks. Near the trees the snow seems to be flowing away.

He freezes in his tracks, mesmerized at the strange sight. Then it comes to him.

"Avalanche!"

As he yells, the snow rushes away and out of sight over the slope.

A quarter of the distance down the run, Jeff is leaning into a turn when out of the corner of his eye he catches a glimpse of snow tumbling, blowing, rolling down. It must be Bob skiing up behind him, throwing up some of the powder, but it does seem like an awful lot.

He edges to a stop and gazes upward. A slope-wide flood of snow is cascading toward him. The forest along the side of the run is too far away. There is only one chance for escape.

He pushes off, dropping into a tuck position to ski as fast as possible, straight down. He takes aim on a medium-size tree in the middle of the slope. The sliding snow sweeps up from behind, lifting him like a wave rushing for the beach. He fights to keep his balance and then lunges for the tree. Locking his arms around the trunk, Jeff crouches behind the downhill side as a thousand snowballs pelt him all at once, tearing at him, trying to pull him away. Every muscle stretches and strains against the deluge pouring off the mountain. He keeps his head down as the snow sweeps over him.

About halfway down the slope, the guide skis to a stop. He waves his girlfriend on by. Elaine, Warner, and Dean continue on as well.

He mentally checks off four skiers. As he looks upslope, scanning for the remaining three, the torrent of snow is suddenly upon him. In an instant he is swept off his feet, careening downhill, tumbling, cartwheeling, bashing through trees, choking on snow.

Dean is the next to catch the movement above and behind. Checking back as he descends, he gets a quick image of the guide rolling in the avalanche down through the scrubby trees. Farther left than anyone else in the party, he races for the edge of the run and the safety of the forest.

Elaine is skiing a few turns ahead of Warner when she stops to take a break about three-quarters of the way down. Turning to look for the rest of the party, she struggles to make sense of the scene. Only yards away, the whole slope is in motion.

Realization and reaction occur in the same moment.

"Avalanche!"

Warner hears her cry. He twists his head to look just as his legs are kicked from under him. A wedge of snow plows downward. Skis and poles go flying. Tumbling like a rag doll in the flowing snow, Warner sees his world go light and dark with each rotation as mountain changes places with sky.

Elaine has a second longer to react. She turns to race for the forest. Catching her out in the open, the snow knocks her flat.

Dean watches from the shelter of the forest, unbelieving, as the avalanche kicks Warner off his feet, then buries his mother. He concentrates on where she disappears, marking the location with his eyes.

The first wave flows around Elaine's body in a liquid state, then instantly solidifies, immobilizing her arms and legs. She can feel the vibrations of a second wave rolling over her. Snow keeps piling up as the light fades.

Fear jags through her mind. Breathing comes fast and shallow as panic rises.

She fights it off, willing herself to breathe more slowly. She can't move to clear breathing space around her mouth or nose. She can't dig for the surface. The weight of the snow presses down.

This is it. I am going to die.

· · · — — — · · ·

Back at the top of the hill, with the snowslide running out of sight, Rob goes into search mode, switching his avalanche transceiver from transmit to receive. Everyone in his group is wearing one. If anyone is buried he can zero in on their position by listening for the signal, a high pitch that gets louder as the searcher gets closer.

Just over the edge of the slope, he skies off the crown. A slab of snow nearly three feet thick has cut loose. A few yards down he finds Bob laid out on the surface. The snow fractured right under his skis. He was able to grab on to one of the stunted trees as the avalanche swept out from underneath him, taking his ski poles with it.

Rob continues down, looking for survivors, as Bob gathers himself to follow.

· · · — — — · · ·

When the snow stops pelting Jeff, he stands to find snow up to his knees. He calls for the other members of the group.

The air is still and quiet.

Am I the only survivor?

Then the yelling begins. Voices cry out from both above and below.

He hurriedly clears the snow from around his feet to find a ski gone. With no time to look for missing equipment, he switches his transceiver to receive. He zigzags down the slope, skiing on one foot, post-holing through the snow with the other, listening carefully for any signal the transceiver might catch. His eyes scan the surface for a glove, a ski pole, anything that might be a sign of someone buried.

He finds a ski from the guide and stabs it upright in the snow to mark the spot. The transceiver isn't picking up a signal, so he continues downhill.

· · · — — — · · ·

When the tumbling stops, Warner is covered with snow. He pushes down with his hands and emerges, balls of ice rolling off his back. His skis and poles are gone. His pack stayed on throughout the chaos.

He looks uphill to find a landmark and get his bearings. The vision in his left eye is blurred, all double images. He can't seem to squint the eye clear no matter how he blinks. Blood oozes from cuts above the eye. If he moves his jaw, he can hear a strange grinding noise.

He calls out. Dean answers from some fifty yards upslope. He is moving across the avalanche debris with his transceiver, calling urgently for Warner to come and help.

Warner snaps out of his haze. Elaine was right in front of him. Now she is nowhere to be seen. He runs up to join the search. The slope, once covered in two feet of light powder, is now a solid surface.

Training is the only thing that keeps Dean and Warner calm and focused as they weave across the jumbled snow in a search pattern, listening for the electronic signal to get louder as a buried victim comes in range. Somewhere beneath the surface, Elaine's life is seeping away with every second. The signal becomes loud and clear. Out of their packs come shovels and probes. They dig like madmen.

Two feet below the surface they aren't finding anything. They hold the transceiver down in the hole. The signal is even stronger. Warner digs deeper, heaving great shovel-loads of snow out of the hole. Dean carefully pushes the long aluminum avalanche probe down through the excavation, working to zero in on his mother under all that debris.

Four feet below the surface, the probe hits something solid.

They both go back to digging like crazy. Snow flies out of the hole. Finally an arm appears. The shovels are thrown aside and they quickly scrape with their fingers, working to uncover Elaine's head. Fear of a second avalanche roaring down drives them harder. They have to get her out and into the safety of the trees.

As they carefully brush the snow away from her face, they can see that her skin is blue. She is unresponsive, and bleeding from a gash in her lip. Blood seeps from a wound on the side of her head.

Dean uses his hands to keep snow from falling in Elaine's face and yells at her while Warner works to uncover the rest of her body.

"Mum, breathe; Mum, you're still alive; Mum, keep breathing, you're still alive."

With her upper body uncovered, Warner grabs under her arms and tries to pull, but it's as if her legs are encased in cement.

He goes back to digging. Dean continues yelling for his mother to breathe.

Suddenly she coughs out a mouthful of snow and blood and takes a breath.

· · · — — — · · ·

The first person Jeff encounters is the guide. He has been spit out of the avalanche and sits on the surface, upslope and out of sight of the skiers below. His leg must be broken, because it isn't working well enough for him to stand. He is alert, breathing, and otherwise uninjured. All his equipment has been swept away. The guide tells Jeff to keep moving and help with the efforts below.

Jeff arrives at the base of the slope as Elaine is pulled from a grave-size hole. Her skin is still tinged blue. She is breathing and conscious, but not talking. Dean and Warner support her as she stumbles across the avalanche path and over to the edge of the forest. They get to work on a fire. One of them pulls a down jacket out of her pack and gets her into it. She starts shivering uncontrollably as her body fights to warm up.

Everyone is accounted for as Rob and Bob arrive and the guide's girlfriend comes up from where she escaped the avalanche in the forest below. The first-aid response begins in earnest.

Rob bounces back and forth, assessing injuries. The left side of Warner's face looks as if he has been hit with a baseball bat. One of the trees must have caught him as he tumbled down the slope. They get a gauze pad over the injured eye and wrap a bandage around his head to stop the bleeding.

The guide's femur appears broken. They splint the leg with a couple of ski poles, dig a platform out of the snow, and try to make him as comfortable as possible.

Elaine's ear is badly torn and her lip punctured, but she seems to be warming up.

When there is nothing left to do except to call for help, they realize the guide's pack is missing, and with it the radio.

When Warner hears that the guide's radio is gone, he realizes why he decided to bring his own along at the last moment. With the guide yelling out radio frequencies from where he lies on the slope above, Dean tries to make contact with rescue authorities. The signal is just not getting through.

There is a base radio back at the hut on the mountain above them. Jeff is the strongest member of the party. He and Bob will have to break trail back up the mountain, try to make contact from the hut, and then bring the rescue sleds. The group may have to get out of this mess without any help.

Not long after Jeff and Bob disappear into the woods, Dean is spinning through the different frequencies when he picks up a radio voice from down in the valley. His call for help is quickly relayed out to the authorities, and the rescue machinery is thrown into motion.

Two hours later the first helicopter arrives, circling over the avalanche slope.

The pilot doesn't want to set down at the accident site. He is concerned about the unstable snow. Over the radio he tells them he will land on a nearby lake, frozen over in the dead of winter. They will have to climb up and meet him there.

Dean takes off, breaking trail through hip-deep snow to clear a path for Elaine and Warner.

Elaine has warmed up and seems to be getting stronger.

Warner is faring much worse. With the crisis past, his head injury has begun to sap his strength. The two of them struggle through the forest, following Dean's path as they climb two hundred feet up to the waiting chopper.

A medic meets them halfway, administers oxygen, and leads them to the aircraft. Before long they are flying out and down to the community hospital in Kaslo, B.C.

Jeff and Bob make it back with the litter in time to help haul the guide downhill to a lake below the avalanche, where an additional helicopter has landed.

After picking up the guide, the second chopper drops into the scene, hovering just long enough to load the extra packs and other equipment lying around for transport back to the hut.

By ski and by helicopter, the remaining members of the party arrive back at the hut before nightfall.

· · · — — — · · ·

The staff at the small hospital in Kaslo takes one look at Warner's broken face and Eileen's shredded ear and both of them are placed in an ambulance headed for Trail Regional Hospital in the city of Nelson.

While Eileen spends three hours in surgery to repair her ear, Warner is diagnosed with five fractures of his left eye orbit. He is shuttled to Kelowna for surgery.

The guide is found to have a fractured femur and spends several days in Trail Regional Hospital as well.

The rest of the group flies out of the mountains as scheduled the day after the avalanche.

They all recover to ski again. But all have stepped back a bit from the aggressive backcountry skiing they used to pursue.

To this day the six friends wonder at how easily they gave away so much of their personal safety. For a few brief moments they set aside all their knowledge and training to rely on the judgment of a single person they didn't even really know. They had the tools to evaluate risk, but even then there was no real guarantee.

Looking back on the incident, two things remain clear. The urge to ski can overpower logic in borderline conditions. The price to pay may be more than most can afford.

His mind stumbles for an explanation as he is pulled under in a blind confusion of frothing, foaming water.

CHAPTER 6

OUT OF THE BLUE

E arly on an April morning along the Oregon coast, a part-time surf bum, part-time surfing filmmaker, and part-time heavy equipment operator named John is southbound on Highway 101. A clear blue sky arches overhead and the first real warmth of spring is chasing off the damp chill of a long Northwest winter.

As his car motors over the crest of Spanish Head south of Lincoln City, the scene through the windshield is a surfer's dream. The blue-green Pacific is as smooth as a sheet of glass to the horizon. A steady, even swell rolls in from the west, angling toward the coastline. Powerful waves crest and curl down a long, straight stretch of sand beach.

These are rare days and John can barely contain himself as he pulls in to the parking lot above Gleneden Beach. About a hundred yards offshore, out beyond the breakers, four or five surfers are catching rides.

He steps quickly from his car, pulls on his wet suit, grabs a sleek, black long-board, and jogs down off the bluff to the beach. The white sound of surf mixes with salt air as he wades into the ocean to begin the long paddle out through the breaking waves, to the set zone where only the biggest rollers crest and the best rides begin.

Joining the other surfers offshore, John finds a friend, Randy, one of the locals. They float together astride their boards, catching up on surf talk, always watching for incoming rollers. Seagulls hover here and there, screeching away. Seals occasionally surface, curious about their human company. Both men ride a few waves, then Randy calls it a day and heads in to go to work.

The other surfers head in as well and for a while John finds himself surfing solo. Perfectly shaped rollers rise up off the western horizon. No one else is in sight. John catches any wave that suits him, dropping off each crest to race the curl down the beach, snapping a quick turn out as the wave collapses in a wash of foam.

Taking a break between sets, John sits up on his board, riding the swell up and down. The surface of the water swirls nearby.

Just a seal, he says to himself.

Not far off, a school of fish jumps out of the water.

With no warning a viselike grip clamps John's right thigh to his surfboard. He has a millisecond to wonder, *Why is this seal attacking me?* Then he and his board disappear below the surface.

His mind stumbles for an explanation as he is pulled under in a blind confusion of frothing, foaming water. The white heat of pain shooting up from his thigh snaps him into action. He begins hammering his fist down on whatever has sunk its teeth into his body.

Four or five feet down in the blurry darkness, as he pounds on the unseen something, the pressure on his leg suddenly releases. John thrashes back up to the surface. Breaking out into open air he gasps for breath, paddling to stay on the surface. As his eyes clear, a large gray back surfaces at his side. In an instant he recognizes the triangular dorsal fin. He can't see the head or tail. With adrenaline pumping and his heart hammering, he does the only thing he can think to do. He beats on the shark with his fist. Three or four times he brings his fist down on the sandpaper skin.

With a flick of its massive tail the shark submerges and is gone.

Dazed from the attack, John floats in the open water, thanking God that the shark has left.

Then he is yanked under again like a puppet on a string. The leash that runs from a strap on his ankle to his surfboard has gone taut, pulling him down as the shark dives with the cord still in its mouth. A roar of bubbles fills his ears as John fights to hold his breath, the light fading as the surface recedes. He struggles to double over so he can tear the strap from his ankle and escape. Between the damage to his leg and the overwhelming pull of the submerging shark, John cannot reach the strap tab. As he is pulled deeper and deeper a sudden calm comes over him. The tension in his body dissipates. His final thoughts are of resignation: *Well, this is the way I am going to go.*

As he relaxes into death the leash snaps, severed by the shark's teeth. The will to live screams through his brain and he fights his way to the surface a second time, his lungs bursting. Breaking out on the surface he frantically searches for his board, spotting it twenty feet away, upside down. There will be no waiting for the shark to return this time. He strokes over and in one motion flips the board and pulls himself up on top. There are no waves to help him make the run across more than one hundred yards of open water back to land. Fear and adrenaline course through his body as he pulls for the beach with a strength he's never felt before.

· · · — — — · · ·

When the waves are good, word travels fast in the surfing community. Friend and fellow surfer Ali received a call from John last night giving him a heads-up on what promised to be one of the best surfing days yet this year. Within hours Ali had enlisted Parish, another surfing buddy. They both arranged to take the morning off and head for the coast.

Arriving at Gleneden Beach, they immediately recognize John's car and know who the solo surfer is out there on the water. After watching John carve a few waves, Parish needs no more convincing. He pulls on his wet suit and heads down the path to the beach.

Ali stays up on the bluff to study the waves a little longer. His gaze shifts back and forth, looking for riptides or obstacles in the surf, always returning to John. Then John and his board disappear beneath the waves.

Ali stares hard at the spot where John vanished. A few seconds pass, then he screams down to Parish, "Don't go in the water. Don't go in the water!"

Parish is wading knee-deep in the surf when he hears the yelling and turns to see Ali pointing out to where John was surfing.

As Parish hesitates, Ali sees John reappear, his board surfacing nearby.

By the time John makes it back to shore, Ali and Parish have waded out to help as he staggers from the ocean. Blood oozing from gashes in the thigh of his wet suit tells the tale even as John answers their unbelieving looks, "It was a shark, a shark bit me!" Parish grabs the surfboard, and he and Ali support John between them as they struggle out of the water and up the beach toward the parking lot.

They ease John into the backseat of his station wagon, wrapping a towel around his injured thigh, blood smearing on the seats.

With Ali at the wheel and John yelling for him to drive like hell for the hospital, the car roars out of the parking lot and up Highway 101 toward Lincoln City. Soon a police cruiser is in pursuit, sirens wailing and lights flashing.

"Screw them and get to the hospital," John bellows from the backseat.

But Ali slows down enough for the cop to pull alongside.

"What's going on?" the officer demands.

John yells through the open window, "Hey, I just got bit by a shark, you bastard!"

A few more words pass quickly between the cars. When it becomes clear that the speeding station wagon is carrying an injured man to the emergency room, the cop pulls ahead. Ali presses the accelerator all the way down and they roar through Lincoln City, now with a police escort.

· · · — — — · · ·

Dr. Bruce Watanabe's routine at his orthopedic clinic in Lincoln City is interrupted by a call from North Lincoln Hospital. As the surgeon on call, his help is needed with the victim of a shark attack.

Arriving in the emergency room he finds John lying on the gurney, giving hurried camera-angle instructions as Ali captures the injuries on video. The emergency room doctors have stabilized the wound, and John can't pass up the opportunity to grab some footage for his surfing video business.

Shooing Ali away, Watanabe inspects the series of deep punctures encircling John's upper right thigh and buttock. The bite narrowly missed severing the femoral artery because the shark had clamped down on the surfboard at the same time. The surfboard saved his leg, and his life. John is truly a lucky man.

· · · — — — · · ·

Three days and fifty stitches later, John is out of the hospital and recovering at home. A shark researcher, after measuring the circumference of the bite marks in John's board and the distance between the teeth, estimates the shark to be around eighteen feet long.

John's surfing buddies point to John's black surfboard as the cause for the attack, saying it looks just like a seal in the surf. John disagrees.

Anybody on a surfboard, he says, "looks just like a seal to something that is looking up. Whatever they see is backlit. Sharks and most fish don't see in color anyway."

"Everybody had this attitude that I was asking for trouble, so after the attack, just to prove a point, I had my next board painted with a gray and black spotted pattern, like a harbor seal. Then I put these big goo-goo eyes on the bottom just for fun."

John still surfs the Oregon coast near his home in Lincoln City and hasn't seen a shark since.

With nobody to tell him he is crazy, he grabs
the branches and swings over the edge.

CHAPTER 7

UP A CREEK

Walking the high routes in the Olympic Mountains of Washington state is to experience a balancing act on a tightwire of trail. This land, where dense primeval forests climb steep mountainsides to crumbling, craggy summits, rarely feels the footsteps of human visitors, and much of it never will. To leave the trails here is to experience terrain that is dangerous and difficult, that is only for the most foolhardy or determined.

Paul Nelson, poet, promoter of the spoken word, and radio show host, heads out on a Friday afternoon in early September for Olympic National Park, a three-hour drive west of Seattle on the Olympic Peninsula. The park is a spiritual place for Paul, and this pilgrimage is becoming an annual event. All his cares float away on this warm Indian summer afternoon as he savors the coming week of backpacking just the way he likes it—no real itinerary, no plans, just take things as they come.

Paul's partner and customary backcountry companion, Stephanie, could not join him due to a teaching commitment. When they first met, they had an instant connection, a mutual love of wilderness. Initially Stephanie, a seasoned backcountry hiker, assumed that Paul was equally experienced in the outdoors. On their first trip together into the Olympics last September, she was surprised to learn that he had started backpacking only a year before.

Before leaving, Paul outlined for Stephanie his general plan for the week. He would drive into the park by way of the Elwha River entrance and hike in to Boulder Creek Campground for the first night. From there his route would take him over Appleton Pass to the High Divide and maybe up to the Blue Glacier on Mount Olympus, a place they had visited together on last year's trip.

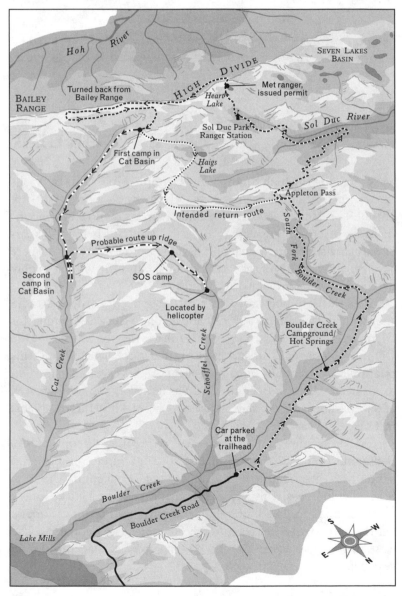

60

Stephanie was a little concerned about Paul hiking solo, but he had been to most of these places and they are on popular routes. There would be other hikers around.

"When should I expect you back?"

"Next Wednesday, Thursday, Friday at the latest."

• • • — — — • • •

Parking his car at the Appleton Pass trailhead, Paul is on familiar ground as he hikes the two and a half miles to the Boulder Creek Campground and Olympic Hot Springs. Setting up his tent, he strikes up a conversation with other backpackers. He is in his element reciting poetry, sharing food, and discussing life and the finer aspects of the local thermal pools as the afternoon turns to evening.

Paul is up early Saturday morning for a quick soak in the hot springs. He declines the breakfast offered by two of his acquaintances from the night before and leaves them with a copy of a favorite poem. Under a lowering gray sky he shoulders his pack and heads south, deeper into the park.

Four miles down the trail, with a misty rain beginning to sift down through the trees, Paul opts not to risk the exposed heights of Appleton Pass. He sets up camp in the forest just below the final switchbacks.

Sunday morning the weather is still questionable, so Paul leaves his tent and most of his gear in camp while he hikes up the switchbacks to reconnoiter.

At the high point of 5,100-foot Appleton Pass, Paul finds a place to sit and watch the clouds weave wreaths around nearby peaks. As he recalls previous visits to this, his favorite Olympics locale, two hikers march by. Their massive packs are loaded with ice axes, crampons, and other equipment that labels them as serious mountaineers. Paul hails them over. A short conversation reveals their destination to be the Bailey Range, a day or two farther into the park down the High Divide Trail.

Paul has heard of this celebrated group of mountains, roughly in the center of the park. Veteran Olympics adventurers know them as the centerpiece of the largest trackless expanse in Washington state. The idea of exploring untrammeled wilderness calls to Paul just as it has to so many before him.

Before he has a chance to ask more, the hikers move on as the clouds begin to lift. The ice-covered massif of 7,168-foot Mount Olympus, the highest peak in the park, becomes visible to the south. Paul takes this as a good sign and heads down off the pass to pack up and get back on the trail.

Late afternoon finds him setting up camp in the upper reaches of the Sol Duc River Valley. The lightweight tent he purchased for the trip is up, with his gear inside. His food bag is safely stored for the night, hanging on a bear wire strung between two trees. Paul sits next to Bridge Creek filtering water, easing into the evening hours, after a day of rambling down rocky paths from the heights of Appleton Pass.

A backpacker striding down the trail catches his attention. Eager for conversation, Paul asks about his destination as a second backpacker appears.

"Where are you headed?"

Stan and Ken are heading to the Bailey Range for a few days of off-trail exploring.

This is too much for Paul. "Oh man, I am envious."

"Why don't you come along?"

"I don't know, I just set up my camp."

"Come on, how many times are you going to get an offer like this?"

The two books Paul has brought along flash through his mind: Walt Whitman's *Leaves of Grass* and Calvin Hall's *Primer of Jungian Psychology*. Jung coined the term "synchronicity" to describe a belief that meaning can be found in seemingly coincidental events. In *Leaves of Grass* Whitman also discusses the topic. *Aha! The Bailey Range for a second time today. Here it is,* he thinks to himself, *synchronicity. I can't pass this up.*

"Okay," Paul says, "can you wait until I take down my camp?"

They say they will meet him at Heart Lake, about a mile down the trail toward the High Divide.

Paul hesitates. The least they could do is wait for him, but the power of synchronicity and the excitement of visiting the Bailey Range shove his misgivings aside. He hurriedly takes his tent down, retrieves his food, and starts off after his newfound companions.

Not far down the trail, Paul encounters a wilderness ranger based out of the Sol Duc Park Ranger Station.

"How are you doing?" she asks.

"Good, good."

"Just making my rounds. Do you have a backcountry permit?"

The idea of needing a permit to enter public land has never set well with Paul. Call it a form of civil disobedience. He feigns ignorance.

"Oh, I paid at the front."

She is a patient ranger. She informs Paul that the main reason for the permit is to let her know where to start searching for him, or his remains, if he does not make it out as planned.

Bagged, tagged, and only slightly delayed, Paul catches up with Stan and Ken at Heart Lake. He mentions that the ranger wanted to know if the two of them have a permit.

"Oh yeah, yeah, some guys ahead of us have ours," Ken chuckles, then raises his hand to point: "Turn around and take a look." Above them a herd of elk ranges across the mountainside, grazing in the twilight.

Stan and Ken are ready to get moving as well.

"Come on, we know of this great campsite on the High Divide."

With the day, and his desire to keep walking, fading fast, Paul follows them down the trail.

Bruce's Roost is their destination, a perch high above the Hoh River Valley that looks across to a sky-filling view. The north face of Mount Olympus seems posed to spill its glaciers right into camp. They arrive to find the site taken. Salutations are exchanged with the two people camped there, then Stan, Ken, and Paul move farther east to an alternate site. As night falls and stars begin winking in the cool blue of a late-summer sky, they share food and talk in excited tones about bushwhacking into the Bailey Range in the morning.

· · · — — — · · ·

Monday dawns and it is not long before Stan, Ken, and Paul are heading east on the High Divide Trail. Stan and Ken are not letting up on the pace. Paul is left behind once again. Blown-down tree trunks lace like intertwined fingers across the trail. While clambering through the tangle, Paul smacks his head hard.

Stunned, he stops for a moment and puts his hand to his head, feeling for blood. His hiking partners are nowhere to be seen.

Paul finally catches up with Stan and Ken at the eastern end of the High Divide Trail. From where they sit, the going becomes notoriously treacherous along an unmarked route with stomach-fluttering drop-offs.

Stan and Ken take off and Paul is left to fend for himself once more. With the mountainside dropping off precipitously to the south, the slightest misstep sends little adrenaline shots into Paul's bloodstream. Somehow, as he scrambles hand over foot up and down the steeps, pushing through brushy wind-warped trees and stumbling on ankle-twisting rocks, he loses his wristwatch and then his diamond-stud earring. As he moves out onto the razor-edge ridge known as the catwalk, connecting Cat Peak with Mount Carrie, his walking stick, inscribed with carvings from past adventures, slips from his grip and tumbles off down the mountainside.

As he watches the walking stick career into the valley below, Paul hesitates. It occurs to him that he could fall and that Stan and Ken probably wouldn't know for half an hour that he was missing. They might never know. The Bailey Range is not worth killing himself over. With a few choice words for his unseen hiking partners, he decides to retreat.

Moments later, across the distance, he hears a voice calling out to him, "Paul, are you okay?"

Holding back his planned remarks, he answers, "Yeah, I'm turning back. Sorry to hold you guys up."

Back on the High Divide, Paul considers his options. There is a way trail he has heard about. It's not an official trail so it doesn't show up on any maps, but it would save him from backtracking through the Sol Duc River Valley. He's pretty sure the route starts nearby, cuts down and across Cat Basin, and then climbs up to Appleton Pass, where he can connect with the route back to his car.

Just then he encounters the two hikers who were camped at Bruce's Roost the previous evening, and he asks them about the Cat Basin route.

"Oh yeah," one of them says, "there are plenty of trails down in Cat Basin, many trails."

This cinches the deal for Paul. No more bushwhacking. If there's a trail, it's going to be easy. With his plans coming together quickly, Paul heads back west along the High Divide Trail, thoughts of Stan, Ken, and the Bailey Range fading fast in his mind.

· · · — — — · · ·

Tuesday morning finds Paul camped along the trail into Cat Basin, about half a mile from the High Divide. Sunlight filters through the fir trees, chasing the chill out of the air. Inspired by the pristine wilderness surrounding him, he sings a welcome to the day, taught to him by a Native American mentor.

The sound attracts a passing hiker and a conversation ensues. The man knows the way trail to Appleton Pass. He has hiked it from north to south, and he remembers a little cabin not too far down the trail.

Now Paul has a landmark to help him find the way. He packs up his gear, slings on his pack, and continues into Cat Basin. Not long afterward, the remains of a cabin come into view, a ruin of wood collapsed after many winter snows. Confident that he is on the right route, Paul follows the trail past the cabin and into the trees beyond.

The trail fades quickly but Paul continues trending to the north-northwest in the direction he feels he needs to go. As the bushwhacking becomes more difficult, Paul veers off slightly to the northeast, forced in that direction by dense thickets.

He comes across a creek flowing northeast. He looks at his map.

This creek doesn't make any sense to him. The only stream he can find on the map near his location would be the upper reaches of the Sol Duc River, but it flows due west. This just doesn't seem right according to the map, but at this point it is probably best to keep moving. Sooner or later he will come across the trail and it will lead him back toward the west. With unswerving faith Paul follows the creek down into Cat Basin.

Tuesday evening, with no trail in sight and the sunlight fading, he finds a level spot by the creek. He's not really sure where he is, but there's water and there's firewood. He smooths out the sand alongside the creek for better sleeping, sets up camp, has a meal, hangs his bear bag, and falls asleep to the sound of water rippling over stone.

· · · — — — · · ·

Wednesday morning Paul wakes up energized, trying to find the positives in his situation. He is on his own in the wilderness, finding his way, surviving, bushwhacking where few people have gone before.

As he begins the day's trek, the brush gets so thick he puts on gloves to protect against the palm-shredding thorns of devil's club. He follows the creek because it creates a path of least resistance through a forest so dense it is like being trapped between solid walls of vegetation. Sometimes he has to cross the creek on logs, other times he wades up to his waist.

He hasn't come across the trail yet and the creek is still trending northeast. He needs to go northwest but the thick brush along the creek won't allow an escape.

Finally an opening in the forest leads to a talus slope on the west side of the basin. Paul climbs out of the claustrophobic creek bottom.

If I can make my way up the west side of the basin I will see the path, he tells himself.

So he begins to climb. When the talus slope tails off into a thicket, he grabs the branches of mountain alder and cedar, using them like ropes to pull himself up through the brush. At times his feet cannot reach the ground, so he steps on bent-over tree trunks like the rungs of a ladder. On steep rock faces he swings over open space, hanging onto tree limbs to keep from falling, climbing higher, hand over hand. It is exhausting work and soon he realizes he is not going to get to the top this day. On the uphill side of two ancient cedar trees, he finds a flat area large enough for his sleeping bag.

Paul makes a dismaying discovery: His trail map is missing. He recalls that he made many notes in his journal during the day as he prayed to find the way. The journal and the map shared the same cargo pocket in his pants. Apparently one of the times he pulled out the journal, the map came with it and fell to the ground. In all the brush and sweat and climbing, he failed to notice.

The thought that he might be seriously lost dawns in his mind.

Not to worry, he tells himself. *The weather has been warm and clear. I have plenty of food. If I keep climbing to the west, sooner or later I'll spot the trail.*

A magnificent harvest moon rises into the night sky, the most incredible full moon he has ever seen. The view from his perch is surreal, the rugged landscape of rock and forest illuminated with silver moon-glow as he lies beneath the cedars, alone with his thoughts, high on the western edge of Cat Basin.

· · —— —— —— · ·

When Wednesday evening rolls around and Paul does not show up at their home south of Seattle, Stephanie is not concerned. She remembers him telling her to expect him back "Wednesday, Thursday, Friday at the latest." She figured he would go crazy being by himself and come home as soon as possible, but he probably found other backpackers to hang out with after a day or two.

· · —— —— —— · ·

On Thursday morning Paul continues his climb up the western side of Cat Basin. He complements the couple of handfuls of granola that he had for breakfast with mountain blueberries. Stephanie taught him about mountain blueberries on a previous trip, and he is thankful for the tasty distraction as he pushes his way higher and higher through the tangle of trees and brush.

Cresting what he thought was the high point, Paul finds much more of the mountain above him. Under his breath he repeats what has become his mantra over the past two days—*Let me be safe, let me find the way*—and keeps climbing.

High on the ridge, his ascent ends at the base of an impassable band of cliffs. As he traverses to the north across a steep, rocky ridge, stones kick loose and rattle down the slope. Thoughts of the catwalk come back to haunt him.

Suddenly his right calf begins to cramp. Paul ran out of water this morning. Now his body is showing the early signs of dehydration. Even if he can spot the trail from the top of this ridge, there is no telling if the muscles in his legs will hold out long enough to get him there. He has to find something to drink fast.

The cliff band ends and he limps up to a saddle. A small snow-field on the far side glares white against the gray rock. *Melt snow to get water,* he thinks to himself as he climbs down off the ridge, looking to soothe a parched throat and fatigued body.

At the snowfield Paul quickly discovers that a pile of snow melts down to only a few cups of water. He begins to wonder how long his fuel supply will last.

There is no question now that he is lost. Without a map Paul can't even guess where he might be, and the elusive trail is not to be seen from his current perch in a rocky cirque.

It occurs to him that a rescue effort must have started by now. *I said I would be back Wednesday or Thursday, and it's Thursday afternoon.*

A log lying in the snowfield catches his attention. A vague memory of an episode from the old *Gilligan's Island* TV show gives him an idea. If he dragged two more logs up here and put them at angles to the first, he could make a rough letter S. A few more logs and some rocks and he could create a complete SOS.

It doesn't take long to form the message in the snow. For a finishing touch, he adds a small cross at the top. Paul figures he needs all the help he can get.

This is all right. I could stay here. I'll ration my food. I've got snow for water. I can find a flat place to sleep.

Setting up camp, he finds his tent missing. Somewhere on that last climb up through the brush it must have fallen off his pack. Fortunately the weather is still warm and clear. He sets his self-inflating pad and sleeping bag out under the open sky.

In the afternoon, with time to spare, he climbs to a saddle above the snowfield. The view is stunning: wild country, high rock ridges, and steep talus slopes, but no sign of a path. Disheartened yet still upbeat, he settles on a plan. He'll just hang out for a while back by the snowfield, finish the book on Jungian psychology, start reading Walt Whitman, and wait for the helicopters.

· · · — — — · · ·

When Paul does not come home on Thursday, Stephanie is surprised but not worried. Normally Paul likes to give himself a day before easing back into the working world as host of a Saturday morning jazz program on the radio, but he may really be enjoying himself.

. . . —— —— —— . . .

Friday passes slowly for Paul. He remembers Stephanie showing him how to use the mirror on his compass as a signaling device. He tries to reflect light from the sun at airplanes that pass in the distance, thinking they might be searching for him. He finishes his Jung book and decides to climb to a second saddle.

From the high point he sees the same craggy mountain landscape spread out before him and no sign of a trail.

Boy, I am really in trouble.

On his way back to the snowfield he comes up with a second plan.

What I have to do is get back down to the creek in Cat Basin, backtrack upstream, go west, and then I'll find that way trail.

That night, as the seriousness of his situation becomes clear, he thinks of his nine-year-old daughter and of Stephanie. He has to survive for them. He prays to his God, *Have some compassion for this arrogant, ignorant man who thought he could do something that was beyond his capabilities.*

. . . —— —— —— . . .

When night falls on Friday and there is still no word, Stephanie is very concerned. Paul has never missed his Saturday on-air shift at the public radio station in Tacoma.

She calls Doc, Paul's business partner at their spoken-word performance lab, a center for live poetry performances and writing classes, south of Seattle.

"Maybe he didn't plan well," Doc says. "He was too far in and realized he couldn't hike out in the dark. He probably is planning on getting up really early tomorrow morning to hike like mad and then drive like mad to get to the radio station."

Stephanie hangs up the phone, hoping this is true. As the night wears on she decides to call Olympic National Park. The park office is closed and no one answers the phone.

· · · — — — · · ·

On Saturday, despite his new plan to backtrack, Paul holds out hope for helicopters. His patience lasts through a long day with no aircraft sightings. When evening rolls around he is completely disgusted.

Forget it, he says to whoever might hear, *I'm just gonna go.*

He packs up what is left of his gear and starts off down the hill. Not far from camp his boots slip on the steep, brushy slope. In an instant he is sliding down toward a cliff edge. Thrashing around in fear for his life, he makes a last desperate grab. A lone blueberry bush stops his fall.

Breathing hard, Paul gathers himself above the cliff that would have been his end. He considers this a message from the gods: Stay one more night near the SOS.

Back at the snowfield, as he climbs into his sleeping bag for a ninth night under the stars, he makes a pact.

If the weather isn't clear enough in the morning for a helicopter to fly, then I have to head back to Cat Creek and find my own way out and not be a coward. I am going to save myself and not be a coward.

· · · — — — · · ·

Stephanie wakes up Saturday morning and calls Olympic National Park. She is routed to the Eagle Ranger Station in the Sol Duc River Valley. The ranger on duty begins the process of filling out a missing-person report. A few questions into the interview, the ranger, named Linda, recognizes this missing person. She had come across Paul last Tuesday while on duty at the Sol Duc Park Ranger Station.

"He hadn't registered for a backcountry permit," Linda says over the phone. "He was following these two other guys who eluded me." She relates how she issued Paul a permit that had him camping on the High Divide for the next three days, with a return over Appleton Pass and out the Boulder Creek Trailhead by Thursday, two days ago.

"He said he might not stick to the itinerary because the two guys ahead of him offered to take him to the Bailey Range."

Stephanie has her maps out. At the eastern end of the High Divide Trail she finds the Bailey Range. She doesn't see any trails. "Oh God."

"Well, you know the Bailey Range has been socked in with fog for the last two days," Linda says. "They're probably just hunkered down waiting for the fog to lift."

She goes on to explain that when hikers are thought to be in the Baileys, a twenty-four-hour grace period is often applied before they are reported overdue. The time it takes to get out of this remote area is easy to underestimate.

Stephanie makes the point that Paul's radio work is not like an everyday kind of job. He hasn't missed a show in twenty years, and according to the permit he should have been out of the Bailey Range well before the fog came.

Linda is noncommittal. She says the first thing they will do is check the trailhead to see if his car is still parked there.

The hours tick by Saturday morning as Stephanie debates what to do. Maybe Paul has shown up at the last minute. She calls the public radio station in Tacoma. When they tell her he is a no-show, her last hope is gone.

If the rangers are not going to take this seriously, she might just have to pack up her gear and go look for him herself.

She calls back to the ranger station to see if they have found his car yet. They are short-staffed and haven't had time to check. She is passed to another ranger. She talks with him for a few minutes, and once again there is a noncommittal response. Yes, Paul is overdue, but at this time any search is a low priority. We just don't have enough people, the ranger tells Stephanie; we will check the parking lot for his car; our rangers in the field will ask hikers if they have seen him. Stephanie e-mails this ranger a photograph of Paul.

Stephanie works the phone all day Saturday, trying to find someone at the park who will take her seriously. As far as she can tell, they are treating her like a hysterical housewife whose husband didn't tell her what he was doing. Finally one of the rangers gives her an after-hours number. At 7 P.M. she calls and talks to a dispatcher. The search and rescue operations chief, a fellow named Dan, calls her back.

It all spills out, all the information she has been offering to anyone who would listen earlier in the day. Paul did not show up for work. His friends, co-workers, and family are very concerned that he is in trouble in the backcountry. She relates what it was like when she and Paul were in the Cascade Mountains in July. Paul would just walk down a trail without knowing anything about it or checking out the topography. He wouldn't check his location at trail intersections or make sure he knew where he was on the map.

Dan listens to her. He asks a lot of questions about Paul—about his physical appearance, his equipment, the way he thinks. Stephanie tells him everything she can remember—the clothing he took with him, the compass she purchased for him, the stove, his tent, the food he packed.

She is bluntly honest when asked for a psychological profile. "He can be impulsive," she says, "He doesn't always think before he acts, but he has a lot of energy and he does have common sense, lots of it. He has a very good sense of direction, but he is not good at reading a topographic map. He doesn't know how to navigate with map and compass, but he will kick in when it is a question of survival."

Dan tells her he needs to gather more information from the rangers in the field. He will call her back in a few hours.

At 10 P.M. Dan calls to tell Stephanie they found Paul's car at the trailhead. He will start the search and rescue operation the following morning.

· · · — — — · · ·

Sunday dawns overcast and misty. As far as Paul can tell, visibility is far below helicopter standards. He packs up and heads out from his snowfield for the second time. Today's plan is to backtrack to Cat Creek and retrace his steps. He works his way down into the drainage, losing altitude quickly.

A twenty-foot-high drop-off stops his descent. Pacing back and forth above the edge, Paul can find only one way down. Tree branches hang over the edge. A second tree is just out of reach midway down. He could lower himself over the edge with the top branches, let go, grab the second tree on the way down, let the second set of branches stretch out, and then drop the rest of the distance.

With nobody to tell him he is crazy, he grabs the branches, swings over the edge, and makes the tree-grabbing descent without a hitch. Within minutes Paul is down at a creek drinking the finest water he has ever known.

Rehydrated and ready to go, he starts walking south, in his mind backtracking up Cat Creek. Turned around, confused and without a map, he has no way of knowing that he is walking up Schoeffel Creek, a completely separate drainage just west over a ridge from Cat Creek.

The terrain just isn't as he remembers it from his trip down Cat Creek. When an unfamiliar waterfall blocks his path, he leaves the creek bottom and climbs the west side of the basin. Entering dense vegetation, he pushes through scrubby trees and bushes, leaves and branches slapping his face, up to someplace where he might see something.

In the midst of the thicket, completely hidden from view, he suddenly hears the sound of rotor blades echoing around in the basin.

There is no way to get out in the open. He fights his way to a small clearing. The helicopter is across the drainage and way up high, by the snowfield SOS. The aircraft passes nearby three times. In desperation Paul tries to signal by wrapping toilet paper on a stick and lighting it on fire.

With the afternoon light fading, the helicopter is forced to leave after searching the area for only a few minutes.

Paul finds a place to camp.

They will be back in the morning, he tells himself. *I will get out where they can see me, and they will be back in the morning.*

· · · — — — · · ·

Dan checks in with Stephanie late Sunday afternoon. "They haven't found him."

All of the hope she had been carrying washes away in a wave of despair. She breaks down and sobs.

Dan tries to reassure her. "He did one smart thing. He turned back from the Bailey Range."

Dan tells her they have talked with other hikers who came across Paul on Monday and Tuesday out on the High Divide. He had turned back and was last seen heading for a way trail to Appleton Pass. Rangers are on the ground now in Cat Basin, looking for clues.

Stephanie is not sure this is good news. She tells Dan that Paul has never been off trail before. She recalls a line from a poem Paul wrote about a scramble they did on their last trip to the Olympics: "Bushwhacking at 6,000 feet / What were we thinking?" That had just been a short walk above the tree line.

Her darkest imaginings flash visions across her mind of Paul lying in a tangle of forest—injured, unable to get water, or worse yet, dead.

· · · — — — · · ·

The rangers on the ground have been tracking Paul into Cat Basin since Saturday. On Saturday evening they found his campsite next to the creek where he slept Tuesday evening. On Sunday they followed his tracks along Cat Creek through dense brush and incredibly rugged terrain.

When they check in with search and rescue headquarters Sunday evening, Dan tells them an SOS was spotted. While returning to base late in the afternoon, a search helicopter just happened to see the letters on a snowfield high in a remote cirque on the ridge that forms the western boundary of Cat Basin. Dan thinks Paul is up there.

"Camp for the night and first thing tomorrow cut along the base of that slope for footprints. Find a route where he went up that ridge."

A short debate over the SOS ensues. Paul's tracks have been leading in a steady direction to the northeast along the banks of the creek. Although the rangers are impressed with the obstacles that Paul has been able to surmount on his way downstream, it just doesn't make sense that he is up in that cirque.

The head ranger in the field tells Dan straight out, "I tell you I am standing here looking up at the ridge and I don't believe he could have climbed it."

Dan is insistent.

The rangers set up camp for the night along the creek so they can be ready to go first thing in the morning.

• • • — — — • • •

Stephanie lies in bed Sunday night wracking her brain. Maybe there is some little thing, some clue that she neglected to mention. She calls Dan one last time.

"Good news," he says. "We found an SOS on a snowfield at the head of the Schoeffel Creek drainage." Dan says he has a feeling that Paul will be found in the morning.

The hope comes flooding back in. She hangs up the phone and goes back to her maps. To get to that snowfield Paul had to cross a high, rugged ridge on the west side of Cat Basin. From the remote snowfield she traces the flow of Schoeffel Creek with her finger two miles downhill, right to where it empties into Boulder Creek, only a quarter mile from the trailhead where Paul's car is parked.

• • • — — — • • •

Monday morning dawns and Paul is sitting out in the middle of a rock field, waiting. Forty-five minutes go by with no sign of a helicopter. He decides to go back to the creek for more water.

Relocating to a large boulder in the middle of Schoeffel Creek, Paul sets up where he can easily be seen. He prepares a meal as he waits. It occurs to him that the media may be involved at this point, so he does a little laundry. The least he can do is look decent.

In the midst of his chores, with half his laundry drying and half still in the wash, he hears the *whup whup whup* of an approaching helicopter. He quickly stuffs all his belongings in his backpack and signals the helicopter with his compass mirror.

With nowhere to land in the rugged drainage, the helicopter hovers over him. A weighted yellow banner is tossed down.

Paul retrieves the banner and finds a message: "Stay here, help will come soon."

The helicopter leaves. Paul goes back to drying his laundry.

Moments later the chopper returns and a bag is lowered to him on a cable.

He unhooks the bag from the cable and the chopper pulls back to hover nearby. In the bag Paul finds a two-way radio wrapped in padding. A voice is broadcasting through the speaker.

"Paul, Paul. Are you okay? Just press the button and talk."

He finds the button, thumbs it down.

"Yeah, I'm okay. I just want to say I am really sorry for putting you guys through this as a result of my stupidity."

"Don't worry about it. We're glad you're okay. We need you to sit tight for a while. We can't pick you up where you are with our helicopter. We have a helicopter coming up from Fort Lewis."

A few hours later, courtesy of the United States Army, Paul is winched up through a windstorm of downwash into a Blackhawk helicopter from Fort Lewis, Washington.

The helicopter deposits Paul in Port Angeles, where he is questioned at rescue headquarters. Much to Paul's relief, they don't beat him with sticks. They tell him his brother is waiting to do that. Paul is able to call Stephanie that afternoon to let her know that he is okay and he loves her.

He walks away from the experience with a few minor scrapes and bruises.

When asked what sustained him during the time he was lost, Paul quotes a line from a poem, the line he says kept him alive: "Those who love each other shall become invincible."

"Thinking of my daughter and my partner. That is what sustained me. I knew I was going to see them again."

Headlines flash through her mind, announcing a mother and daughter's cold, lonely deaths in the mountains.

CHAPTER 8

SWALLOWED UP

Spring in the Puget Sound region of Washington state: a time when hundreds of families are eager to get outdoors after a long, damp Northwest winter in the confines of their mildewed homes.

The Brunke family is no different. In late May, Mark and Shirley, with their fifteen-year-old daughter Louisa and ten-year-old-son Willy, gather with a group of friends and neighbors to camp in the Mount Baker National Forest along the North Fork of the Nooksack River.

Saturday morning finds the families stuffing lunches and light jackets into day packs. Everyone is excited to get going. Today they are hiking up to Heliotrope Ridge with plans for a picnic in the sun overlooking what they have heard is a prizewinning view of Mount Baker.

At the trailhead the weather cooperates with scattered clouds and a light breeze. Warm rays of sun filter through the overarching limbs of cedar and fir trees. The children race back and forth across a lively stream, balancing on logs and rocks. Laughter echoes through the forest as they start down the path.

Eventually the trail takes them above timberline, climbing through alpine meadows into a high, barren basin. They walk up slopes of shattered gray rock, crossing the hummocky remains of old glacial moraines and an occasional snowfield. To the east, Mount Baker looms over them, an immense white pyramid filling the sky. Draped across its western flank, the Coleman Glacier spills off the summit, flowing down the mountainside to hang along the upper reaches of the basin like a frozen white wave, tinged blue in the shadows of crevasses and icefalls.

They stop for lunch alongside the trail, on a rocky ridge that looks out to the mountain. Mark Brunke, always looking for a smile, offers trail-mix handouts to other hikers passing by the happy hikers.

Shortly after lunch the party separates into two groups. Some of the adults and many of the children want a closer look at the terminus of the glacier, about a half-mile away over snowfields and tumbled rocky terrain to the east. Mark, Shirley, and Louisa have climbed far enough for the day. A chilly breeze puts them in a mood to head back down the trail.

With promises to meet back at camp, the larger party moves on as the Brunkes pause for a last look at the mountain. A sloping snowfield just east of the trail catches their eye. Sliding down the snow would be much faster than hiking. Besides, it would be fun.

They have done this before on other hikes, and this looks like a fine place for sliding. They pull plastic trash bags from their packs for makeshift sleds and position themselves at the top of the run.

Shirley and Louisa are the first off. They ride together toboggan style, leaning back for speed, shrieking with laughter as the snow flies up behind them in great rooster tails, ice crystals glistening in the afternoon sun.

Mark is a little slower getting started. As he gains speed he suddenly has second thoughts about the snow depth. There could be rocks just under the surface. He yells for Shirley and Louisa to stop, but mother and daughter are out of sight over the crest of the hill.

The snow is perfect for sledding, melting just enough in the afternoon sun for a smooth and fast ride. Halfway down the snowfield, as Shirley and Louisa accelerate to full speed, Louisa catches a glimpse of what looks like a small ditch cutting across their path. She has a fraction of a second to react, and then they are falling.

Their world of sunlight, laughter, and excitement flashes into a tumbling, somersaulting horror, bodies banging off rock and ice with sudden violence as mother and daughter plunge into darkness. Their ears fill with a thundering roar. A strange blue light envelops them, and then comes a final stunning impact.

Mark stops his slide to stand up and walk down the hill. Gazing far down the slope, he cannot see Shirley or Louisa anywhere.

They couldn't possibly have made it all the way to the bottom in that short time, he says to himself. *That just couldn't be.* Looking for answers, his eyes trace the shallow groove etched in the snow by mother and daughter.

Unseen from above, the melting snowpack has pulled away from the mountainside, forming an open trench in the middle of the snowfield. Shirley and Louisa's trail leads right to the edge of the trench. Mark's mind fights to comprehend the scene. It's like a fist ramming into his gut when he realizes they have fallen in.

· · · — — — · · ·

Perry and Seana met just recently through their work with Outward Bound's wilderness school in the Pacific Northwest. This weekend of climbing and skiing on Mount Baker is one of their first dates. Last night's summit attempt had to be scrubbed due to bad weather, but this morning the conditions are glorious. The sun is out, the snow is silky smooth, and the spring skiing is supreme.

Perry leads the way as they carve turns down from high camp. The snow gets sloppy below the glacier and Perry stops to take off his skis. He slips them into the sides of his pack and begins to stride downhill in search of the trail.

At the sound of whooping and laughing he turns to see two women slide past on the snowfield, sledding on a piece of plastic. When they disappear over a break in the slope, there is a sudden silence. Perry is struck with an immediate unease.

Following an instinct developed over a lifetime in the mountains, he jogs over to gaze down the snowfield. He has to take a second look. In all his years of climbing he has seen nothing like it. The track left by the women ends at a mouthlike trench melted through the snowpack. The sound of a subsurface torrent of meltwater roars from the opening. If the fall has not killed them, their chances of survival in the ice-cold water are decreasing by the second.

As Perry surveys the scene, Mark arrives breathless, stunned. Perry is dressed for mountain travel. He carries a pack loaded with climbing equipment. Mark has a glimmer of hope; this man knows what to do.

The two of them call down into the trench, pausing to listen for cries of help. Nothing but the roar of water rises from below.

Fighting panic, Mark turns to Perry: "What should I do?"

"Get to the ranger station down in Glacier. Tell them we need a helicopter with a winch, specifically a winch, for an evacuation at the 5,800-foot level of the Coleman Glacier on the Deming Route."

Feeling helpless, with only a belt pack containing the remains of lunch, Mark latches onto the one thing he can do: go for aid.

· · · — — — · · ·

The adults and children heading for the glacier have not gone far when they hear a voice calling from across a ravine behind them. They spot Mark among the rocks, waving his arms, yelling for them to come back. At first they think it is one of his jokes, until they realize something serious has happened to Shirley and Louisa.

"There has been an accident," he tells them. "I am heading down to get help."

The adults split up. The main group starts off for where they last saw Mark, Shirley, and Louisa. Two stay with the children, including Mark's son, Willy. Then one of the adults remembers a climbing group he saw setting up camp on a snowfield above. They may have much-needed equipment and experience. He heads up the mountain to find them.

· · · — — — · · ·

Cold, damp stone sucks the heat from Louisa's body. Her fall has ended on a rock ledge behind a torrent of falling water. An intense roar echoes from all directions. The air vibrates with the sound. Meager light filters down through snow and ice, casting her surroundings in a dull blue glow. Her first reaction is pure instinct: Get in control and get out.

Her gaze turns upward. All she can see of her former world is a tiny crack of sky far above. Down in the cold gloom, with the white noise of plunging water filling her ears, a sense of doom settles in. There is no way out of here.

Shirley is only a few feet away in the darkness, her body broken. Unable to move, she lies on the ledge dazed, trapped directly under the torrent. In a haze of shock and trauma, she notes the progression of frigid meltwater through her windbreaker, then sweatshirt, then T-shirt. Even with adrenaline pumping through her bloodstream she feels the pain. Moaning seems to help as she lies there, water hammering down from far above.

The human sound snaps Louisa out of hopelessness. With all the noise it is hard to tell what direction the moan is coming from, or if she really heard anything. Searching for the source, Louisa crawls to where the waterfall hits the ledge before crashing off into blackness below. Peering through the spray, she can see her mother pinned under the deluge.

As Shirley lies there, movement catches her eye. She looks up to see a hand reaching down through the water. Her daughter's voice cuts through the roar.

"Grab my hand, Mom. I have to pull you out away from that water."

"I can't, Louisa."

"You got to, Mom."

When she feels her daughter's fingers tighten around her wrist, Shirley summons all her strength. Using the toes of her hiking boots to push off the rock ledge, and with Louisa pulling, Shirley is able to crawl out from under the water into the relative dryness behind the falls. Out of the torrent, she collapses, flat on her back, exhausted.

Other than a few cuts and scratches, Louisa feels okay. She is somewhat dry, warmer than her mother.

Shirley's arms aren't working. Her pain is intense. She is sopping wet, getting colder by the minute. Yet as they huddle in the darkness, Shirley does her best to reassure her daughter.

"We have a chance," she says. "Remember those mountaineering people we saw hiking up the mountain? They must be nearby. They might have the equipment to get down here and save us." They both begin to yell for help.

· · · — — — · · ·

Eric had been waiting for many weeks to lead this group of his fellow students from Western Washington University to the summit of Mount Baker. The weather couldn't be better. Clear skies and warm spring sunshine mix with cool mountain air to fire up a desire, even in the most jaded alpine veteran, to stand upon a high peak. The snow-clad summit beckons only five thousand feet above them—close enough to touch, it seems.

After setting up camp on a snowfield just below the glacier, members of the college group pull their gear out of their packs for a practice session. For the past hour they have been working on glacier travel techniques, ice-axe arrest, and crevasse rescue. Just as the session is wrapping up, a lone hiker approaches from below.

His words make them all pause.

"Does anybody here know mountain rescue techniques?"

Eric and his fellow instructors have never done more than practice, but now is not a time to debate experience. Two people are in trouble below. They gather their gear and follow the man back down the mountain.

· · · — — — · · ·

Seana is concentrating on her telemark skiing technique, working to carve perfect turns in the soft snow, when she hears Perry yelling out a warning. Cresting the hill, she finds him standing on the downslope edge of a trench melted into the snowfield. She skis out wide and pulls up next to him. It's a quick conversation, and then they turn to the task at hand.

As they search through their equipment, working to put together some kind of rescue, cries for help filter up from below. Perry quickly straps sharp-pointed crampons onto his boots. Maybe the two women are close enough to reach. Maybe he can just pull them out by hand. He works his way down, a boot spiked into either side of the trench. The footing is treacherous. Unstable ice, snow, and rock form uneven walls. Ten feet below the surface, he can go no farther. Peering down into darkness, he yells, "Are you okay?"

Below his stance the trench walls have melted around ledges of rock protruding from the mountainside. The flood of meltwater gushes from underneath the snowpack, obscuring anything or anyone that might be down there. Perry can hear cries from below, but he can't make out the words. It is just not safe to go any farther. He climbs back to the surface.

· · · — — — · · ·

After Shirley and Louisa look up to the narrow opening far above and begin calling for help, it's not long before a figure appears near the top of the trench. A voice filters down, garbled through the water noise. Overcome with hope, Louisa yells back, "Yes, we have two conscious people down in this hole, we are going to be just fine."

Just as quickly the figure disappears from view.

· · · — — — · · ·

Struggling to come up with a plan, Perry and Seana hurriedly stuff dry clothing into a waterproof bag. With the frigid meltwater pouring into the hole, the people below are fighting not only injuries and shock, but also the fast and fatal effects of hypothermia. If Perry and Seana can lower warm clothes to them, it might buy some time to complete a rescue.

· · · — — — · · ·

As Louisa shivers in the gloom next to the waterfall, wondering what is happening up above, a bag descends by rope down through the water. She grabs it with hands stiff from cold. Try as she might, she cannot open the bag. Her fingers just won't work. As suddenly as it arrived, the bag is pulled back up to the surface.

· · · — — — · · ·

When Perry pulls the rope back up, he can tell the bag has been handled but not opened. Redoubling their efforts, Perry and Seana are at work on what to do next when reinforcements begin to arrive. The Brunke family's hiking partners are on the scene, as well as other passersby heading up the mountain. The climbing group from Western Washington University arrives with Eric at the lead.

Somehow this thrown-together group of strangers clicks immediately and begins to work as a well-trained rescue squad.

Seana directs preparations for first-aid efforts. Platforms are carved out of the snow for a place to treat the victims. Perry works with the other climbers to set up an anchor with his skis so a rescuer can climb down into the hole, safely belayed by a rope. Sleeping bags, ropes, insulating pads, and ice axes come out of backpacks.

· · · — — — · · ·

Down on the rock ledge, Shirley can feel her body getting colder and colder. Shock and hypothermia are taking their toll. As she hovers on the edge of consciousness, her first thought is for her daughter.

"Louisa, I am not dying, I am just passing out."

At the sound of her mother's voice, Louisa turns to find her unresponsive. Headlines flash through her mind, announcing a mother and daughter's cold, lonely deaths in the mountains. She begins to cry as waves of despair wash over her in the blue gloom.

· · · — — — · · ·

Mark Brunke is in a state of disbelief as he races for the trailhead. It is all he can do to focus on where his feet are hitting the trail so he does not fail in this mission.

The scene replays over and over in his mind as his legs carry him down the mountain. He sees his wife and daughter sledding together, happy, laughing as they head out of sight down the hill.

Then silence. The tracks leading into that horrifying trench in the snow; water roaring from beneath the snowpack.

What should I have done? he asks himself. *What could I have done?* Trees flash past. He leaps over roots and works his way across the stream where his group had been laughing and joking only hours before.

He prays for his wife and daughter. Prays that they will survive. Prays that he will see them again, alive.

· · · — — — · · ·

In minutes everything is ready. But no one among the dozen rescuers now gathered is eager to descend into the trench.

For the afternoon practice session he had been leading, Eric had fully outfitted himself with climbing bib and jacket, climbing harness, and plastic mountaineering boots. Fate has now come his way. Someone has to descend into the trench immediately, and he is the one ready to go.

Eric ties into the rope and pulls on his gloves. Someone hands him a headlamp. He looks down into the darkness, toward the roaring flood of frigid water. He feels as if he is preparing to die. He locks eyes with Perry.

"Just make sure you get me out."

Eric climbs downward, methodically planting his boots on opposite sides of the trench. The belaying team feeds him rope as he works his way past the ledge where Perry was forced to stop. He squeezes around pinch-points between the rock and snow. He ducks his head as he descends into the torrent.

Even through multiple layers of waterproof clothing and insulation, the icy water is paralyzing. His hands begin to stiffen and his arms become heavy with cold. He can hear nothing from below through the roar. Thoughts stream through his mind of being trapped in the flood, unable to breathe, washed under the snowpack to a dark, watery death. His headlamp projects a weak pool of light as he climbs deeper into darkness.

· · · — — — · · ·

Louisa crouches on the ledge next to the waterfall, all hope gone. Her mother's body lies prostrate behind her. Louisa doesn't want to move. Her vision swims as though she could pass out at any moment.

Out of the corner of her eye she catches a flash of brightness, then darkness, like a cloud passing over the sun. She looks up as a figure descends. A man drops down onto the ledge next to her, and she stares with disbelief.

"Why are you here? Are you here to save us?"

· · · — — — · · ·

Mark reaches the trailhead after the toughest run of his life. Jumping into his car, he fires up the engine and drives like a madman down the winding mountain road. He waves frantically at each vehicle he passes, until it pulls over.

"Got a cell phone?"

Then he is off again, gravel flying, when his question is answered in the negative, every time.

Pulling up to the Glacier Ranger Station, he runs inside. Before the door can close behind him he is yelling breathlessly at the uniformed people behind the counter.

"We have an emergency! My wife and daughter have fallen into a meltwater trench in the snowpack at the 5,800-foot level of the Coleman Glacier on the Heliotrope Ridge trail. We need a helicopter rescue!"

The rangers behind the desk put aside what they are doing and ask Mark to slow down and give them all the details. With thoughts of his wife and daughter caught in that trench and the hopelessness that he felt up on the snowfield clouding his mind, Mark carefully recites everything he can remember, including Perry's request for a helicopter with a winch.

When the rangers finish taking down the information and start phoning for help, Mark turns to head back to the mountain. The rangers stop him.

"You need to wait for the mountain rescue team and give them directions to the accident site."

· · · — — — · · ·

Eric has brought a climbing harness and the end of a second rope, for pulling Louisa and Shirley out of the hole. His hands are numb from the climb down through the water, and his useless fingers cannot fit the harness to Louisa. Precious seconds pass as the cold saps his strength. Running out of time, he drops the harness and forms a sling around Louisa's upper body with the rope.

Perry has stationed himself partway down in the trench to help as the victims come out of the hole. When he feels Eric's tug on the rope, he signals to the rescuers above. With plenty of hands on the retrieval line, Louisa is quickly hoisted out of the hole.

Seana is relieved to find Louisa conscious, talking, accurately answering questions about her name and what day it is. Louisa is untied from the rope, stabilized for possible spinal injuries, and carried over to one of the first-aid platforms.

With Louisa up and out, Eric spots Shirley for the first time. She is lying still, back in the darkness, no color in her face. *She's dead,* he says to himself.

He moves over, cradles her head gently in his lap, and waits.

When the rope returns, he carefully loops it around Shirley. She begins to stir. Rousing out of unconsciousness, she fights to push him away, then relaxes and begins talking. Eric struggles to get her tied in, and then she is pulled out of the hole.

Shirley emerges sopping wet and cold yet speaking clearly. She thanks the rescuers as they stabilize her and carry her to the second platform. They exchange her wet clothes for dry and put her in a sleeping bag. She goes suddenly silent. Her body begins convulsing. She is foaming at the mouth, an animal look of fear in her eyes. She wants to get up, escape, go somewhere. It is all they can do to hold her down. Her body is freezing cold to the touch. Seana has two of the rescuers lie next to Shirley for added warmth, then all three are layered with sleeping bags. There is not much more they can do as Shirley struggles to stay alive.

Eric is the last to come up. He is quickly wrapped in sleeping bags as he sits on the snow, waves of deep, uncontrollable shivers wracking his body.

With the victims out of the hole, Perry sends a second messenger down to the ranger station. The remaining rescuers huddle around Shirley and Louisa, doing their best to treat their injuries and keep them warm.

· · · — — — · · ·

Hours later dusk approaches with no sign of a helicopter. The temperature drops. Clouds gather, and the wind picks up. Perry and Seana consider their options.

Louisa is alert and, other than scrapes and bruises, seems to be uninjured. She might be able to walk out.

Her mother is barely conscious. Even with two people in the sleeping bag with her, she is not warming up. The odds of Shirley's making it through a night on the mountain decrease with every hour. As Perry and Seana search through the inventory of available equipment one more time, hoping to form a plan that will get both mother and daughter off the mountain alive, a silver helicopter suddenly appears out of the gray sky.

The rescuers stand together, in near awe, as a Sikorsky Sea King from Whidbey Island Naval Air Station circles for an approach. With the flight crew checking out the rescue site, the rescuers scramble after loose equipment in preparation for rotor downwash.

The next few minutes go by in a blur. The chopper pulls into a hover over the accident site. Two crew members with a litter are lowered by cable. There is no time for conversation, with rising winds putting the helicopter on the edge of flying limits. The crew members perform a fast medical evaluation as they prepare Louisa and Shirley for evacuation.

The helicopter pulls back into a hover over the site. Louisa is the first to be winched up. Shirley is next, offering no response as she is hoisted into the helicopter. The two crew members go up last.

As quickly as it appeared, the helicopter is gone.

The rescuers are left in silence, subdued and exhausted from the past few hours. They slowly gather their equipment, say good-bye, and head their separate ways.

• • • — — — • • •

Down along Highway 542 in Glacier, a crowd is gathering at the rescue staging area. A medical helicopter waits along with several ambulances.

Two hours have passed up on the mountain since the second messenger arrived to tell Mark that his wife and daughter had been pulled out of the trench alive. He knows they must have been seriously injured. The knowledge that two hours is a long time without professional medical attention has not made his wait any easier.

When the Navy helicopter lands, Mark has only a moment to see Shirley as she is transferred to a medical helicopter for the trip to St. Joseph Hospital in Bellingham. Shirley seems to be responding to treatment from the Navy medical technicians. She is talking, but not completely lucid. He kisses her quickly on the forehead, then stands back as the helicopter takes off.

Louisa is transferred to an ambulance for the ride into Bellingham. She is speaking cheerfully and is doing remarkably well, complaining a bit about being strapped onto a back board. Mark rides with her. For the first time in hours he feels as though he can finally breathe.

• • • — — — • • •

Shirley arrives at the hospital with a dangerously lowered body core temperature of 92 degrees Fahrenheit. She responds to the efforts of the emergency room staff and slowly begins to warm up.

Beyond Shirley's obvious cuts and bruises, the doctors find seven broken ribs, a broken collarbone, and a broken shoulder blade. The surprise comes when Louisa is found to have a burst vertebra in her upper back.

It takes the better part of a year, with Louisa in a back brace, for mother and daughter to recuperate from their injuries.

Today, Shirley and Louisa suffer no visible effects from their brush with death. It is clear to both mother and daughter that sheer luck and the selfless courage of strangers are all that stood between them and death on that day.

Shirley points to a photograph taken just before the incident. "That would have been the last picture of me alive."

Mark sums up the experience: "We have done lots of backpacking in our lives. We have done things similar to this garbage-bag incident and had happy endings. Of course we will never do that again, even if we see a snowfield that looks perfectly lovely, because you just don't know. You just never know."

Mike says it first, and Johnny agrees—
"This is not good."

CHAPTER 9

RIVER WILD

I t all starts on a warm evening in July. Mike is sitting on his sofa, watching a fishing show on a cable TV channel. The images capture his attention. The river looks beautiful, calm, idyllic, cutting a cool path through a forest of tall evergreens. A drift boat floats downstream. One man is at the oars as two others, one in the stern, one in the bow, cast into deep pools. They are catch-and-release fly-fishing for native cutthroat and rare bull trout on the Lewis River in Washington state.

The Lewis River, Mike says to himself. *That's just south of here.*

He's never seen anything on his fishing trips in Washington that quite compares with the scenes flashing across his TV screen. Feisty trout seem to beckon from every pool. Panoramas of nearby Mount St. Helens are woven in for local color. This looks good.

When the program ends, Mike, thorough as always, does follow-up research on the show's website. He learns that the North Fork of the Lewis River is 135 miles of blue-ribbon fishery where the endangered bull trout is protected. There haven't been any fish planted since 1997. The river is medium-size with generally easy wading. And there's another photograph of the same drift boat on that beautiful river.

He's sold. He has nothing going on this weekend. Well, there's that Saturday-night party his girlfriend mentioned—but he's just going fishing for the day. He'll show at the party when he gets back. Mike's plans for a solo road trip to check out the Lewis River begin to take shape.

It's not long before Johnny, a fishing buddy at work, catches wind of the plan. He wants to go as well.

With two cars they can take their pontoon boats, leave one of the cars downstream, and float the river. This way they can cover far more of the river, faster, in search of the premium fishing grounds.

Johnny has a neighbor in his early twenties, David, who has been bugging Johnny for a long time to take him fishing. Somehow David finds out about the Saturday trip and the next thing Johnny knows, David is over at his house.

"Come on, take me fishing with you guys."

David just keeps at him; he won't drop the topic. Johnny now owns an additional one-person pontoon boat, which David could use. So Johnny relents and invites him along.

· · · — — — · · ·

Early on Saturday morning the three men meet outside of Seattle and drive several hours south on I-5, turning east on Highway 503 at Woodland, Washington. They stop at a Forest Service office long enough to buy a couple of trailhead parking passes. Johnny strikes up a conversation with the ranger and asks if the North Fork of the Lewis River is floatable.

"Oh yeah," the ranger says, "people float that all the time."

Reassured, the three men get back on the road.

Driving upriver past Swift Creek Reservoir, they pull out their Washington state gazetteer, with topographic maps showing all the logging roads, campgrounds, fishing locations, paddling routes, and such. They turn to page 34 and search for the river.

Yep, there it is, the North Fork of the Lewis River, accessed by Forest Road 90. They can leave a car below where the road crosses the river near the falls of Curly Creek. On the stretch of river above that, they can see the canoe icon indicating canoe trips and the little fish icon for fishing. This is it.

They leave a car at the Curly Creek take-out, then drive a winding logging road to a spot on the map that looks to be about six miles upstream and just below Lewis River Falls. This is where they will launch.

It's around noon as they unload their gear at the put-in. Johnny and David then drive back to the take-out; David left his reel in the vehicle there. Mike stays at the river to assemble the pontoon boats.

Each single-person craft consists of two inflatable pontoons about fourteen inches in diameter and eight feet long. The pontoons support an aluminum frame that carries a seat, oarlocks, and foot pegs. These little boats are ideal for floating down smaller rivers, where their modest size, light weight, and maneuverability allow a lot of flexibility for pulling up at choice fishing holes.

With the job done and no sign of his two partners, Mike decides to test the waters. He wades into the river just below the bridge and lofts an orange stimulator dry fly out over a choice pool. It floats down onto the surface a few times. In just moments he hooks two fish, one after another, boom, boom.

Now this is what I am looking for, he says to himself as a smile spreads across his face.

· · · — — — · · ·

It's not long before Mike, Johnny, and David are floating off down the river on what is promising to be a stunning July day. The sky is as blue as can be. The air is warm. An afternoon of fishing remote and secluded blue-ribbon trout territory lies ahead. It doesn't get any better than this.

Johnny starts off with a small elk-hair caddis fly. Right off the bat he lands a couple of eight- to ten-inch native cutthroat and releases them, gently, back into the clear, cold water.

The river carries them away from the road and deep into the woods. All three men concentrate on fishing, working pocket water behind boulders, slowing up at the larger pools.

Around a bend in the river they look downstream. The water drops out of sight between two rocks. This wasn't on the TV show. They pull over to scout the drop.

It turns out to be only a two- to three-foot waterfall, dropping off into riffles and another long stretch of quiet water.

Just the price of admission, Mike thinks to himself as he walks back to his boat.

Johnny and David go first. Mike brings up the rear, lining himself up with the drop. At the base of the falls his pontoons sink deep below the surface. Water splashes up to roll harmlessly off his chest-high waders.

Johnny hangs back just below the falls as the two other men row on by. The small pools here look promising. It's hard for Johnny to steer and fish at the same time in the current. Suddenly one of his oars catches a rock and tips the raft up at a steep angle. He has to throw himself up on the high side to keep from capsizing. His boat hangs up for an agonizing second, then rolls off and rights itself, but the aluminum oar comes loose and disappears.

Stowing his rod, Johnny quickly paddles into an eddy with his one remaining oar. He swirls around for a while, searching the river for the lost oar, before he spots it floating by. With his one oar he chases after the escapee, and several hundred yards downstream he scoops it out of the current. It's bent into a rough C shape.

When Johnny catches up to his two partners, they all pull over. Johnny has a look on his face that makes them both say, "What?"

He shows them the oar. They bend the oar back into shape on the riverbank while giving Johnny a hard time.

The river seems to be a little more than they had expected, yet no one wants to put a damper on the trip. They laugh off their troubles. But after almost dumping his own boat, Johnny is starting to worry about David.

They get back to fishing, hoping the worst is behind them. They catch a few more fish, stopping wherever they want to cast into clear pools and along the edge of riffles.

Around another bend, the water disappears over a falls again. Mike has to row like crazy to hit the drop on center. He bounces through, spray flying, hands gripped on the oars, the fly rod clenched in his teeth.

They fish another stretch, dropping flies into the slack water behind boulders, then drift through a long pool.

Meanwhile, Mike begins to do a rough calculation in his head. The float distance they estimated off the map, six miles or so, seems to be way off. The map didn't give a clear indication of the meandering channel. Near as he can tell, the actual river miles they are traveling could easily be double what they expected. That would make it more like twelve miles to the take-out.

From past experience Mike has developed a rough formula. One mile on the river equals one hour of floating. He hasn't been paying close attention to the time, but at least a couple of hours have passed since they set out around noon. With the new mileage estimate, this means they are far less than halfway.

When his two partners float down to him, he gathers them up for a conference. They need to pick up the pace. Mike lays out the strategy.

"We are going to have to just fish from the boats. We can't keep stopping to fish like we have been doing. Let's just see the turf while we move as fast as possible."

The river isn't cooperating. If they are not in a pool or going over a waterfall, their boats are bumping through shallow rapids. The three men are frequently forced to drag their boats over the riverbed to make any progress.

. . . — — — . . .

Not long after their riverside conference, Mike is in the lead when he comes to a bend in the river. A sweeper log extends from shore, right at the waterline, across the deep water and reaches into the shallows. The log bounces menacingly in and out of the water as the main current piles up on the upriver side.

Mike has plenty of time to work his way into the quiet water on the inside of the bend and to beach his boat. Johnny is not far behind and soon both men are standing in the shallows, scouting the rapids below.

As David approaches in his boat, Mike yells to him to watch out for the sweeper.

Before either man can react, David is swept into the log. His boat capsizes, throwing him into the river. The pontoon craft pops over the log and heads downstream. David is left clinging to the bouncing timber, fighting to keep his head above water. Every time the log bounces, he loses a little grip and is dragged further under by the force of the current.

Neither Mike nor Johnny can do anything with their boats without risking the same fate. The current is running strong, the water ice cold, and the river looks very deep out there where he is trapped.

A second passes and then Mike wades in without hesitation. Using the log like a rail, he makes his way out along the downstream side to where David hangs on.

The water comes up to Mike's waist as he reaches David. He talks to him calmly.

"I am going to reach under the log. Just lock your elbow around my arm, then let go and bob your head under the surface. I will pull you out on the other side."

David releases his death grip on the log and comes flailing out the other side. His grip on the log is replaced with a grip on Mike. They are both in danger of being dragged under as David scrambles to climb out of the river and up on Mike's shoulders. Mike is trying to fight him off as he yells into the young man's face.

"Stand up!"

David is freaked out. He isn't hearing. He keeps struggling.

"Stand up, man!"

David is out of his mind, freezing in the water, fighting to live.

"Stand up!"

Finally the message gets through. David lowers his legs to find the water less than four feet deep. Mike walks with David back to shore, gripping the log.

David has lost all his gear. His waders were swept off by the current and are gone, lost on the river bottom. His fishing gear, gone. His capsized craft, both oars still attached, is wedged in the rocks on the opposite side of the river. He stands on the riverbank, soaked to the skin, wearing only nylon sweatpants, T-shirt, and white cotton socks, yet he's extremely happy to be alive.

* * * — — — * * *

Mike's waders filled with water when he bent to pull David free. Now he lies upside down on the bank to let the water drain out.

This is not looking good, Mike thinks to himself, staring up at the sky. *We are deep in this canyon, it's going to be dark soon, and we don't really know how much farther it is to the take-out.*

They had a map but left it in the car. After all, they were just floating down the river. Why would they need a map to follow the river?

After drying off and calming down, they regroup at the river bend. Fishing is definitely off the schedule now. They will have to paddle like madmen just to get to the car before nightfall.

Mike rows across the river to retrieve David's boat. Because everyone is a little nervous after the sweeper incident, they wade through the next set of rapids, pulling their boats behind them. Mike and Johnny wince as they watch the young man sliding from rock to rock in his stocking feet. Reaching the next stretch of calm water, they launch into the current and begin rowing.

Only a short distance downstream, the river takes a sharp bend and drops through some of the worst rapids yet. It twists through foaming zigzags, slashing its way between polished rocks that pinch the flow into treacherous pour-offs.

Nobody is in the mood to run whitewater at this point. They pull over and begin dragging their boats along the bank. David struggles, placing his feet carefully with every step.

Halfway through this section, a boulder the size of a Volkswagen van on end blocks their way along the bank. A similar-size boulder rises on the other shore, and the river squeezes between the two monoliths. The only possible route to the other side of the first boulder is up and over.

Weary but determined, the men manage to climb up the river-polished boulder. A rope is used to pull the boats and equipment, hand over hand, up the rock and back down the other side.

Last in line, Mike pulls his valuables off his boat, ties a rope to it, then kicks it out into the main flow to bang down through the rocks. It seems easier than hauling the cumbersome thing over the top.

They gather at the base of the rapids and Mike fetches his beaten but still afloat craft out of the river. Everything is lashed back on the boats and the three men are treated to a long, calm stretch of scenic river through the kind of meadow most people see only on calendars. Then the water starts getting shallower and shallower.

The canyon is all in shadows when they get to the next bend in the river. The sun is long out of sight. The river disappears around the corner, running into another canyon.

Johnny and Mike pull their boats up to shore and walk downriver to scout the route. The river quickly narrows to about a third of its width as it roars down into a gorge. This time the rocks are school-bus size. Then the river makes another turn, and they can't see any farther.

Mike says it first, and Johnny agrees: "This is not good." While it is still light, they need to gather up what they have and make themselves a camp for the night.

Back on the calm stretch of water, the three men pull their boats up at a place that is high, dry, and protected by the overhanging branches of a tree. Before long a big stash of firewood has been gathered.

Johnny sets up his butane stove and starts chili to cooking in a cast-iron pan. Mike pulls out matches to start a fire. Once the fire gets going, they hang David's clothes over the flames to dry. Mike has a water filter and begins to refill their water bottles. The little bit of trail mix and beef jerky he stashed away for the day also help supplement the menu.

Darkness is complete that night down along the river, surrounding the men where they huddle around the fire. Johnny is worried; his wife will be expecting him back. And Mike won't be meeting his girlfriend at the party.

Even though it's July, the night air is chilly. All they have for pajamas are T-shirts and waders. For David, it's his nylon sweats and a spare long-sleeve polypropylene shirt borrowed from Mike. Furnishings are lean as well—dirt for beds and moss for pillows—but nobody complains.

Mike stays awake long enough to admire an almost full moon before dropping into a comfortable sleep. Johnny and David spend a long night shivering and feeding the fire.

· · · — — — · · ·

Shortly after dawn on Sunday the men debate their next move. They have three options: They can get back on the river and finish the float; they can hike straight up the side of the river canyon and find Forest Road 90 way up on the rim; or they can search along the river for a possible trail.

No one is ready for an attempt at the rapids below camp. Looking for a river trail seems to be the best move. Mike had seen a couple of hikers near the river yesterday, indicating there could be a trail to follow out. Mike crosses the river to search the north bank. It takes a while to find a way up, but once he is above the river he quickly finds a well-worn trail paralleling the stream.

He returns to camp with the good news. Now they just have to figure out how to haul all their gear to the trail.

The first plan of action is to eat all the food; that way they don't have to carry it.

When breakfast is done, Mike and Johnny search out a route that will allow them to haul the boats up to the trail. Guessing that they are about halfway down the river between their two cars, it's a coin toss on which direction to go. Down seems easiest, so they scout out the trail downstream a short distance. It's also a chance to see how much trouble the rapids below camp might be.

Viewed from above, the river doesn't look so bad past the huge boulders that stopped them yesterday evening.

Maybe that's the last of it, they think to themselves.

The water smooths out and the current seems to slow down. So they continue to walk to a vantage point in the trail, where they can look farther downriver.

The smooth water runs between increasingly sheer cliffs, only to pile up and roar as it siphons beneath a massive logjam completely choking the canyon. A pontoon boat would be sucked in and crushed among the old-growth logs like a tin can in a trash compactor. The occupant would have only seconds to react before being forced under and wedged somewhere in the strainer of trees below the surface.

If they had pushed their luck last night and continued down the river, there would have been no escape.

It's a sobering sight. If there was any question of how they were going to get out, it has been vaporized now. The trail looks great, it's dry, and the likelihood of drowning up here is very low.

Back at camp they begin packing up their equipment for the walk out. Mike's boat suffered yesterday. When he pulled it out of the water, he found the aluminum frame was cracked. He can buy a new one for three hundred dollars when he gets back, or carry scrap metal out today. The boat is shoved under a tree and out of sight, along with Johnny's cast-iron pan and the anchor he likes to use for stopping to fish midriver.

They deflate one of the boats and lash the frame and pontoons on top of the other boat. Next, they engineer two carrying harnesses between the pontoons at both ends of the boat. It looks something like a pontoon rickshaw, with one man on either end.

The remainder of the gear goes back into the watertight bin that had been carried on Johnny's raft. David offers to pack that out.

Wading across a shallow section of water, they climb up the riverbank. Mike and Johnny stumble and sweat up the slope, pushing and pulling the pontoon boats through brush and rocks while wearing waders and felt-bottom wading shoes. Balancing the bin on his head, David follows, gingerly picking his way along in stocking feet.

Once on the trail heading downstream, they don't really know how far it is to the parking area. The trail is fine for walking, mostly on dirt and fir needles, but it's narrow. Maneuvering two forty-pound boats plus fishing gear through the trees is difficult. Johnny is still worried about his wife, who undoubtedly is worrying about him.

Mike soon heats up with all the physical effort. He calls a stop to strip off his waders and to convert his T-shirt to harness padding. Then they are off again, with Mike marching down the trail on one end of the pontoon rickshaw, wearing only wading shoes and boxer shorts as steam rolls off his body in the cool morning air.

The day stretches into a long, exhausting slog, following the trail through old-growth forest. Occasionally the trail comes back to the river, but they never think twice about staying on dry land. David soldiers on, never complaining, his socks now dark with mud.

At one point late in the day they cross paths with a few people camping near the trail, and judging by the amount of gear the campers have, the trailhead has to be near. But it turns out that it's still another two and a half miles to the parking lot. One of the men loans David a pair of river sandals.

"Just leave them in my truck at the trailhead."

· · · — — — · · ·

Finally, close to four hours after they started walking, the men stumble into the parking lot where they left a car only the morning before. Moments later, as they sit exhausted in their car, a Forest Service vehicle pulls up and the ranger rolls the window down.

"Are you the guys that own the black Ford Explorer up the hill?"

"Yeah, that's us," Johnny answers.

"We've been getting calls from your wife," the ranger says. "She is really worried about you. Would you mind calling her and telling her you're still alive?"

The weary men drive home. A few days pass before Mike is able to convince his girlfriend that he didn't purposely dodge the party.

David still lives next door, but he has yet to ask Johnny to take him on another pontoon boat fishing trip.

As for the river and its unexpected challenges, most of the fishing and drifting normally takes place on the stretch below the three men's proposed take-out—not above it. The point where Mike, Johnny, and David planned to end their float is the point where most people begin, and from there they drift a few calm miles down to Swift Creek Reservoir. Sometimes, even with the best intentions, maps are inaccurate, television doesn't present the full picture, and the locals don't give the best directions.

When morning dawns on his second full day
lost, he climbs out from under the stump
with a plan.

CHAPTER 10

THREE NIGHTS TO BULLWINKLE'S

Bob Wells had lived in Juneau when he was younger, and he had a sister who still called the Alaska state capital her home. He flew up one year from the lower forty-eight with his girlfriend and one of her friends for a late-summer visit. One day the three of them decide to hike up Perseverance Trail right behind town, up along Gold Creek to Granite Creek Basin.

It's one of those clear days when the mountains look to be only an arm's length away. The air is smooth and pure in Bob's lungs. He has been gone far too long from Alaska and now he feels the need to make up for lost time.

"Man, this place is just beautiful," he bellows out as they hike the trail.

When they finally stop for a rest, way up in Granite Basin, he studies his Forest Service guidebook to the trails around Juneau. If they climb up and follow the ridge to the north, the trail eventually loops back around and they can return to the trailhead down the Mount Juneau Trail.

His girlfriend and her friend don't want any part of it. "This is a big, long hike back here," one of them says. "This is good enough."

But Bob has mountain fever and can't let the idea go. The view from the top of Mount Juneau will be spectacular on this clear, sunny day.

Finally they agree to a compromise. "Okay, okay, go ahead without us. We'll meet you later."

He estimates the amount of time the loop will take and asks them to pick him up at the trailhead around eight or nine that evening. The long summer days this far north will give him plenty of daylight to find the route.

They part ways and the two women return down to the Perseverance Trail, following Gold Creek back to Juneau.

· · · — — — · · ·

Half an hour after leaving his companions, Bob is just getting to the top of the ridge when fog blows in and obscures the surrounding mountains. Bob is familiar with the lay of the land from his previous years in Juneau, and he still has hopes for a view, so he searches out the trace of a trail and starts walking in the direction of Mount Juneau.

The route meanders through a mist-shrouded alpine landscape of small meadows and rock scree. In an effort to conjure up recognizable landmarks from his childhood memories, Bob recalls a large metal container that was left on top of Mount Juneau from a tram project several years back. He shouldn't be able to miss that, even with the mist.

An hour or so passes as Bob traverses the high country. The fog doesn't let up. Eventually the ridgeline leads him up to a rocky summit. There is no view, just a white fog bank for 360 degrees.

Things aren't looking quite right. He hasn't found the metal container that should be here somewhere. And there is no sign of a trail leading off the mountain. Not knowing the way down, Bob decides it would be best to backtrack and return the way he came.

As he walks back down the ridge, the fog parts occasionally and he can see off the high ridge and down into a valley to the north. He recognizes Salmon Creek Reservoir, exactly where it should be. Maybe he should hike down there. There is a trail down in the basin that will lead him back to Juneau. Not to the trailhead he left this morning, but at least he can get back to town.

Nah, he decides, that's too far out of the way. Besides, it would be a long, cross-country trip down a steep and unfamiliar mountainside. He sticks to the ridge top, retracing his steps.

At some point the fog clears a second time. Finally Bob recognizes a landmark. Way down below he can see the big rock he passed earlier in the afternoon as he climbed up from Granite Basin.

He was getting a little concerned. Now, with the rock in view, he has his bearings. The path leading along Granite Creek, back to Perseverance Trail, is just below. He should be able to make it out to the trailhead with time to spare. Bob starts working his way down off the ridge and out of the fog.

· · · — — — · · ·

Bob's girlfriend and her companion have a pleasant hike back down the trail. Taking the car, they spend a few hours in town. The afternoon passes, and at 8 P.M. they drive back to the trailhead. There is no sign of Bob.

Nine o'clock rolls around and he doesn't appear.

The weather had been really nice earlier in the day, but now clouds have formed and rain cannot be far behind. They wait and wait.

When the clock reads midnight and he still hasn't made an appearance, they call the police.

"He was supposed to meet us," they say. "We waited several hours past the prearranged time. Something has happened."

The next day the search begins as the Juneau Search and Rescue folks and the Southeast Alaska Dogs Organized for Ground Search, SEADOGS, go out. It's cloudy, and the weather is not cooperating. They can't get any helicopters up looking on the mountain.

It isn't a massive search, but it is a pretty good effort for a first day. With the addition of a few Alaska State Troopers there are maybe ten, twelve people out looking.

They don't find any footprints. They don't find anything at all. That night the state troopers call all the search groups.

There is a hiker missing. He's been gone for about twenty-four hours, doesn't really have rain gear, doesn't have much food. He has a small day pack. He might have a sandwich in there, a water

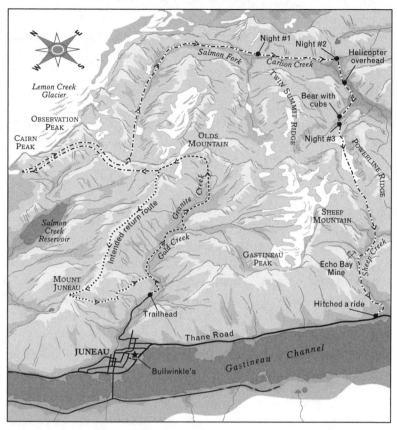

bottle. When he was last seen he was wearing jeans and a cotton or fleece sweatshirt.

The second day there is a massive search. The Alpine Club, Juneau Mountain Rescue, Juneau Search and Rescue, SEADOGS, the Civil Air Patrol, the National Guard, the Forest Service, and the Coast Guard join the effort. Some people just show up and volunteer.

Mount Juneau covers a lot of territory, and the search area is spread out along the whole ridge leading back to Granite Basin. The Coast Guard helicopter scans the terrain with an infrared device most of the afternoon. The National Guard is flying a Blackhawk helicopter. A local tour company, Temsco, has a helicopter in the air.

105

Juneau Mountain Rescue, the group that does high-alpine technical retrievals, is scheduled for a flight into the area. They will be let out on the ridge between Mount Olds and Mount Juneau, at a saddle that is wide enough for an easy helicopter landing, right about where Bob would have come up out of Granite Creek Basin. They will spread out and check all likely locations, sweeping the ridgeline route to Mount Juneau.

As the mountain rescue team is flying up, their lead is looking down at the landscape and thinking, *So where did this guy go? He is up here on this ridge and he is lost. He has been out two nights and a full day. He's not wearing much. He could be dead just from hypothermia.*

Following a hunch, he leans over to the helicopter pilot and points out the window. "Why don't you fly down this creek?"

A man lost in this area would be likely to follow one of the many creeks out of the mountains, down to the saltwater passage known as Gastineau Channel. Once on the channel he could follow the paved road back into Juneau.

The pilot drops down the back side of the ridge and follows the creek drainage off the heights, flying low and slow for several miles. They see nothing.

The mountain rescue guy wants a second look. "Can you fly back?"

"You know I have other people I need to pick up for this search," the pilot answers. "I've got to get going."

So the pilot wheels the red and white chopper around, gaining altitude fast, and heads north on a more direct route back to the search area. The mountain rescue team is dropped off on the ridge, and the helicopter takes off to ferry more searchers.

As the sun sets on day two the massive effort produces no results. Not a clue has been found to the missing man's fate.

On day three the operation continues. Everyone is still searching and the helicopters are still flying, but they can't find Bob.

· · · — — — · · ·

That night the search coordinators hold a gathering in a big banquet room at a Juneau restaurant. A state trooper conducts the meeting. Maps and overhead graphics are set up and all the search teams assemble. It's an intense session, reviewing where people have searched. Each team points out its search areas on the overhead projections.

Everybody is helping. Everybody is talking. And nobody can figure it out.

What the hell happened to this guy? He just disappeared. It's as though aliens came down and beamed him away. The search teams combed the area. They found every pop-top can and beer bottle that had been left on the mountain. But no sign of the missing man.

A member of the mountain rescue group asks the state trooper, "Did this guy have an insurance policy or something? Where did he go? He either had to fall in a river and drown, or he is in a mine shaft somewhere."

The whole area was scanned with an infrared scope from the Coast Guard helicopter. A missing person would have shown up as a distinctive heat spot even if they could not be seen through the tree cover. The state park ranger who was using the scope is right there as a witness, and he didn't miss a thing.

"Yeah, now I know where all the deer are hiding."

He saw bears through the scope as well, but no lost hiker.

They pause for a moment to consider the bear factor, but even if Bob had been mauled by a bear, there would be something left.

There is one steep face high on the ridgeline. Maybe he fell off there.

You can tell what the trooper is doing. The search has been going for three days without finding a trace. He is trying to make sure everything has been covered. Is there anything more they can do?

They debate other likely possibilities. Someone brings up the account of a hunter reported lost outside of Sitka not that long ago. The search stretched over several days. The searchers were finding signs that the missing man was in the area but they never could find him. Word spread that, more than likely, the hunter, even though he was lost, wasn't going to let himself be found because women ran the search group and he was too much of a man to be rescued by a bunch of females.

"This guy is not like that," the mountain rescue guy says, and a huge groan ripples through the room, echoing the thoughts of many. *Oh man, how much longer are we going to search and how far out are we going to go?*

Just then a waitress enters the room and catches the attention of the trooper.

"There's a phone call for you."

The trooper leaves the room. He's gone for a couple of minutes and everybody is chattering away in their separate groups.

Then the leader of the SEADOGS is also called out in the hall.

The room is buzzing with curiosity. "What's up? Something is going on."

· · · —— —— —— · · ·

After finally sighting the route back into Granite Creek Basin, Bob made his way down out of the fog. He lost elevation quickly, watching his footing, working around rocks and the occasional clump of scrubby trees. It was not until he was all the way down that he realized the big rock he was using as a landmark was not the big rock he remembered. Looking around, it's obvious that he is not in Granite Creek Basin.

Not a problem, he thinks to himself. *All these bowls feed into where we started hiking this morning in the Perseverance area. I'll just keep going down, pick up the trail below somewhere, and follow it back to the trailhead.*

So he keeps walking down and down and down. The trees begin increasing in size. The canopy closes in over his head. Before long the dense undergrowth forces Bob onto the only route he can find: trails worn through the brush by the many bears that ramble down this rugged valley.

The only sign of human presence he can find is an old mining claim-marker, a white post standing out from all the green deep in the woods. A cold drizzle is seeping down out of the sky.

Late in the afternoon, pushing through the overhanging branches on one of the bear trails, he steps in something. Looking down, he finds his foot immersed in a huge pile of berry-filled dung.

A chill runs down his spine. From what he can remember, in Southeast Alaska most of the big brown bears, the local version of a grizzly, are out on the islands. He recalls a few locations on the mainland that they have been known to frequent. By the size of the pile, this might be one of them.

With senses now on high alert, he continues down the valley.

When the light begins to fade, Bob finds himself along a river he cannot recognize in the middle of a forest he does not know. The Forest Service guidebook he has is worthless. It offers only patches of map that follow the trails behind the city of Juneau. Nothing is shown of the surrounding areas.

The drizzle has changed to a steady rain. His orange and half a sandwich are long gone by now. There is little else in his day pack that can help him.

Bob's disposable lighter is damp from moisture in the air and won't light—not that there is anything dry around that he could start a fire with anyway. His clothes, denim pants and a polyester fleece hooded pullover, are soaked through.

Along with his other troubles, the mosquitoes are relentless. When darkness falls Bob curls up in a sheltered spot on the riverbank, pulls his hood tighter over his head, and tries to fall asleep.

Throughout the night he lies there, rarely sleeping, always shivering. His mind is filled with thoughts of hungry bears following his scent through the forest. In the darkness, his hearing becomes highly sensitive. The background sounds are a chorus of water. Waterfalls, rivers, creeks, rivulets, and raindrops, thousands of gallons of water, pouring off the surrounding mountainsides to run down the valley.

Beyond this natural noise, his hearing picks out an occasional slap or popping sound from nearby. He strains to hear, trying to obtain direction or some clue as to origin. His eyes are wide in the darkness, searching for movement, or any sign of something coming to get him.

• • • — — — • • •

The light of dawn is a huge relief. Bob stands to stretch the kinks out of his body. Walking in the approximate direction of the strange sound he heard in the night, he discovers a beaver pond. What he thought might be an approaching bear had been merely a beaver slapping its tail against the water.

There is no question in Bob's mind that he is lost. It's damn embarrassing, but people are probably looking for him by now. He decides it would be best to get out in the open where he can be seen and wait.

Not far down the river he comes across a sandbar at a wide spot in the river where the trees open up. Bob grabs a stick and scratches a big arrow in the sand as a visual signal to searchers in airplanes or helicopters. The drizzly rain continues, but as long as he is up and moving, he can keep relatively warm.

It's not long before he sees his first helicopter. Over the course of the day, he spots about thirty of them. The problem is that they are simply commercial operators carrying passengers down Gastineau Channel to Taku Lodge or some other tourist destination.

These helicopters are miles off down the valley, flying just under the clouds at fifteen hundred to two thousand feet in elevation—too distant to see his sandbar or arrow.

Bob waves his arms whenever he spots a helicopter. But even if people aboard were looking right at him, from that distance he would be barely a dot in the woods, blending into the landscape in his dark green pullover.

When night arrives again, he finds a stump and crawls under it to get out of the rain. His shivering keeps him awake. Every shadow thrown by every bush seems to move, mimicking a large carnivore ready to pounce.

· · · — — — · · ·

When morning dawns on his second full day lost, Bob climbs out from under the stump with a plan.

Yesterday he watched helicopters follow the same route all day. They all fly out of the heliport on the outskirts of Juneau. Following the helicopter route in reverse will take him right back to town.

Bob strikes out down the valley, on a line that will intersect the distant flight corridor. The river offers a path of least resistance through a wide valley flooded with beaver ponds.

The early hours pass uneventfully until Bob finds himself on another sandbar. With little warning, a helicopter suddenly appears almost directly overhead and only about five hundred feet up.

Bob tears his shirt off and waves it wildly, yelling. The red and white chopper is right there, right above him. Suddenly it wheels around, gaining altitude fast, veering off to the north, and quickly disappearing from view.

He waits, hopeful. It doesn't come back.

Pulling his shirt back over his head, Bob starts out again, angling for the mountains just to the west, over which the tour helicopters have been flying.

He passes a long, exhausting day walking across the valley and then climbing the mountainside in what he hopes is the general direction of Juneau. Occasionally he finds huckleberries and salmonberries to eat, but it's late in the season and the pickings are lean.

Working his way through more bear tunnels in the brush, it occurs to him that any bear he meets might be a little angry at having to share what berries are left. Luckily he avoids any close encounters and, high on the mountain, he emerges from the claustrophobic paths to find himself in a meadow.

Just as he sits down on a rock to take a break, he spots a sow bear with two cubs a short distance away.

Bob starts edging away, hoping to escape without a confrontation. As soon as the bear spots the movement, she is gone in a flash, her two cubs trailing quickly behind.

The scene brings a chuckle, finally something to laugh about. What a relief to note that they were black bears, generally far less dangerous to humans than the brown bears he has been fearing.

With the sun setting on his third night out, the meadow looks as good as any place to sleep. He edges under a rock for shelter. Rain drips down on him all night long.

· · · — — — · · ·

In the morning Bob continues walking west. A knee starts to bother him after he climbs down a cliff, but there is nothing to do but keep moving.

After crossing a high, flat valley he scrambles up another ridgeline. Finally he recognizes the landscape. Gastineau Channel is visible only a few miles away.

Bob can hear a crew at work just below, in what he can clearly see is the valley of Sheep Creek. The crew isn't visible from where he stands, but the sound of men and tools filters up to the ridge. *It must be the Echo Bay Mine, and those are the guys who can give me a ride back.*

The last remaining obstacle between Bob and civilization is a verdant, vegetation-choked mountain side. Without hesitating he heads off downslope. Descending is like fighting a shoulder-to-shoulder army of spiky devil's club plants reinforced by regiments of interwoven mountain-alder branches. The low-growing alder holds him at bay, almost pushing him back, while devil's club thorns tear at his clothes, skin, and face. His feet search blindly for footing when he can't see the ground.

Scratched, beaten, exhausted, and soaked to the skin, Bob eventually emerges at the bottom of the valley, crosses a stream, and stumbles onto the Sheep Creek Trail. By the time he arrives at the mine, everything is locked up and the crew is gone for the day.

· · · — — — · · ·

The state trooper and the SEADOGS leader are out of the search and rescue meeting for only a few minutes. When they walk back in, they don't say a thing.

"What's going on?" everyone wants to know. "What was that phone call about?"

The trooper is hesitant. "I don't know if we can really say yet. We have something we have to check out."

"Well, what?"

"I don't even really want to say. We get things like this. We get a lot of weird phone calls from people. Some guy just called from Bullwinkle's downtown and he said, 'My name is Bob and I am hungry and I am cold and I am tired.'"

"What? He's in Bullwinkle's? No way!" is the unified retort.

· · · — — — · · ·

Bob stands there at the mine, his feet killing him, his hopes for a ride with the crew dashed. He considers breaking into the mine building to use the phone.

"Oh, the hell with it. I've been this far."

He starts walking.

In a little over an hour, Bob limps out to Thane Road along Gastineau Channel, about four miles south of Juneau.

He's dirty, dripping wet, ragged. His hair is hanging in his face as his only defense from mosquitoes. Standing on the shoulder of the road, he's waving his arms, trying to get a car to stop.

The driver of the tourist bus coming back from the salmon bake declines to pull over. Soon enough, though, a car stops. When Bob opens the door, the young man at the wheel puts a raincoat on the car seat so Bob won't soak the upholstery.

"What happened to you?" he asks.

"I went out hiking," Bob replies. "I got lost, been out for a few days. I have to get to a phone."

"Hey, you're the guy they have been looking for over the last three days!"

"Yeah?"

"Oh yeah, there's this massive search going on for you."

He points out the window. "They're all over there. What are you doing over here?"

All Bob can say is, "Man, my girlfriend is going to be pissed off, my sister is going to kill me, and as soon as the cops get me they're going to want to know all kinds of stuff. I'm starving. I have to get to a phone and let everybody know I'm okay."

The young man gives him a ride into Juneau, but they can't find a pay phone. Finally the driver remembers.

"There's a pay phone at Bullwinkle's Pizza."

So they drive to Bullwinkle's. Bob walks in and the pizza chef is right there.

"Wow, you look pretty funky. Are you out there helping search for that missing hiker?"

"No," Bob says as he pulls a soggy twenty-dollar bill out of his pocket, "I *am* that missing hiker. Here, make me some pizza."

He finds the phone and calls his sister's house. Nobody answers.

He makes other calls. Nobody answers.

Of course, it occurs to him, *they're all out searching.*

Finally Bob gets through to a state trooper, who tells him to wait right there. Just then his pizza arrives. He hangs up the phone and devours half the pie as he waits. His stomach has shrunk too much to eat the other half.

• • • — — — • • •

The state trooper running the meeting eventually gets everyone to quiet down after the announcement that the object of their search may be at Bullwinkle's.

"We're sending the Juneau Police Department to check on this because we get these weird calls, you know. There are a lot of really twisted people out there."

Everyone sits, fidgeting impatiently in their seats. Ten minutes later a man walks in to announce that the report has been confirmed. They got an ID on the guy at Bullwinkle's, it's Bob, and he's okay.

Everybody looks at each other like, "You gotta be kidding." Then the room breaks out in applause and cheering, people jumping up and down. But everyone is wondering how the heck this happened.

A couple of nights later, Bob gathers all the searchers together in a classroom at the local middle school—the classroom where his sister teaches. Of course he orders Bullwinkle's pizza for everyone. Then he lays out some maps and tells the story of how he walked off the wrong side of the mountain, far away from his intended route. While the search concentrated on where he said he would be, Bob was walking in almost the opposite direction.

That's why, just as the state troopers were on the cusp of either calling off the search or expanding the effort, Bob showed up a few blocks away at the neighborhood pizza joint.

When the flames part briefly, the men
sprint through the smoke toward the sound
of voices.

CHAPTER 11

SAVED BY THE BELL

T his was a banner year for forest fires in the West. The smoke
jumpers out of the aerial fire depot in Missoula, Montana,
broke records for jumps, number of fires manned, and everything
else over that summer. There was just one flight after another.

As an advance guard, smoke jumpers play a key role in forest
fire control. Sent out at a moment's notice, they parachute on small
fires, far from any road, and snuff them out fast. Their task rarely
stretches past a few days. They complete the work, hike out or are
picked up, and return to base for the next assignment. In a busy
season they keep the lid on the nuisance fires, freeing up the
ground troops for the big battles.

The jump call on August 4 begins no differently than any
other. The temperature at the airfield that morning is more than
100 degrees Fahrenheit. A DC-2 with twelve jumpers takes off
from Missoula.

It's a close-knit group. Only the people who really want to be
jumpers make it through the training. Most know each other from
attending college in Missoula. Firefighting over the summer season put these men through school.

The foreman, Fred, is a full-time Forest Service employee and
veteran firefighter. There are few things that disturb his focus on
the fire line. In his mind, the safety of his crew is foremost.

Darrel has returned to jumping after nearly a ten-year break. His seasonal Forest Service work surveying roads didn't come through this year. With a wife and six kids, he makes good use of his summer Forest Service income as a welcome supplement to the salary he earns as a schoolteacher. Darrel wondered if he could still hack it as a smoke jumper. What a pleasant surprise to find the parachutes greatly improved, with a larger canopy for a softer landing.

Tom is only a first-year jumper, although it's not from lack of trying. As Fred's college roommate, he applied over several seasons and passed everything but the eye exam. After a few years in the Army, he returned to Missoula to find a new director at the smoke-jumping base who was unaware of Tom's vision problems . Tom got a copy of the eye chart, memorized the lines, and passed with flying colors.

The fire they are heading for was started by a lightning strike. It's burning in a roadless maze of rugged country straddling the Idaho-Montana border, in the Selway-Bitterroot Wilderness. Eight jumpers out of Grangeville, Idaho, are already on the ground, flown in at 8 A.M. aboard a Ford Tri-motor.

By noon the DC-2 with the Missoula crew circles over the drop zone. Fred works with the pilot and a spotter to designate a landing zone for the jumpers. The cargo of firefighting tools will be dropped closer to the fire. The air is calm, the sky clear.

Below them the fire drapes like a smoking blanket across the upper elevations of a ridge that descends off the north side of 7,298-foot Freeman Peak. The fire is small, a few acres at this point, burning along the ground up through a helicopter landing zone carved out of the forest on the ridge top at about 7,000 feet. The flames, primarily on the west side of the ridge, threaten to expand into two basins just below the summit.

The jump is smooth. The cargo falls right in place.

Now with a combined force of twenty, Fred sends five men to work the eastern flank along a rocky promontory just over the crest of the ridge. The other fifteen men begin work on the main body of fire by cutting a fire line across the ridge and then south along the western flank.

The plan is to encircle the fire while it is still small. Borate bombers will be called in to drop retardant and help knock down the flames. Then the men will attack the remaining fuel sources, break up the heart of the fire, and extinguish the blaze.

For an hour and a half the crew works along the edge of the fire. They cut brush back, clear burnable materials out of the way, dig down into mineral soil with their half-hoe, half-axe Pulaskis. The swath of bare dirt they unveil stops the ground fire from spreading. A few of the men have power saws to cut downed trees. It's sweaty, dirty work with an August sun blazing down. Hot air parches dry throats.

Just a week earlier they were issued experimental shirts, new equipment for Forest Service firefighters. The bright orange fabric is stiff, loaded with some kind of fire retardant, and doesn't breathe like the work shirts they normally wear. Nobody complains. When you're working to pay the bills, a free shirt is a free shirt.

As the line extends up the ridge and the fifteen men move higher, Fred pulls Tom aside and tells him to hang back and watch the tail end of the line. They can't take any chance that the fire might creep across the line and begin burning below and behind them.

• • • — — — • • •

The breeze that begins around 2:30 that afternoon would be a blessing on most summer days. To the firefighters it means trouble. Wind delivers oxygen, feeding and fanning the flames. As they look up they can see the leading edge of the fire begin to advance rapidly up toward Freeman Peak.

Their opportunity to encircle the blaze is slipping away. All they can do now is fight to keep what fire line they have from being lost while working to keep any new flames from circling behind.

As the blaze intensifies, a spot fire ignites downslope behind them. In a quick scramble, the fire line is readjusted and the men's personal gear is moved into a rock-slide area away from the flames.

An hour passes and the best they can do is hold the flames around them at bay. Just after four o'clock a weather front begins to form. Stratus clouds gather in the sky. High winds suddenly lash out of the west, buffeting the forest, fanning the flames. The fire rages upslope, whipping into the crowns of the trees, roaring as the tinder-dry forest explodes.

As the jumpers retreat down the fire line back toward their drop zone, the winds reverse and the fire burns back toward them, flanking both sides of the original burn. A flaming snag is blown over and across the line, igniting a fire that burns downslope, cutting off their escape.

The firefighters' first instinct is to head down and get below the blaze. After taking a few steps off the fire line, Darrel watches, stunned, as the fire runs downhill for hundreds of yards with incredible speed.

At the other end of the line, Tom can do nothing as the flames suddenly sweep across the firebreak and began burning new material downslope. Rather than be cut off, he runs through the flames to rejoin the crew.

With winds of fifty miles per hour feeding the fire like a blast furnace, Fred leads his crew in the only safe direction left: uphill through the burned forest to the helicopter landing spot on top of the ridge. Maybe they can find shelter in the cleared-out area above.

It doesn't take long to find the landing zone. Fred is first on top and Tom is not far behind. About half the crew has time to sit down and collect themselves as they wait for the rest of the men to arrive.

Tom remembers the personal gear bags stashed just below, down the crest of the ridge. He has a new camera in his pack, along with his glasses, a jacket, and other items.

"You know, our personal gear bags are just down about thirty yards away," Tom says. "I'm going to go back and get mine."

Fred doesn't pause to consider. "No, you are staying right here."

With the words still hanging in the air, the wind reverses again and the western slope of the ridge explodes in flames. The heat is immediately intense.

Darrel is bringing up the rear with his squad of men as the burned-over forest reignites around them. They hesitate in a pocket of air surrounded by flames. Heat, smoke, and ashes are swirling. They can't see which way to run. The men soak handkerchiefs in water from their canteens, each man holding a wet cloth over his mouth to ease breathing. When the flames part briefly, they sprint through the smoke toward the sound of voices ahead.

Emerging into the clearing, they find the rest of the crew soaking T-shirts and handkerchiefs with water from two five-gallon cans. They cover head and face with the wet cloths as protection from the heat and smoke. Wind, oxygen, and fire mix in a swirling maelstrom as the forest seems to ignite all at once in a ball of fire.

Above them a thunderhead forms over the conflagration. The smoke cloud mushrooms thousands of feet into the atmosphere. Lightning rips down out of the blackening clouds. Flames whip high above the treetops, then lash into the clearing, forced down by the wind.

In the swirling winds the crew dodges back and forth across the ridge top to escape blistering heat and waves of fire. They lie next to each other on the ground in pairs, head to feet, faces close to the earth where the air is cool enough to breathe, watching each other's legs for flames. If they stand up, the superheated atmosphere will sear their lungs. They watch for the snags that burn through and crash into the clearing. Blasts of scalding air roar over the ridge top, singeing skin and clothing. One man's pants catch fire, only to be pounded out by other crew members. Flying firebrands land on their clothes to be slapped away. Wind snaps off the burning crowns of trees. Other trees blow apart as the pitch expands in the intense heat. Fire thunders around, deafening, like a hundred freight trains roaring by. Steel hard-hats and canteens become too hot to touch. Dense smoke chokes lungs and burns eyes. The men can barely see in the acrid smoke. There is no escape as the fire incinerates the forest around them.

· · · — — — · · ·

For three years now, Rod has been a pilot with Johnston Flying Service in Montana, hiring on after a tour of duty flying helicopters in Alaska for the U.S. Air Force. On August 4 he and his Bell 47G-3 helicopter are based out of the Moose Creek Ranger Station, contracted to the Forest Service for fire duty in the Selway-Bitterroot Wilderness. The aircraft is a little over a year old, the first civilian model from Bell Corporation with a supercharged engine and the power needed for flying in the mountains.

Early this morning he and the head ranger, Bill, had flown out to check on reports of a lightning-strike fire. Before long they spotted the smoke plume rising lazily in the calm air and hovered into a landing on a small plateau. Less than a mile away they could see a little brushfire burning hungrily under the trees up toward the crest of a ridge just below Freeman Peak.

The day was shaping up to be as hot as they come, the forest tinder-dry. The smoking ridge was surrounded by thousands of acres of densely treed terrain. The conclusion was obvious. Airplanes should be called in to bomb the blaze with fire retardant before it had a chance to spread. A few minutes later they lifted off and returned to the ranger station.

Later that afternoon Bill is ready to head out with Rod to take a second look at the fire. The Borate bombers are unavailable, tied up fighting other fires. Once in the air and en route, he tells Rod that smoke jumpers have been dropped on the fire. He wants to check on their progress.

When the ridge comes into view, the lazy plume of morning has been replaced by huge, billowing smoke clouds. The brushfire has exploded, engulfing the ridge top. Whole trees are going up like torches.

With the helicopter bucking stiff headwinds and severe turbulence, Rod and Bill fly back and forth, peering down through the dense smoke. There is no sign of the twenty men sent to battle what had been a small burn just hours before. Running low on fuel, they are forced to return to Moose Creek.

Fighting off their worst fears, Rod and Bill are back over the fire within the hour. The westerly headwind, clocked at more than fifty miles per hour, has not let up. Waves of hot air billow up off the burn, shaking the chopper violently as they strain eyes and crane necks to spot any signs of life.

Suddenly, high on the east side of the ridge, Bill catches a glimpse of orange shirts through the smoke. Five men are trapped in the middle of a rock scree slope surrounded by flames. Immense plumes of fire lap over the crest toward them, pushed by the howling winds. With the fire raging out of control, it doesn't look as though they can survive much longer.

Rod and Bill scan the eastern slope. If they can find an opening in the fire, maybe they can get down there and lead the men out, or direct them somehow with the helicopter. There is a possible route through the flames, but it leads down to the east. If a spark or firebrand lands somewhere in front of men fleeing in that direction, the resulting fire would roar back up the slope and trap them between the two blazes. Yet there seems to be no hope if the men stay where they are.

Seconds tick by as Rod searches for a better option. Staring down into an area of intense fire, he spots an open space among the flaming trees. The smoke clears for an instant and he can see more men in orange shirts, huddled below in the open space on top of the ridge. Smoke and flames are swirling ferociously. It's hard to keep the men in sight. The winds and updrafts are severe, and he can barely hold the helicopter in place.

There is no more thinking now, only doing. The only way to save the men below is to get into that clearing with the helicopter and tell them to run for the opening that leads down the east side of the ridge.

Circling back around, Rod drops through the smoke, aiming straight down for the clearing. As soon as the chopper gets below treetop level, the turbulence shakes the helicopter violently. Billows of smoke erase any view of the landing zone. He pulls up and out to look for a better approach.

On his second attempt, he approaches sideways—sliding along the ridgeline, nose into the western wind. Maybe he can duck in quickly and drop through the turbulence.

Once again, gusting updrafts and the roaring headwind eject the aircraft, with Rod fighting to control the chopper.

Backing off from the fire, Rod can see the westerly wind is forming a rotor, cresting like a wave over the ridge. This creates a dangerous reverse tailwind, and all that unstable air is right where he needs to land. The western approach is far too dangerous, coming in over the fire. Running out of ideas, he tries to back into the clearing with the chopper's nose to the east. The ridge top is completely obscured with smoke. Rod can't see to land. He pulls out again.

Maybe if he flies nose in, really fast from the east, he can catch enough of a headwind to land safely.

As he enters the smoke a fourth time, the intense turbulence flings the helicopter up and away like a flake of ash on the wind.

As Rod circles out from the conflagration, he turns to the ranger. "There isn't any way we are getting in there today."

But the vision of those men surrounded by fire is burned into his mind. He can't stomach the thought of leaving them trapped.

Dropping into the valley to the east, he lines up for one last attempt. It's a gamble, but he might be able to sneak up through the turbulence from below. Ground effect—the downwash of the rotors—should catch the helicopter before it crashes into the landing zone.

Ascending at top speed up and out of the valley, Rod takes a final bearing on the landing zone. As he crosses into the fire, smoke envelops the aircraft, visibility goes to zero, and the bottom drops out. The helicopter free-falls toward the ridge top.

· · · — — — · · ·

For an hour or more, the men have continued fighting to live, dashing back and forth to avoid the flames and heat waves lashing into the clearing. Blowing ash obscures everything beyond a few paces. The flames roar in their ears.

As they hunker down in one spot, eyes burning from smoke, a helicopter suddenly drops through the smoke, plummeting toward where they lie. At the last second, they dodge out of the way. The chopper stops its descent mere feet from the ground.

The clearing becomes a hurricane of whirling ash and burning debris. Everything aflame glows red hot in the downwash of the rotor blades. When the helicopter sets down amid the burning stumps and logs, a ranger jumps out. He tells Fred he will lead the crew out.

No one is willing to follow. They have managed to keep alive so far, and the last thing they are going to do is walk off into the burning inferno.

With tanks of helicopter fuel heating up over the red-hot ground and no time to waste, Rod agrees to try and ferry the crew out. As two of the men with the worst smoke-damaged eyes are strapped in next to him, Rod wonders if he can get the helicopter back in the air, let alone control the aircraft as they fly out of the fire.

Rod pulls back, the clearing whips into a hurricane of blowing ash, and the helicopter slowly lifts off. As it rises above the clearing, the turbulence and heat catch the aircraft and fling it up and away. Within seconds the smoke is left behind as the helicopter flies out into open sky. Cool, clean mountain air soothes his passengers' smoke-parched lungs.

Rod drops the two men off in a nearby safe area below Free-man Peak. They step off into an alpine meadow with a stream flowing under a clear blue sky. It's as close to being delivered from hell to heaven as they have ever experienced.

Rod flies right back to the fire, repeating his approach, fighting through the turbulence and zero visibility, to drop back on the land-ing spot. He looks out at what seems like a hundred men milling around his aircraft. How is he going to get all these guys out?

This time two men get inside the helicopter and two men are instructed to climb into the trays—aluminum boxes mounted on each skid that are normally used for carrying equipment. There is no way to tie the men in. They will just have to hang on and tough it out. Once again, straining the helicopter and working the updrafts, Rod catapults out through the firestorm.

Over the next hour he returns four more times through the smoke and fire. Smoke-jumper etiquette calls for the crew to be first out, before the supervisors. Fred, Darrel, Tom, and the ranger are the last men left when Rod comes on the final trip. With Fred and Darrel buckling into the seats, Tom and the ranger roll into the trays and hold on as best they can. Minutes later they join the rest of the crew in the meadow and wash the smoke and soot from their eyes as dusk begins to settle over the mountains.

· · · — — — · · ·

The next day the men are flown out by helicopter and transported by truck to Missoula. Twelve of the jumpers are treated for smoke-burned eyes at St Patrick Hospital and released that day. The remainder of the crew walk away with no injuries.

Five hundred firefighters are eventually brought in to battle what turns into a major fire.

The helicopter pilot directs all praise toward his aircraft. From what Rod's instruments told him, the conditions over the fire cre-ated an air density similar to flying at 12,500 feet. He doesn't think any other helicopter of the time could have done the job. When he first dropped out of the sky, he came close to doubling the redline maximum for manifold pressure in order to stop the aircraft from hitting the ground. Every liftoff was life or death, with the helicop-ter straining far past its known limits.

The next day, when the mechanic arrived to check out the aircraft, he couldn't find anything wrong. He changed the oil and Rod kept flying.

The fire-repellent shirt fabric proved itself as well. All of the crew's clothing showed burns, except for the orange shirts.

Darrel and Tom were not alone in feeling that they were very lucky to escape with their lives. Fred credits the training of his crew for their survival. "They stuck together and followed directions. Not one man panicked. They were a good crew, good guys."

Shivering, tired, Larry makes his peace
with the world and prepares to die.

CHAPTER 12

IN DIRE STRAITS

U p in the northwest corner of Washington state, the San Juan
Islands beckon like a paradise just out of reach. Situated in
the rain shadow of the Olympic Mountains, they enjoy a warm,
dry, and inviting climate that is rare in the region. The many small
islands, inlets, channels, and pocket beaches are ideal for kayak
exploration.

As always, there are obstacles to reaching paradise. The
current-filled and occasionally cantankerous waters of Rosario
Strait guard the entrance to these islands. The crossing of this
strait, not for the faint of heart, is best done quickly, between the
tides, and in calm weather. It is always waiting as the final barrier
back to civilization.

Saul and Larry are good friends from college. They have kept
in touch, and now, a few years out of school, Saul has a week off
between jobs. He decides to spend a few days kayaking in the San
Juans. Larry wants to come along.

Both are accomplished athletes, former collegiate running
teammates, still training every day and competing in races around
the Pacific Northwest. Saul has been sea kayaking for a couple of
years, including several previous trips in the San Juans. Larry has
handled kayaks before, mostly on freshwater. They are young,
strong, confident in their athletic abilities.

Saul has all the equipment: two kayaks, paddles, dry bags, life vests, safety equipment, and the camping supplies. All Larry needs to bring is his sleeping bag, clothing, and personal gear.

They agree to meet at the Washington Park boat ramp west of Anacortes on a Friday afternoon in November. The plan is to paddle just under four miles the first day across the open water of Rosario Strait, north to tiny Strawberry Island. The next couple of days will be spent exploring Orcas Island and maybe west to Blind Island State Park before returning to Washington Park.

On the day of departure Saul is ready and waiting at the ramp. Larry doesn't show. Hours pass before his car pulls up in the parking lot.

"I was caught in traffic coming out of Seattle," he says. "I totally underestimated the time it would take."

Saul has little patience at this point. He throws a dry bag to Larry.

"Stow your stuff in the green boat."

When Larry is ready, Saul gets him settled in the kayak, adjusting the foot pedals and showing him how to handle the rudder. The spray skirt that keeps water from splashing into the cockpit fits a bit tight around the coaming. Larry might have a hard time pulling it loose if the boat were to capsize and he needed to bail out. He tells Larry to stash it under the deck. Saul himself is more comfortable without one, having learned a paddling style that keeps errant waves from splashing inside his boat. By the time they finally paddle away for the beach, it's 9 P.M.

The sun has set hours before on this late fall night, yet it is easy enough for Saul to see the far shore across Rosario Strait. They paddle for Reef Point on Cypress Island. Blakely Island is off to the northwest. Farther to the north, Mount Constitution on Orcas Island is an easily recognizable landmark.

The water starts out choppy but manageable. As they make their way farther from shore, wind-driven ocean waves rolling up Rosario Strait undulate in from the south. With no horizon to focus on in the darkness, Larry begins to feel a little seasick. Before long the black hulk of Cypress Island rises above them, and they decide to take a break so Larry can get his equilibrium back.

They ride the waves onto the shore of Cypress, crashing on the rocks but pulling themselves up on the beach without too much

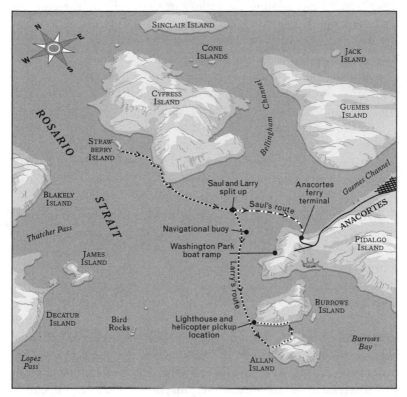

trouble. The night air is cold. The sound of surf surrounds them, white noise in the darkness. The lights of Anacortes glow to the east.

Saul is feeling a little uneasy; the paddling conditions are more difficult than he had expected. If he is feeling uncomfortable, then Larry is definitely a little over his head. Neither of them has much to say. Saul pulls out his dry suit and tells Larry to put it on. Saul settles for the shorty wet suit he brought along as a spare.

Back on the water, it's hard to judge the powerful currents in the darkness. As they approach Strawberry Island, the beach sweeps by before they can make it to shore. With few landing options left and no chance of fighting against the tide, they are forced to surf up on a wave-washed section of rocks.

Saul is first in. His kayak hangs up on a submerged outcrop and spins parallel to the waves. Larry is right behind, and his kayak spears Saul's boat amidships. Suddenly Saul finds himself upside down, staring out at a blurry underwater scene lit by the glow of his headlamp. It occurs to him that this trip isn't going well.

They bail out of their boats, and waves wash over the men as they wrestle with the swamped boats in the darkness. Finally, out of pure frustration, they use brute force to pull and heave the boats, fully loaded with equipment and what feels like a hundred pounds of water, off the rocks and up the steep slopes of the island.

As the equipment is pulled out to set up camp, they discover that the hatch seals on Larry's kayak have leaked. Seawater has seeped into the storage compartments. In the rush to get paddling, Larry wasn't sure how to seal the dry bag Saul gave him. His clothing, his sleeping bag, everything is soaked.

They get the tent set up, no easy task in darkness with wind blowing, and crawl in. Giving his sleeping bag to Larry, Saul puts on all his extra clothes for the night. As they lie there trying to get comfortable, the rain starts and the wind begins to pick up.

Staring up in the darkness, watching the tent roof flex and cave with each gust, they talk about what they might be able to forage if they have to wait out the weather past their three-day food supply. Saul noticed some wild onions while they were hauling the boats out. The wild strawberries are long gone. The remaining selection is a little lean: lichen on the rocks, dry grass, a few fir trees and red bark madrones; maybe some seaweed is washing up on the high-tide line as they speak.

Late that night the temperature drops into the thirties. The rain turns to sleet, pelting the tent in the driving wind.

· · · — — — · · ·

At first light on Saturday, Saul is down on the beach to check the weather. Wind and waves continue to buffet the island. Gray clouds crowd out the sky, hanging low over the water. The weather radio is crackling out a report of small-craft advisories, with southwest winds fifteen to twenty knots.

Saul finds a hole in his kayak from the previous night's rough landing. While scraping together a patch using tent seam sealer, he considers their options. They could stick to their plan and ride the wind and tide north to Orcas Island. This would mean crossing another four miles of open water.

Or they could paddle the half-mile to Cypress Island and find someone to help them. He can see a cabin over there, with smoke rising out of the chimney.

They could also paddle to Cypress and backtrack, hugging the shore around to the east side, then make a dash across a mile-wide channel to Guemes Island, where they could catch a ferry ride back to Anacortes.

Or they could stay put until the weather improves.

Larry joins him and they both look north to Orcas Island. Between them and their planned campsite for the second night, sailboats competing in a regatta heave through frothing whitecaps that would bury their kayaks in sea foam.

Cypress is an easy paddle, but they would have to find someone with a powerboat to give them a ride back to the mainland. This seems like a lot to ask.

Paddling around to Guemes is a long way off-route. Their situation just isn't that desperate.

In the end they decide to stay put and wait. Larry's gear isn't going to dry out. The trip is over. Now they just have to get back.

· · · —— —— —— · · ·

By the afternoon the clouds are breaking up and the wind seems to be tailing off. From their vantage point, the four miles of water between Strawberry Island and Washington Park doesn't look that bad.

Saul goes over the tide charts and sets a departure time for a return crossing with the slack tide. Getting across at slack is critical. When the ebb tide starts, the waves will become much worse as the current pushes water against the wind.

They pack up their kayaks and launch at the designated time—Larry in the dry suit, Saul in the shorty wet suit, spray skirts stowed below deck. They retrace their route, paddling strong, riding the waves like a gentle roller coaster. It feels good to be back on the water, going somewhere. Maybe the bad times are behind them and they have finally found their stride.

As they come around the southern end of Cypress, a southeastern wind, unnoticed in the shelter of the island, is whipping up whitecaps out in the channel. Saul is confident he can handle the waves. Larry follows, and they make good progress. But one mile out into the channel with another two miles to go, Larry begins falling behind.

Out away from land, the wind is tearing off the tops of waves. As the wind crashes into the rollers at an angle, the water heaps up into frothing crests that assault the kayaks from two directions. The waves build until Saul and Larry lose sight of each other as their boats fall into the troughs, salt spray lashing through the air.

Larry's boat is taking on water as waves break over his kayak and splash into the cockpit. Saul yells across the distance, coaching Larry to angle with waves and ride out the swell. Larry's kayak feels too unstable. He rides the waves sideways, turning head-on into the larger ones. The technique keeps him afloat but takes him south, off-route, away from the landing place. At one point Saul tries to tow him but the rope is too short. The kayaks crash into each other in the steep wave troughs.

Caught in this wild water, all they can do is paddle to keep from capsizing. The wind and waves hold them in place, slowing their pace to a crawl. Fear pushes down on their backs. Hunching over to fight for balance, they pray they won't overturn.

For forty-five minutes they stay together, making little progress against a six-foot swell and forty-knot winds from the south and southeast. At the turn of the tide they are less than halfway across the channel. Saul calculates that their progress is less than one knot against a two-and-a-half-knot tide. Whether they continue forward or turn back at this point, the result will be the same. With the ebb tide picking up speed, they will be swept south through Rosario Strait and into the twenty-two-mile-wide Strait of Juan de Fuca.

As they drift farther apart, Saul makes a difficult choice, then yells across the waves to Larry: "I'm going for help." Saul starts pulling for the Anacortes ferry terminal across a mile and a half of wind-whipped water. On each wave crest he looks back to see Larry farther away, his kayak slowly disappearing into the white spray whipping off the water.

Before long a fishing boat passes within a hundred yards, tossing on the rough sea. Larry has flares, but they are stored below deck. In the time it would take to pull them out, the waves would capsize his kayak. He keeps to the paddle as the boat fades into the distance.

By the time he reaches the shoal west of the ferry terminal, the tide is running like a river at flood. He pulls with everything he has left to keep from being swept back into the open water. Exhausted, Saul drags his boat up on shore. He climbs over a cyclone fence to get to the terminal and a phone. At 4 P.M.. his call for help is answered by Skagit County 911 dispatch.

Within minutes the Anacortes Police rescue boat is on the way. When it hits Rosario Strait, the storm-driven waves threaten to capsize the small craft. It is all the crew can do to don survival suits and head back to the marina.

Saul is taken to the Coast Guard office in Anacortes. He gives them a description of Larry, the boat, and where they were when the two men became separated.

Forty-five minutes later a Coast Guard helicopter out of Port Angeles is on the scene, flying search patterns. Coast Guard boats from Seattle and Bellingham are dispatched for the search.

Darkness falls and there is no sign of Larry. The search continues with civilian watercraft, fixed-wing Coast Guard aircraft, and a helicopter from the Whidbey Island Naval Station.

· · · — — — · · ·

Locating a dark-green kayak, at night, in a three-mile-wide expanse of salt water whipped to froth with wind and waves is an almost impossible task. The search area is in constant motion, foaming white, washing green. Noise from wind and helicopter blades drowns out all other sound. Darkness narrows the search to the beam of a spotlight. But as the chance of finding Larry alive decreases with each passing hour, the crews on the water and in the air never slacken their efforts.

Communications are difficult. Having no direct contact with the search crews, Saul can only listen to the radio traffic from where he waits at the Coast Guard office. So many thoughts are running through his mind. Will they ever find him? What is he going to tell Larry's parents?

At midnight the radio traffic picks up. A Coast Guard boat has sighted something washed up on the beach of an uninhabited island two miles south of Washington Park. With the water too rough for a landing, they send a swimmer in to investigate.

Through the lashing windstorm the swimmer radios from the beach to the Coast Guard boat just offshore. The Coast Guard boat radios to Seattle, and Seattle calls Anacortes. Saul is handed the phone. They have found a green kayak.

Saul waits patiently as information is passed through several relays. When they describe the kayak, he can confirm that it is the green kayak Larry had been paddling. Then there is more waiting as additional information works its way back and forth.

The paddle is with the boat. That's a good sign.

More waiting.

The sleeping bag is missing.

That's another good sign. Larry must be alive. He was swept south and somehow fought against current and waves to paddle in to the island. At this minute he is probably somewhere up in the forest, hunkering down, trying to stay warm in the sleeping bag.

This is great news, wonderful news. Saul has to call Larry's parents in Seattle. He had been putting it off, not sure what to say.

When Larry's parents pick up the phone, Saul pours out the story. He tells them they just found Larry's boat pulled up on a beach south of where they became separated. Searchers are heading out to the island. Larry is sure to be found within the hour.

When Saul hangs up, the Coast Guardsmen run him out to the Anacortes airport. Two search groups are gathering there for the flight to the island. They want to know what Larry looks like, his habits, anything and everything that might help them to find him as fast as possible.

· · · ▬ ▬ ▬ · · ·

Saul is then taken back to the Coast Guard office, where he waits by the radio for news. Voices rattle back and forth. It is a difficult search in darkness on the steep slopes of a rugged island. There are plenty of nooks and crannies for a person to crawl into for shelter out of the weather.

An hour and a half passes as the teams work their search grid across the island. Saul hears an offhand comment filter through the radio static—something about the paddle found with the kayak. Then it hits him.

That sounds like the emergency paddle!

In a flash he is punching the numbers for the Coast Guard in Seattle. He has to talk to the swimmer, the guy who found the kayak.

As he waits for all the parties to be connected, an awful dread tightens his chest.

Slowly, carefully, he questions the swimmer.

"How many hatches are on the boat?"

"One," the answer comes back.

"How many cockpits?" The seconds creep by.

"Two."

"What color was the paddle?"

"Red."

"What bags are with the boat? Please, just dump them out and describe them."

The swimmer finds the food bag, a flashlight, and the flare bag, among other things.

It's like a punch in the gut.

The swimmer, unfamiliar with sea kayaks, had mistaken the opening to a storage compartment, its hatch cover missing, for a second cockpit. The red paddle is a spare lashed to the boat for emergencies. Larry's white fiberglass paddle is not there. Even if he had made it to shore without the paddle and without the hatch cover, he would have taken at least the food, the flashlight, and certainly the flares.

It's 2 A.M. Saul has to call Larry's parents and let them know.

· · · — — — · · ·

Larry stuck with Saul as he led the way out into the wind-whipped channel. When waves started to build, he tried to angle into them the way Saul told him to, but the kayak felt ready to roll at any second. The wind was whipping salt water into his face. Some of the bigger waves broke over his boat, spilling water into the cockpit. His kayak began riding lower in the water, making the paddling slower and the boat more unstable than ever. He just couldn't keep up.

As Saul got farther and farther away, Larry began to yell from the crest of each wave for Saul to wait up. But his words were stolen by the wind. He could see Saul yelling something back, but he couldn't hear with the wind roaring in his ears. Then Saul was gone, paddling south toward land.

Alone now, Larry continues struggling toward shore. With the cockpit almost swamped, the boat actually seems a little more stable. He makes some progress, though the wind and waves never let up.

As time passes, the rocky western shore of Washington Park seems to come closer. The swamped kayak is sluggish, hard to steer. Larry judges the distance to land to be less than a mile. He has swum such distances before in competitive triathlons. The dry suit should keep him warm in the water, which is at 50 degrees Fahrenheit. As he debates abandoning the kayak, a wave rolls the boat, making his decision for him.

With powerful strokes Larry begins swimming for shore, feeling more comfortable, more in his element now that he is out of the kayak. It is not long before he notices the shore slipping by at a rapid rate. The ebb tide is sweeping him south down the strait.

He turns into the tide, swimming for all he is worth, working his way across the current toward land. In the midst of his fight against the tide, a sightseeing boat passes within fifty yards. He can easily see human figures in the windows as he waves and yells. They give no sign of hearing or seeing him.

Before long he sees that he is approaching a red navigational buoy. Maybe he can grab on to the maintenance ladder and pull himself out of the water. Swimming full out, Larry gets a sense of the current's power as the buoy races by, far from reach.

A cold reality settles in as the buoy recedes from view. *I'm not going to make it. I am going to drown.*

· · · — — — · · ·

When darkness falls Larry is still being carried south with the current. Several miles to the north he can see a helicopter scanning the water with a searchlight. He waves, yells; the helicopter is too far off.

Hours have passed and even with the dry suit on, he is becoming cold, beginning to shiver. From his work with a volunteer fire department, he knows the stages of hypothermia.

A lighthouse comes into view as the tide carries him by an island on the eastern shore of Rosario Strait. Maybe it has a light keeper. With renewed hope he swims within one hundred yards before the current sweeps him past.

It is completely dark now. He can see the lights of more search crews working the water and shoreline far to the north. Shivering, tired, Larry makes his peace with the world and prepares to die. Floating along, calm in the face of death, he hears the sound of crashing surf over the water. Turning toward the sound he can see the dark outline of another island, closer than the last. Gathering the last of his strength, he fights off the cold and strokes for shore.

It is a battle through surf and rocks, but it seems the current has finally released its grip. Numb from cold and exhaustion, Larry pulls himself out on the shores of Allan Island and thanks God for giving him this chance to live. Standing out in the open, he notices that the air seems colder than the water. He works his way into the forest to get out of the wind. Finding shelter under a tree, he alternates between exercising and covering himself with fir branches to stay warm.

Throughout the night he refuses to sleep. Whenever a boat or aircraft passes nearby, he sprints onto the beach to wave his orange life vest and yell. At one point a search boat cruises by within a hundred yards. Larry does everything he can to get their attention, yet they are scanning the water with their lights and never check the beach.

In the early-morning darkness the boats and helicopters leave the area. Larry tries to rest; surely they will be back when the sun comes up.

* * * — — — * * *

First light finds Larry scrambling across the rugged island. He wants to be as close to last night's search area as possible when the crews return today. The route is difficult, over steep slopes, rocky outcrops, through thick trees and brush, but the effort warms him up.

Arriving at the north end of the island, he sits on the shore to rest and gaze across the channel to Burrows Island. He can see the lighthouse that evaded him last night. An hour passes with no sign of search boats or helicopters.

If the search has ended, the only source of help in sight would be the keeper at the lighthouse. Larry strides down to the water to study the third-of-a-mile crossing to Burrows. He tosses a stick in the water to judge the current. It looks slack. He wades in and starts swimming.

Larry makes the swim and climbs up the cliffs to the lighthouse, only to find that it is now automated and has no keeper. As he stands there, figuring his next move, the sound of a helicopter captures his attention. Turning to the south, he sees a Navy helicopter searching the island he just left. He runs out onto the lawn in front of the lighthouse, waving his arms and yelling.

This time the crew spots him.

· · · — — — · · ·

Saul has spent a restless night at the Coast Guard building, wracked with grief and guilt, with no hope left for Larry. When the search begins in the morning, the Coast Guard is operating on radio silence. They need to concentrate on the job at hand while keeping the media from complicating the effort. Preset flight patterns will let the rescue crews on the ground know what is happening.

Around 7 A.M. a Navy helicopter flies over the Coast Guard building where Saul waits inside for bad news. The Coast Guardsman on duty has a close eye on the flight path of the chopper.

He turns to Saul. "They have picked your guy up. He's alive and they are taking him to the hospital."

When Saul arrives at the Anacortes hospital emergency room, people there are cutting Larry out of the dry suit that saved his life. The two men have never been happier to see each other. The atmosphere is giddy; they laugh and give each other a hard time. They know they are lucky to be alive. Larry is then warmed up, and he walks out of the hospital only a few hours later.

On their drive home, the wind is still ripping through the trees and frothing the waters of Rosario Strait.

When Saul looks back at that day, all he can do is shake his head and wonder, "Exactly what was I thinking?

"One of the first things I did when I got back was to buy a pair of waterproof VHF radios. I bought the smaller flare sets you can fit inside your life jacket. I worked out rigging on all of my boats to keep paddle float bags and other safety equipment topside instead of below decks where I used to keep it.

"That day has made me aggressively cautious as a trip leader. It's one thing to kill yourself; it's another to get your friends killed."

He smooths a place in the snow to scratch out a last will and testament.

CHAPTER 13

BURIED ALIVE

A high-speed roller-coaster run through a winter landscape buried in a cushion of pristine powder snow. Weightlessness on earth, dropping off steep hillsides in free fall, power-sliding around curves, weaving through trees, gliding across wide-open meadows. A smooth, effortless ride.

These are the reasons why Ken and Bill are the first to pull into the snow-park lot south of Greenwater, Washington, just off Highway 410, on a Wednesday morning in February. Snow has been piling up in the Cascade Mountains and they know there is no better way to beat the crowds than snowmobiling midweek.

Ken and Bill are partners in a home-building business and have been riding together for years. Last winter they logged three thousand miles on their machines. This year, with powerful new snowmobiles built for hill climbing in deep snow, they have already racked up eleven hundred miles on the odometers.

They throttle up Forest Road 70, breaking trail through two feet of fresh powder. The morning is promising: warm temperatures, a blue sky overhead. The few times they stop to talk, their snowmobiles sink deep in the snow.

Shortly after noon they arrive on the crest of the Cascade Mountains at Government Meadows, just east of Naches Pass. Across the meadows to the east they motor down to a narrow bench at the upper entrance to what local riders call the slough.

138

This ravine fills with snow over the winter months and becomes a trail for riders coming east or west over the Cascades. Today's plan was to ride the low hills to the east, but as the day has warmed up the snow has become heavy and the snowmobiles more difficult to maneuver. They weigh their options and decide to backtrack, hoping for cooler temperatures and lighter snow up high. First they have to run down the slough and find enough room to pull a U-turn.

Ken takes the lead, standing for better balance as he drops over the edge. Bill follows close behind, his sled almost steering itself in the two-foot-wide trench of a trail Ken is cutting through the deep snow.

Not far off the top, Bill's snowmobile begins to shift as the snow on the right begins to move. The trench made by Ken's trail-breaking is pinching shut. At first it's funny. Bill laughs as his snowmobile is pushed off the trail to the left. Then, as he looks up and across the gradual slope above them, a crack opens in the snow sixty feet upslope. In an instant the crack widens, paralleling their route, running hundreds of feet both in front of and behind them.

Ken can see it now and cranks his throttle wide open. The snowmobile roars as he tries to outrun the slab avalanche. As Bill moves to do the same, the snow slides into the ravine, doubling over like a wave. Slowly but relentlessly a wall of snow pushes him off his sled. He grabs for a small tree as the snow pours into the narrow ravine, filling in up to his waist and then creeping up his body. One second it flows like sand, the next it solidifies as hard as concrete. Suddenly his legs are clamped in an icy vise. Bill can hear Ken's machine winding up to high speed, then another wave pours in from behind.

In a panic Bill starts shaking the tree as the snow fills in over his head. He has to make room to breathe, has to keep the snow from trapping his upper body. He fights to stay calm, knowing that if he stops moving he will die.

Thoughts flash through his head: *If I don't come out of here, my kid . . .*

Fighting, fighting, seconds seem like hours buried in the darkness underneath all that snow. The tree is his way out. He keeps shaking the trunk because there is nothing else he can do.

Finally, when he is close to exhaustion, two feet of snow above his head collapses, flooding light and air into the hole.

He can see up and out. The panic fades.

I'm gonna make it. Ken will pull me out of here.

He yells for help.

Ken will come running right over and get me out.

No one answers.

Bill yells for all he is worth, calling out and up to the small hole of sky. There is nothing but a cold and lonely silence in return.

Shaking the tree did keep his upper body free, but there is little room to spare in the hole. He can't get his hands down to dig his legs out. One of his boots is tied loose enough so that he can move his foot slightly. He begins working the foot back and forth, pushing at the snow. Minutes pass. Sweat rolls off his forehead. He makes enough room to begin moving one leg up and down. He keeps working, pushing, pulling, straining.

Half an hour passes as he fights to escape, and then the other leg has a little room.

When his hips come free, he gathers what remains of his strength and lunges upward, digging his fingers into the top edge of the hole. With one last heave, he pulls himself out of the icy trap and collapses on the surface, exhausted.

$$\cdot \; \cdot \; \cdot \; - \; - \; - \; \cdot \; \cdot \; \cdot$$

As his breathing slows, Bill sits up. *Ken has got to be somewhere nearby. Any minute now he will climb back up from below.* As he looks across the jumbled surface of the avalanche, surrounded by a deep silence, reality comes home like a slap across his face.

Ken is buried. All their emergency gear is buried as well, eight feet below in the trunk of his snowmobile. Then he remembers that avalanche victims have only fifteen to twenty minutes before they suffocate.

He jumps to his feet and searches frantically in the snow where he last saw Ken. He stumbles around, digging with his hands, sifting through the snow, working his way up and down the ravine, hoping for something, anything, that will allow him to save his friend's life.

An hour passes. He finds nothing.

With few options left, Bill says a prayer, putting Ken's life in God's hands. He turns his back on the avalanche and starts hiking toward their truck, sixteen miles away up and over the Cascade Crest. It's a struggle climbing back up through the slough in the deep snow. Sometimes he crawls. Sometimes he sinks in up to his waist.

Three hundred yards out, he hesitates.

Ken wouldn't leave me. He has to be down there somewhere.

He heads back down, saying another prayer: *Okay, God, the joke is over, let me find him.*

He covers the same ground again, searching across the jumbled snow, yelling out Ken's name, digging down here and there but finding nothing.

He leaves again, only to come back two more times.

Finally, with evening approaching and snow starting to fall, he tears himself away for the final time. He has to save himself, get out, and find help.

It takes an hour of crawling and thrashing to get back to Government Meadows. Sometimes he has to back up and take a running start to plow forward and make any progress in the waist-high drifts. Exhaustion is taking its toll. With every step it feels like a knife is being rammed into his thighs.

He comes to the Forest Service cabin in the meadows. This would be a good place to stay and wait for someone to come up tonight or maybe tomorrow, but the thought of Ken buried will not let him rest. He refuses to give up as long as he can keep walking.

He makes his way another mile. The going is a little easier, following the compacted trail their snowmobiles made. Yet his body is at the edge. He can barely pick up his feet to walk. His legs are wobbly, his muscles like rubber. Approaching the trail junction that leads down to their truck, he recalls that there is another twelve miles to go. He falls to his knees.

God, you are going to have to send me some help because I just can't go on anymore.

A moment passes. Then a distant sound filters through the forest. Snowmobiles coming up the road!

One hundred yards away the trail splits. The left branch leads to the Naches Trail. The right branch passes by him on the way to

Government Meadows. He cannot take a chance of missing these riders. With a sudden burst of energy he runs, limps, drags himself through the snow, racing the sound that is coming closer and closer, and then stumbles out into the path of the oncoming snowmobilers.

Bill has kept it together up to now, but when they ask him what is going on, he loses it—babbling, crying, going on about the avalanche.

"When did it happen?"

"Well, what time is it?"

They tell him it's close to 4:30.

"It was like 12:00, 12:30, about four hours ago."

"Is he still down there?"

"Hell yeah, we lost our. . . . I lost him, I can't find him."

They calm him down enough to get him on the back of one of their machines, then turn around and go all out for the snow-park lot below.

Two miles from the lot they come across a second party of snowmobilers heading up. One of them has a cell phone. They immediately call 911 and are patched through to the Pierce County Sheriff's Department.

Bill wants to head back up with the cell-phone group, but the sheriff wants him down at the parking lot to meet the search and rescue crew and help them locate the site of the accident.

They quickly agree on a plan. The cell-phone snowmobilers will head up and try to follow Ken's trail to the avalanche site. The first snowmobilers will continue down with Bill and wait with him at the parking lot for the search and rescue crew.

$$\cdots \ - \ - \ - \ \cdots$$

A tense half hour passes while Bill and the snowmobilers wait at the Greenwater snow-park lot for help to arrive. Bill keeps himself busy unloading another snowmobile from his trailer and gathering gear from his truck so no time will be wasted when the rescuers arrive.

When the lead search and rescue crew pulls into the parking lot, Bill gives them all the details. Their mood is grim. They have bad news. If Ken has been buried for five or six hours, they are no longer looking at a rescue. They are considering this operation a recovery, and there is no sense in bringing in the recovery team at night. They will set up a base camp and head up first thing in the morning.

The word "recovery" hits Bill hard. Reality floods through his haze of shock and disbelief and he starts to choke up. The search and rescue coordinator takes him aside. They want him to call Ken's fiancée. She needs to know that he is gone.

. . . — — — . . .

Troy had been itching to get up snowmobiling for close to a week. Riding solo is not his choice, but he couldn't find anyone to go with him. On Wednesday, with business slow at his job as a car lot manager, he decides to blow off work and head up to Greenwater for some fun.

He arrives at the snow-park lot hoping to find a partner or two, but there are only a few rigs in the lot and no one in sight. He rides up Forest Road 70 following the route to Government Meadows and pulls up at the Forest Service cabin to see if anyone is in the area. Fifteen minutes pass and no one appears. Troy fires up his machine again and heads across the meadow toward the east and the many trails that loop through the nearby hills.

At the top of a deep ravine he pauses. The deep, heavy snow brings back fresh memories of last weekend, when he spent nine hours digging his snowmobile out of a snowdrift west of Mount Rainier. He can see snowmobile tracks leading into the ravine and footprints heading out.

Somebody buried their sled down there and had to walk out, he thinks to himself.

That's enough to convince him. He decides to head back across the meadows to the south and ride the slopes above the cabin. With luck he may still find riding partners.

Half an hour passes before he comes across another snowmobiler. They quickly pull up together. As soon as their machines are shut down, the other snowmobiler tells Troy that somebody is buried under an avalanche. His group had come across the guy's buddy on the road up. He isn't sure where the avalanche happened, but he came up to try and find the site.

Troy doesn't hesitate. "I know exactly where that is."

They both fire up their sleds and Troy heads over to the ravine and the tracks leading down. The other snowmobiler doesn't think his machine will make it back out if he goes down. Troy has a powerful machine with two-inch paddles on the tracks. In a life-or-death situation he is willing to gamble that he can get back out.

He turns to his companion. "I am going in to look around. If I don't come back, make sure you let somebody know that I went down in here."

Troy drops in, following the snowmobile tracks for close to half a mile before they disappear at the edge of the avalanche. Balls of snow, softball-size and larger, have tumbled down, filling the ravine to a depth of more than ten feet for at least one hundred yards downhill.

He shuts off his snow machine and looks out over the scene of the burial.

Oh man, whoa man, if somebody is in there they are in deep trouble.

As the mountain quiet returns, Troy steps off his sled and works his way onto the jumble of snow. The walking is difficult, with his legs post-holing up to his knees with every step. It's a big white field, no sign of any snowmobile, no shred of clothing or piece of equipment. He calls out across the avalanche debris. As the sound of his voice fades, the returning silence is deafening. He continues to follow the snow-filled ravine knowing his task is hopeless, but unwilling to give up. About halfway across he yells again, then pauses to listen to the silence.

The air is suddenly filled with a desperate cry for help. Troy still can't see anything on the surface. He yells back, trying to soothe the frantic voice: "Calm down, I can't see you yet."

He keeps walking, listening carefully to trace the location of the disembodied cry. The voice is yelling hysterically.

He spots something lying in the snow.

"Do you have a black helmet?"

The voice cries back, "Yeah, yeah, that's my helmet!"

"Okay, okay, just calm down. It is going to take me a while to get there."

Troy stumbles through the chaotic piles of snow. As he steps up to the helmet he can see a small opening on the surface. He leans over close to peer in the hole. Several feet below, a frantic face is looking up.

· · · — — — · · ·

When Ken gunned his snowmobile to escape the avalanche, the high revolutions just dug the machine in deeper.

The first mass of sliding snow came from right to left, pouring in around the sled and rising up to his waist. His feet were pushed forward, trapping his legs under the cowling.

A second wave of the avalanche rolled in from behind like water flowing down the ravine, covering him up to his shoulders. He had a momentary thought that he must look ridiculous with just his head visible above the snow. Instinctively he brought his arms up to protect his face.

A third rush of snow covered him completely, the light fading to dark blue. The snow consolidated around him. He struggled to clear a breathing space in front of his face while he could still move his hands. There was just enough time to take one last, large breath before the snow completely solidified.

Trapped, sealed in a blue gloom, snow pressing down heavily from above, he cannot move. He remembers reading that most avalanche victims are buried only one foot under the surface. With this in mind, he figures escape may not be difficult. He knows the most important thing is to stay calm. Panic will kill quickly.

An immediate problem is his snowmobile. It continues to run, leaching carbon monoxide up into what little oxygen exists in the snow around him. He cannot move to reach the kill switch.

Ken finds that he can just barely move his right hand. He begins to work it back and forth, making a space in front of his face. With a little more room he forms a fist and starts to punch upward.

As the open space gets larger, he can bend his wrist and dig. Some of the snow is soft, but some of it is crusty, too hard to dig with his gloves on. Eventually he frees his other hand and pulls his gloves off to use his fingernails. In places the digging is so hard that his fingers feel as though they are going to break as he claws at the ice.

After twenty minutes the snowmobile sputters to a stop, but the exhaust smell won't go away.

Ken continues to scrape and scratch toward the surface. When his vision first begins going black, it's a mystery until he punches upward in desperation. Oxygen seeps from the hollow made by his fist, and his vision clears. He learns to quickly recognize the symptoms of oxygen deprivation and to punch a new hole, lay his head close to it, and breathe deep until he can get back to digging.

When he has enough room to tear the visor off his helmet, he folds it into a digging tool. Now he can reach farther, scraping higher above his head. As the scrapings fill up around him, he compacts them into snowballs and shoves them into holes made by his fist.

He yells for help at regular intervals. The sound is completely absorbed by the surrounding snow.

Buried below the surface, Ken rides the line between life and death with no real notion of passing time. At one point he feels the end is near. He smooths a place in the snow to scratch out a last will and testament while he is still conscious. He has to let his kids and fiancée know that he loved them.

This thought just makes him angry. He's not going to quit now. He makes a vow to fight until he has nothing left and goes back to scratching and scraping upward.

He remembers looking at avalanche transceivers with Bill not long ago. At the time the two-hundred-dollar price tag seemed like too much for a device that transmits a signal so that an avalanche victim can be located quickly. He would be more than happy to write a check for one right now as he strains upward, scraping the roof of his hole, ice and snow falling in his eyes.

Hours pass and he begins to see light filtering down through the snow. He cannot reach any higher, even with his digging tool. His knees remain trapped up under the handlebars of his snowmobile. The snow holds him fast.

His strength is gone, drained from lack of oxygen and the effort of digging. There is nothing left to do but pray.

All I need is a little air, Lord, and I will do the rest.

With those words barely out of his mouth, the six-inch layer of snow remaining at the top of his hole caves in. Cool, clean air and bright light pour into the hole.

The infusion of fresh oxygen gives him renewed energy. Now he can make snowballs and throw them out of the hole, enlarging his space even more.

The surface remains just out of reach. He considers trying to break a leg in order to help himself escape. He broke one leg badly the year before. It may still be weak enough to rebreak the bone and bend it around the snowmobile handlebar.

He yells frantically for help. No one answers.

All he can do is go back to digging. He makes enough room to throw his helmet out of the hole, and then starts excavating down, working to free his legs.

Every time he stops to yell and no one answers, his hopes fade. Yet he will not stop working to free himself, scraping at the snow, pulling and pushing his legs.

More time passes.

He gives up on the thought that someone on the surface might hear him. Yelling for help is ridiculous. There is no one out there to help him. He concentrates on the effort to dig his legs out and escape this trap on his own.

Late in the afternoon in the midst of this final effort, the sound of a voice echoes down into his hole.

He can't believe it at first. He yells back, all his fears and panic lifting the cry out and up.

He exchanges calls with the voice for a couple of minutes, and then a face appears in the opening above his head.

· · · ▬ ▬ ▬ · · ·

It takes Troy ten minutes to dig the hole large enough so that he can reach down at arm's length, grab onto the outstretched hand, and pull the man out. Up on the surface, Ken is punchy and weak from carbon monoxide poisoning and his hours-long effort to dig out. He flops down on the snow bootless, missing one sock and cooling off fast in the open air. Yet he is frantic.

"We have to find my friend Bill. Bill is buried here somewhere."

Troy tells him that Bill is okay. He is down at the parking lot with rescuers. They sit and talk while Troy pulls the leg of Ken's snowsuit over his exposed foot and ties it off. He explains that they have to climb out of the ravine. Ken is willing, but too weak to stand. Troy half-pulls, half-crawls with Ken as they ascend out of the slough. Before long they are met by two other men walking in to help. With darkness falling fast and Ken in no shape to ride out, let alone walk up the steep ravine, the snow makes walking difficult, and the ravine is too steep for both men to ride out on Troy's snowmobile. It is obvious that more help is needed. Upon reaching Troy's machine, they set Ken down.

Troy turns to the men.

"I am going to try and ride out of here. If I make it to the top, I am not stopping. I'm going to go all the way down to get help."

Troy fires up his snowmobile, pulls a tight U-turn, and roars off up the slough, his taillights fading in the darkness.

· · · — — — · · ·

Back down at the snow-park lot, Bill refuses to call Ken's fiancée. Ken can't really be dead.

"He's a stubborn little shit. If anyone can survive, he can."

They aren't going to push him. The search and rescue coordinator lets the issue go.

The command post begins to take shape. Generators are brought out and lights are set up. A table is unfolded. Maps are pulled out. Bill and the coordinator are bent over the maps, pinpointing the location of the avalanche, when a snowmobile races down off the hill.

Troy turns off his machine and yells to the men gathered around the trailer, "We found your guy."

"No! Is he alive?"

"He's alive but he's in real bad shape."

· · · — — — · · ·

An hour later Ken has been moved up to Government Meadows. Flares, flashlights, and snowmobile headlamps illuminate a landing area as a Blackhawk helicopter from Fort Lewis hovers in the pitch-black darkness. Everyone ducks behind snowmobiles when the downdraft from the rotors whips up the snow into a swirling cloud of ice. The pilot touches down without turning off the rotors. Ken is loaded aboard and the chopper is off to Madigan Hospital in Tacoma, just minutes away.

· · · — — — · · ·

Arriving at the emergency room, Ken is quickly stabilized and warmed up. Beyond the poisoning from carbon monoxide, CO, he is uninjured.

He sits in his hospital bed in a moment of calm between coughing fits. A nurse walks in.

"Are you dead?"

"No," he says.

The nurse cranks the valve on an oxygen tank until the flow just about blows the mask off Ken's face.

"You should be. We have corpses come in here with lower CO counts than you have."

After only four hours in the hospital he is given a clean bill of health and released.

Ken says that while he fought for five hours to escape from the snow, he had a lot of time to think about his life. He made a promise to quit being selfish and to spend more time with his fiancée and kids. That same year he sold his snowmobiles and bought a boat for family outings.

Bill gave up snowmobiling for family reasons as well. But he hasn't sworn off the sport entirely.

"Maybe I'll get back into it next year, especially now that they came out with that new 156-inch-long track. That has got to be awesome!"

The gray sky ahead of them begins to blend with the white landscape. Detail, depth perception, and the horizon vanish in the flat afternoon light.

CHAPTER 14

CHOPPER DOWN

T he attraction of helicopter flightseeing is undeniable. The aircraft is like a magic carpet, offering anyone a chance to enter wilderness normally inaccessible to all but the most adventurous. In Juneau, Alaska, it's a thriving industry. Tourists from all over the world step out of their hotel room or cruise ship cabin and within the hour are walking on the pristine expanse of subarctic landscape known as the Juneau Ice Field.

The helicopter experience is dreamlike, cruising above the landscape of saltwater inlets and mist-shrouded forests, through valleys flanked with mountains and filled with glaciers, up and over high ramparts to a 1,500-square-mile plain of ice spreading as far as the eye can see, pierced here and there by lonely spires of rock.

Skilled pilots land their aircraft, open the doors, and let their passengers step out into the middle of a snowbound landscape of unimaginable beauty. Jagged peaks soar into the surrounding sky. A blue-tinged crevasse is always somewhere nearby, providing the perfect photo opportunity.

Richard and Rhoneel, husband and wife, are up from the San Francisco Bay Area of California. They have finished the land portion of their early September Alaskan tour, and now their cruise ship is docked in Juneau on the first leg of a journey through

Southeast Alaska. The three other helicopter passengers—William, his fiancée Deborah, and William's father, William Sr.—are also from the Golden State. They have all opted for what's known as the Pilot's Choice, a helicopter tour to locations away from the standard routes.

From the information they received when booking the tour, they know to bring sunglasses, a warm sweater or jacket, a camera, and plenty of film. Gloves and a warm hat are optional, suggested for people who get cold easily. The tour company provides spiked over-boots for safe walking on the glaciers. There are hooded raincoats in the helicopter as well, just in case wind and rain become a factor.

There is a safety briefing and then they are off, flying over glaciers and rugged peaks mere minutes from the heliport. The pilot points out wildlife on the landscape below.

Thirty minutes into the tour they land midway up a glacier. The pilot lets them out to scramble about and snap pictures of each other standing near yawning crevasses.

Their second landing is up higher on the ice field itself. The vast, blindingly white plain stretches out before them, a frozen sea flooding a mountain landscape. They step down from the helicopter and walk out across the snow to snap pictures, hoping to capture the impossibly immense scale of the place. Humbling, breathtaking, awe-inspiring; they don't want to leave.

Just after noon the pilot rounds up his five passengers for the return flight. As the helicopter descends off the heights down along West Herbert Glacier, all the passengers are craning their necks back and forth, soaking up as much view as possible before the trip ends. The gray sky ahead of them begins to blend with the white landscape. Detail, depth perception, and the horizon vanish in the flat afternoon light.

To the passengers, the change is imperceptible as they snap photographs out the side windows. Rhoneel has a mild sense of altitude loss and leans over to her husband.

"Save a few pictures, I think we are going to land one more time."

Then snow suddenly dashes up over the windshield, their world spins violently, and a massive impact slams them forward.

When all is still, a moment passes as Richard tries to figure out what is pressing against the back of his head.

It's the ceiling of the helicopter.

He's upside down, hanging from his seat belt, his ears ringing as if he was just punched in the face. Reaching up, he pops the buckle on his seat belt, rolls over onto his knees, and crawls out the opening that once held the door.

The body of the helicopter is upside down, crushed from the impact and split at the seams. The instrument panel is ripped out and lying off to one side. All the doors are torn off and scattered around the snow-covered surface of the glacier, dark fragments on a white background.

The Plexiglas windows have popped out. The tail has sheared off and sits vertical in the snow. The skids are mashed backward. The shattered rotors are scattered about the crash site.

The pilot and other passengers slowly emerge from the wreckage, limping and bleeding. They stare at what's left of the helicopter, stunned, dazed, wondering what happened, amazed that they are alive.

Rhoneel has bit through her lip. The pilot is bleeding from a deep cut between his eyes. Deborah and William Sr., sitting in the front seat next to the pilot, slammed their legs in the initial impact. Deborah's left ankle hurts and she can't walk without help. William Sr.'s legs are stiff and painful, but he can get around under his own power. Richard and William Jr. are relatively unscathed.

As the shock and surprise wears off, they put snow on their injuries to slow the swelling and do what they can to stop any bleeding.

The pilot searches through what is left of the aircraft. He pulls out a survival box. Inside are a few thin Mylar space blankets, a small first-aid kit, and a couple of other items. Cuts are bandaged. The hooded raincoats are passed around as everyone cools off in the chill breeze blowing up the glacier.

The radio has been smashed. Communications with the tour base in Juneau are cut off. The best the pilot can do is activate the emergency locator beacon and assure the passengers that the tour company will be expecting them back. As soon as they are overdue, someone will come looking.

A voice perks up, "Hey, does anybody have a cell phone?"

The pilot pulls one out of his pocket and turns it on. No signal. He walks out on the ice away from the helicopter and more in line with the valley that leads down toward Juneau. Nothing. Up here it's just a useless piece of plastic.

An hour passes as they wait at the crash site on the upper reaches of the glacier. With the windchill, the temperature is dropping into the twenties. Bandaged, beat up, and bloody, the five passengers and pilot huddle around the wreckage.

Deborah's ankle is now throbbing with pain. She shivers in the cold. Rhoneel sits with her in the shelter of the wreckage, trying to share body heat.

To pass the time Rhoneel mentions the slide show she and Richard watched only days before, on a rainy afternoon at Denali National Park. There were images of elaborate snow walls that climbers build high on the mountain to protect their tents from wind.

Deborah recalls building igloos as a child and remembers how cozy they were. The subject gets the rest of the group talking.

With no radio to call for help, and no hint of when anyone will come looking for them, some form of shelter would be a good idea.

The container for the emergency kit is just about the right size for forming snow blocks. They dump out the contents and form an assembly line.

Using a couple of the blown-out Plexiglas windows as shovels, some of them dig while others pack the loose snow into the container. The snow blocks are then popped out of the container and stacked to form a wall. The cracks between the blocks are stuffed with loose snow for a wind-tight barrier. They begin to warm up with the physical effort, as the wall stretches around the windward side of the helicopter fuselage.

As the afternoon passes, clouds come and go, dropping down over the glacier for short periods of time, cutting visibility to a few hundred yards, only to lift and blow away. Around 3:30 P.M., with the clouds swirling, they hear an aircraft and look up to see a helicopter from a different tour company flying toward them from far below.

They run out in front of the wreckage, spreading apart so their yellow jackets are more visible against the white glacier. Some of them are waving the flimsy metallic space blankets. Others hold brightly painted pieces of the helicopter fuselage, anything that will show up in that wide expanse of white.

Through the mist they watch the helicopter stop at the edge of the cloud cover. It hovers for a few moments at a distance, then turns and flies away.

· · · — — — · · ·

When the flightseeing helicopter with its five paying passengers doesn't return shortly after noon as scheduled, the tour company begins a radio search. Word spreads quickly among the many other tour companies. Before long all the pilots in the area are scanning the terrain.

By 1 P.M., with no word, the tour company sends a second helicopter with a spotter to fly the route of the missing craft.

By 2 P.M. there is still no word from the missing helicopter. And now the second helicopter has reported mechanical difficulties and is down on the ice field. The tour company sends up a third helicopter, with a mechanic acting as a spotter.

The third helicopter arrives to find the second helicopter upside down on the ice. Both the pilot and his spotter stand next to the wreckage, waving their arms.

When the third pilot lands his craft, the second pilot describes his problems with the flat light. He lost the horizon and couldn't tell where the surface of the snow was. He slowed down, looking for something to judge location, and before he knew it he caught a skid and rolled.

As the third helicopter lifts off from the ice field with the pilot and spotter from the second craft aboard, the two men report that they received a transmission from a nearby helicopter that had sighted survivors at the first crash site.

This first site is just over the ridge and not far away. The third helicopter flies over the ridge and, sure enough, there is the first downed chopper, with six people standing near the wreckage. As the third helicopter heads for the site, the gray overcast blends with the white ice field. The horizon disappears. Depth perception is zero.

The pilot slows the helicopter, losing altitude as he searches for some point of reference in a featureless landscape.

· · · — — — · · ·

The survivors stop their waving and yelling as the helicopter below them, on the edge of the cloud cover, retreats back down the valley. Rhoneel is sure they were spotted. For the first time today everyone is upbeat.

As they gather back at the wreckage, a second helicopter appears over a ridge behind them. Even from a distance, they recognize the distinctive markings of their tour company's aircraft.

Elation and relief sweep through the group. *We've been saved, we've been saved.* They wave their arms and yell as the helicopter flies toward them, descending lower and lower and lower as it slowly flies into the ground, flipping and crashing far off across the ice field.

A shocked silence. Six unbelieving sets of eyes are fixed on the spot where their rescuers have just augured into the ice.

Richard is the first to act. In the clear mountain air the crash site looks close. He heads across the ice to look for survivors. A few hundred yards out, clouds begin to roll in and he hesitates. Raising binoculars to his eyes, he can make out four people standing in the snow around the wreckage. Then the clouds drop, obscuring the crash from view.

He turns around to find his own crashed helicopter barely visible a short distance away. Hustling back through the mist, he can't figure out why a six-passenger helicopter would come to the rescue with a four-man crew.

For the five survivors and their pilot, this second crash is a collective slap in the face. Suddenly their situation becomes very clear. They are stuck on a glacier, in light clothing, with the sun low on the horizon.

They may be only a few minutes' flight from the warmth and comfort of civilization, but the chance of another helicopter arriving before darkness isn't looking good. When Richard returns from his short journey out on the glacier, they redouble their efforts on the shelter.

What was the roof of the aluminum fuselage is pulled loose from underneath the wreckage. Climbing inside, they dig down into the snow to expand the sheltered space. The roof panel is then slipped back in and placed in the bottom of the snow pit as a floor.

The seat cushions are gathered from where they lie scattered across the glacier. They are placed over the aluminum floor of the shelter as insulation. The two-person front seat, torn from its mounts on impact, is carried in.

The snow-block assembly line starts up again and the wall is extended to wrap completely around the helicopter.

The helicopter doors are picked up off the snow and straightened out. Richard pops the Plexiglas windows back in. The doors are hoisted atop the shelter, balanced on the fuselage and the wall, and packed in place with snow to form a roof.

Last but not least, a makeshift door is made from the heavy canvas tie-down covers for the helicopter blades. These are all they have left that might be heavy enough to stay in place against the wind sweeping up the glacier.

As darkness falls and the cold becomes bone chilling, they crowd into the shelter.

Richard and Rhoneel brought knit hats along, just in case. The others wear the helicopter headsets to keep their ears warm. They share a small bottle of water and an apple that Rhoneel had in her purse. The pilot has a large bag of dried fruit. He passes it around. No one is eating much or saying much. They all have the same thoughts.

If the weather gets any worse, we could be here awhile.

How long will that food last?

How long can we last?

With darkness the wind becomes stronger and snow begins to fall. They watch as it piles up on the windows of their makeshift roof. Their collective body heat warms the roof just enough to melt the snow. The flimsy Mylar space blankets make for poor coverings as water drips down from leaky seals around the windows. To get wet now is an invitation to death.

Hours pass. Even crammed together in the shelter, they can feel their toes and fingers going numb. They struggle to stay awake and alive, talking, singing, playing memory games.

Richard does his best to participate, but bears are on his mind. At Denali they had been told that bears are everywhere. He learned that this time of year they are out feeding and fattening up for hibernation.

"Be careful, watch out for the bears," the rangers warned. "They are unpredictable and dangerous."

It's that bag of dried fruit. He can smell it even with the plastic seal closed tight. If his normally insensitive nose can smell it, than any bear within ten miles can smell it. He imagines the sweet smell of dried fruit wafting over the landscape, bears for miles around lifting their noses, snorting at the scent, their stomachs growling as they come searching for the source.

Late in the evening they are talking away when one of them hears a noise. Richard is sure it's a bear, but he keeps quiet. Everyone listens closely as Richard prepares for a growling, snarling, wild beast to tear through the wall of the shelter.

A few minutes pass in silence.

They hear it again.

It's someone calling "Hello," off in the distance. Richard exhales in relief.

It must be the crew from the other aircraft, hiking over to check on them. How are they all going to fit into this cramped space?

The pilot and Rhoneel are closest to the door. They head out into the darkness to call them in.

· · · — — — · · ·

As a member of both the all-volunteer Juneau Mountain Rescue and the Capital City Fire and Rescue team, Doug is on the call list when bad things happen in remote places. His pager goes off around 4:30 in the afternoon. The fire department is calling for an air medevac team, medics, and the rope rescue team.

Arriving at the fire department, he learns that there are ten people stranded high on the West Herbert Glacier. There is much confusion, but what is known is that there is at least one helicopter is down with damage; the passengers have been seen walking around. A second helicopter is down on the glacier apparently due to mechanical failure, and a third one is out of commission and no one can say if it is because of weather conditions or mechanical problems or exactly where it might be.

When Doug and his team show up at the incident response center set up at the tour company, the Coast Guard helicopter is there along with two helicopters from other tour operators. A group of nine rescuers is assembled, including Juneau Mountain Rescue members, fire department emergency medical technicians, and the rope rescue team.

The good news is that they get to ride up to the glacier on helicopters. The bad news: A storm is headed in off the coast, and they could be up there for as long as three days.

They gather together stoves, tents, sleeping bags, ropes, climbing gear, and food. The tour company throws in a few Mustang survival suits normally used for boating, but they also work as insulated coveralls.

Shortly after six o'clock, the three helicopters fly the rescue team up the West Herbert Glacier. Clouds shroud the ice fields, forcing them to be dropped off low. They will move up on foot to the crash sites.

Down on the glacier, the nine rescuers split up into two rope teams. The four fastest climbers are sent out ahead. The five larger men will bring up the rear, carrying most of the equipment.

It's close to eight o'clock by the time they reach the upper levels of the glacier and the beginning of the ice field. Darkness is falling, wind is blowing, and snow has begun to fall. They pull out compasses and check their maps for a bearing to where the search coordinators had thought they picked up transmissions from locator beacons. Headlamps are switched on, and the rescuers head out into the night.

Ten people are out there in an expanse so vast as to make them almost invisible in broad daylight. With the darkness and cloud cover, this search will be guesswork at best.

For a couple of hours the rescue teams trudge across the ice field, cut off now from communications with Juneau by distance and terrain. Led by the compasses of their rope team leaders, the nine men wander in the meager pools of light cast by their headlamps. Their world has become darkness, white flakes swirling, and the unchanging snow-covered surface.

The second rope team catches up as the first team is slowed by knee-deep snow. In the night sky above, a Coast Guard C-130 has joined the effort, circling to provide a communications link back to

Juneau. From down on the ice field, the rescuers relay their GPS position to the navigation crew.

Within a few minutes a message comes back. One of the emergency locator beacons is less than a mile away.

The rescuers move toward the spot, stopping periodically to yell out into the night in unison.

There is no answer in return.

Concerned about the possibility of passing the crash site in the darkness, the two teams decide to keep moving for just thirty more minutes. If they find nothing by this time, they will set up camp and start rotating people out in smaller teams to search throughout the night.

The next half hour passes as they walk farther and continue calling out "Hello." Just as they start looking for a place to set up base camp, a faint "Hello" comes back in reply.

Maybe just an echo.

They yell again.

The answer is the same. The tone seems the same, just a faint "Hello" rolling in from the darkness.

They yell a third time just to check. This time, the high pitch of a woman's voice cuts across the distance.

• • • — — — • • •

When the pilot and Rhoneel step outside the shelter, they can see lights flashing in the distance. The pilot yells out into the darkness, then Rhoneel joins in.

As the voices get closer, the pilot flicks on a small flashlight. The surrounding fog lights up like a halo.

Doug is the first rescuer on the scene. He steps up to Rhoneel and gives her a big hug and says, "Man, are we glad to see you!"

"You are glad to see us?" she replies. "No, we are glad to see you!"

Doug turns to look at the wreckage, looks back at Rhoneel and the pilot, then looks again at the wreckage lit up by his headlamp.

"How in the heck are you walking around? Look at this thing. It's messed up."

Before they can answer, one of the emergency medical technicians is looking them over, performing a quick evaluation. Then he climbs into the shelter to look over the other survivors.

Deborah's ankle looks as if it is broken and she is still in pain, so they splint the injury. William Sr.'s legs appear unbroken but are heavily bruised.

Rhoneel, Deborah, and William Sr. are put in the Mustang suits for added warmth. Additional warm clothes are pulled out of packs and given to the other passengers.

As the rescuers work to stabilize the passengers, Richard tells the two teams about the helicopter crash they all witnessed earlier in the afternoon and the survivors he saw standing around the wreckage.

This is good news for the rescue team. Now the ten people reported stranded can be accounted for in two separate locations.

Four rescuers continue on toward the other helicopter.

· · · — — — · · ·

When the four rescuers arrive at the site of the third crash, they find the helicopter in much better condition than the one in the first location. The four survivors are buttoned up in the fuselage and out of the weather. When the rescuers identify themselves, the men peek out.

"Nobody in here is hurt. We are warm and dry and are not coming out."

With everyone accounted for, and their jobs completed for the evening, the four rescuers dig a trench to get out of the wind, slip their sleeping bags into bivy bags, and settle down for a few hours of sleep.

Back at the first crash site, the rescuers have set up two tents to get some of the survivors out of the weather. William, Deborah, and William Sr. are placed in the first tent for the night. Three of the rescuers climb into a second tent. The remainder of the group climbs back into the shelter.

Admiring their handiwork, one of the rescuers turns to Richard and Rhoneel.

"You guys really have your act together up here," he says. "You put this snow wall up. You grabbed the door and put the bubble

window back in. You guys are all from California. You made your-
selves a California igloo with a sunroof."

· · · — — — · · ·

In the shelter, it's a long, uncomfortable night of talking, huddling
together for warmth, trying to stay dry. They finally are forced to
leave the shelter when the water dripping from the roof threatens
to soak their clothing.

Eight people crowd into the second tent, a four-person model.
They cram together under a few sleeping bags. One of the rescuers
sits in the doorway brewing hot chocolate on a stove to help keep
people warm.

The best anyone can do throughout the rest of the night is
to doze off during the brief times between when someone needs
to get up and go outside. Whenever one person shifts around to
stretch cramped muscles, everyone is bumped or jabbed with a
knee or elbow.

The morning dawns with no improvement in the weather. An
hour after daylight they can hear the sounds of helicopters flying
around, lower on the glacier.

Up where they are, the cloud cover is heavier than yesterday.
With the approaching storm, the chance of clearing is slim. The
best option at this point is to get everyone up and moving, retrace
the rescuers' route back down, and hope for an opening at lower
elevations so the helicopters can carry them the rest of the way.

Deborah and William Sr. will have to be carried out. Everyone
else can walk.

As the rescue crew inventories their equipment in an effort to
engineer two stretchers, the Coast Guard makes contact over the
radio. Their helicopter pilots have located the crash site through
the clouds.

The next few minutes flash by. Flying almost blind, the Coast
Guard pilot hovers slowly in, dropping mere inches at a time from
two hundred feet directly overhead. Radio chatter flies back and
forth between the crew and the rescuers on the ground. In the flat
light the pilot and co-pilot don't have a clear view of where the air
stops and the snow starts.

The rescue crew places climbing wands and broken pieces of helicopter skin out in the snow to give the air crew some perspective.

As the rotor downwash begins to whip up a gale of wind and snow, the crash survivors are lined up and instructed to shut their eyes. A basket on a cable is lowered to the ground. The rescuers lead the five passengers and their pilot, one at a time, to the basket. Ice crystals pepper their faces as they grab on. One after another they are hoisted up.

Above, in the helicopter, the tension is palpable. The pilot and co-pilot are on edge, blind in the fog. Rhoneel is paralyzed with fear looking out at the same whiteout conditions that caused yesterday's crash. When everyone has been brought up and secured, the helicopter eases off hover and slides slowly away in the clouds.

Minutes away from the glacier, they break out of the clouds and into open air. At the Juneau airport, an ambulance waits to take the injured to the hospital.

. . . — — — . . .

All of the survivors are treated and released in a few hours. The most serious injury is Deborah's broken ankle.

The rescue team and the four tour company employees walk down off the glacier and out of the clouds. They are picked up by helicopter that afternoon.

The lack of serious injuries in a day of three crashes is attributed to the reactions of all three pilots. When a pilot lost the horizon, he stayed calm, didn't make any quick moves, and slowed the helicopter while keeping it level. This response saved lives.

The media picked up the story, attributing the accident to the storm that was approaching.

"It was nothing like that," Rhoneel says. "Visibility was great."

The National Transportation Safety Board, NTSB, investigation revealed that flat noontime light, localized light snow showers, and the featureless surface of the ice field combined to create conditions in which the pilots could not judge how far their aircraft was above the ground. Storm conditions were not in effect.

"None of us saw it coming," adds Richard. "None of us. We didn't have time to get scared."

He laughs, remembering that shortly after crashing on the glacier, when they began building the shelter, Rhoneel approached the young pilot with a question.

"Do you think we are going to get half our money back since we only went halfway?"

"The look on that kid's face was worth a million bucks."

The ranger back at the put-in had told them there could be smoke on the river. "It should be nothing to worry about," he said.

CHAPTER 15

RAFTING THROUGH FIRE

Mid-August in a drought year is a tough time to run the Middle Fork of the Salmon River through Idaho's River of No Return Wilderness. Low water means more work, constant maneuvering to find the deeper channels, pushing and pulling rafts off barely submerged rocks. But you can't predict the weather a year ahead, and the lottery for rafting permits means you go when you are scheduled to go.

No one in the group of seven river running buddies and their spouses from Portland, Oregon—Jay, Sue, Brian, Cammie, Dick, Roy, and Bob—has yet to voice any regrets. The reward for their labors so far? Eighty-degree days, clear skies, a succession of shimmering aqua-blue pools, and foaming rapids deep in rocky canyons, lush with greenery along the riverbank. Their evenings have been spent soaking in natural hot springs on the river's edge. At night the white noise of the river lulls them to sleep under a canopy of ponderosa pines.

In the morning of their fifth day on the river, halfway through the hundred-mile float, a slight haze begins to form in the distance. At a footbridge across the river near the Middle Fork Lodge, a ranger flags them down. His words are a warning.

The Forest Service is closing the wilderness area. Forest fires are burning out of control downstream. More than likely they will get into heavy smoke, if not fire.

They talk about their options with the ranger. Walking out is a possibility. The nearest road is at least a couple of days away on foot. This would mean abandoning their boats and most of their equipment. That is not a choice they are ready to make.

The ranger agrees. The best strategy is to stay on the river and take their chances. He just wants them to know that the going may be difficult.

That afternoon they pull up at Cow Creek for the night. The haze has become a dense fog perfumed with the sweet smell of burning grass. A few members of the group hike the riverbank to Loon Creek for a soak in the hot springs. Everyone has the smoke on their minds.

The ranger back at the put-in, five days earlier, had told them there could be smoke on the river.

"It should be nothing to worry about," he said.

The only problem is that his description placed the smoke in the lower canyon. That is miles downriver from where they are now.

That evening chukars, skittish game birds that normally fly at the sight of humans, emerge from the brush to wander about the, campsite, as if disoriented and confused.

· · · ▬ ▬ ▬ · · ·

Thursday morning the rafters wake to dense smoke all around camp. They can't see any flames, but fires seem to be burning both above and below them on the river. They launch their boats and continue on.

After a long, smoky, but uneventful day the Flying B Ranch appears around a bend in the river. This is a popular stop for anyone rafting through the wilderness. A small store supplied by aircraft offers cold drinks and other civilized treats.

They pull up to find the place in an uproar. Chain saws whine; trees are being felled left and right. A crew is working feverishly to clear firebreaks around the outbuildings. Others are watering the roofs and grounds around the lodge. People rush back and forth, loading equipment on a string of packhorses.

Jay stops one of the ranch workers hustling by. He learns that ten days have passed since the last plane was able to make it through the smoke and land with provisions. A fire is burning on the ridge right above the lodge. The workers are making a last effort to evacuate everyone and everything they can by horseback.

Jay asks about conditions downriver. A woman steps forward. Just this morning she took her horse downstream, looking for a safe route out. The fire was burning to the river's edge about three miles below, at Little Pine.

A few commercial outfitters have pulled up in their rafts and are calling out on satellite phones, trying to find planes that can come in and fly customers out. No one can say exactly what is happening. Reports of what the fire may be doing are sketchy at best.

With the mood at the ranch just this side of everyone-for-themselves, the seven rafters from Portland push their boats back out into the flow of the river and head downstream. The whine of chain saws slowly fades in the distance.

Sure enough, three miles downstream at Little Pine, their assigned camp for the night, a ground fire is creeping down the canyon slopes. The campsite itself is not yet burning, but as they look over the location, flames race up a lone ponderosa on the slope above and the tree explodes, roaring in a fury of flames that climb high into the sky. It's only a matter of time before that fire starts a raging blaze in the surrounding dry grass and brush.

A quick vote sends them back on the river. They check the map. Grassy Flat is next.

When that camp comes into view, it seems the fire has just completed its work. The ground is burned black and smoldering. The outhouse is a charred, smoking ruin. The limbs on the mature ponderosa pines are far enough above the ground to escape the blaze, but the trunks have been scorched. Flames fed by pitch continue to burn on the trunks here and there. Using bailer buckets, the rafters douse the flames with river water.

They huddle in a group at the torched campsite, wisps of smoke rising from the ground, the heat of live embers baking up through their river sandals. Afternoon has become evening and they need to get off the river. They debate whether to stay or go.

The campsite has already burned once and it's unlikely to burn again. Maybe it isn't such a bad place to stay, although the smoldering ground doesn't look very tent friendly.

The majority agrees that there has got to be a better campsite downstream. They launch into the river again. Surely if they keep going, the fire will be left behind and the air will clear.

Dusk is coming on. The smoke is thicker than ever. Members of the group who know this river are thinking about the class-3 and class-4 rapids downstream. When the sun goes down, the night will be pitch-black. No moonlight is going to shine through this haze. If they can't get off the river soon, they will be rafting blind through serious whitewater.

Before long they come to Survey Creek, with its big camping area on a bench above the river. Limbs of large ponderosa pines arch over sandy tent sites. A grove of smaller trees make a brushy backdrop that climbs up the canyon slope behind camp. Normally there would be a large party here, usually an outfitter. As they look at the location, a guide from a commercial group camped across the river paddles over to speak with them.

"I don't mean to scare you folks, but there's a fire burning on the ridge just above this camp, with seventy- to eighty-foot flames shooting into the air."

They walk out onto the gravel bar at the river's edge and look up. High above, the fire is clearly visible, burning up on the rim of the canyon.

He tells them the outfitter assigned to this camp has already been here and left. He watched him walk up the hill to get a better look, then depart.

Once again the group is left to debate whether to stay or go. Jay decides to reconnoiter. He will check out the extent of the fire behind the campsite and report back. Grabbing Brian as backup, he walks to the upriver end of the bench. The two men push their way up and through the grove of smaller trees.

Two or three hundred yards uphill, Jay and Brian break out onto an open grass slope that runs another half-mile up to the canyon rim. Just ten feet away, creeping slowly downward, a front of low flames is blackening the grass, igniting small trees and bushes here and there.

With the flames just paces away, Jay turns to Brian. "If we can put this out and stop it from getting in that timber below, then I think we will be okay staying here."

Brian hesitates. "Jay, I have never fought a fire."

Jay snaps off a limb from a pine tree, "Come on. Grab a branch."

With no time to warn the others or call for help, the two men start pounding on the flames. They work their way across the hillside, kicking and scooping dirt on the more intense areas of the blaze. In time their impromptu fire line extends two hundred yards, then three hundred yards, across the slope.

On the downriver side of camp they come to a ravine filled with trees. The fire is no longer burning on the ground. Thirty feet above their heads they can see flames slowly skipping from treetop to treetop down the ravine, far beyond their reach.

. . . — — — . . .

Back at the river, close to an hour has passed and the two men have failed to return. The five remaining members, watching the flames above camp, are more than a little concerned. Two more men head upslope to see if they can find Jay and Brian.

Following the same route up, they step from the brush to find the ground fire extinguished. The crude fire line and footprints lead across the slope. This distinctive trail ends when they come across two dirty, smoky-faced men scraping at the ground and pulling out brush in a ravine on the downriver side of the camp.

Jay and Brian are digging the last of their fire line under the trees when Dick and Bob arrive.

"What in the heck are you guys doing?"

Jay gives a quick summary of their firefighting efforts as his friends snap pictures. No one will believe the work these guys have done without photographs.

With the fire line finished, there is no reason to linger in the fire zone. The four men retreat back to the river. Passing through a grove of pines they spot a four-foot-long bull snake, panicked by the fire, trying to climb a tree by wedging itself into the furrows of the bark.

When they arrive back at the campsite, the group gathers to make their decision. They have at least two more days of floating before the take-out. Jay and Brian's fire line should buy them some time for now. The guide from across the river told them that his group will be taking shifts throughout the night, watching for sparks or firebrands that might start a blowup nearby. If it looks as if the fire is getting too close, they will send someone over to warn them. With the sun setting and fire both above and below them on the river, they are going to have to make their stand here, at Survey Creek, for the night.

Everyone will sleep out in the open. No tents. If the fire gets down to the campsite, they will move out on the gravel bar. If things get really bad, the rafts and canoes are right there. Just toss their stuff aboard, make sure everyone is in a boat, and go.

After darkness falls, with all the smoke and the fire so near, no one is ready for sleep. For hours they sit on the beach sipping whiskey while watching the main fire rage half a mile above them on the ridgeline overlooking their camp. Immense ponderosa pine trees explode in roiling balls of fire, flames whip one hundred feet in the air, sparks swirl even higher into the night sky. Tree trunks burn through to fall with a roar and crash. The night sky is aglow with flame and embers. The moon glows a dull blood red through the swirling smoke.

One by one the rafters break away from the show, head over to the campsite, lie down, and try to sleep. Coughing from the sooty air, they are awake more often than not. Bleary eyes are always checking for flames nearby.

The air stays calm, no wind. The fire concentrates on the high ridges, burning upslope far faster than down toward the river. Jay and Brian's hour of effort on the fire line keeps the rafting group safe through a long, restless night.

. . . — — — . . .

It's hard to tell when the sun rises Friday morning. The smoke has cut visibility to a few hundred feet. The air is thick. With each breath comes a dull pain in their chests.

It is a grim group that climbs from the sleeping bags. The fun is definitely over. Any hope that they would eventually float out of

169

the smoke is long gone. As breakfast is set out, the flames finally work their way around the fire defenses and creep within thirty feet of camp. They decide to flee rather than fight. What little gear they have out is packed up quickly, and they push off into the main current.

The sun appears over the rim of the canyon as a pale, sooty disk in the sky. The smoke screens out all warmth. For the first time on the trip there is a chill in the air.

It is almost impossible to judge distance traveled or location except by the passing of time on their watches. The fire has to be very close because the smoke is the thickest they have experienced. Yet no flames can be seen. Throughout the day they pass through a deathly still, burned, smoking, otherworldly landscape. The atmosphere has a surreal yellowish hue. Normally a highlight, the big rapids on this stretch of the river are more work than play with smoke-stung eyes and lungs tightening with each breath of sooty air. At noon it is dark, almost like a solar eclipse. A feeling of doom pervades the day, as if the end of time has arrived and they are the only ones left.

As evening approaches, the fire reminds them they have yet to escape. Ash begins falling from the sky. Taking no chances, they pull up for the night on a sandbar in the middle of the river. For fire protection they could do no better; their five tents are completely surrounded by water.

· · · — — — · · ·

On Saturday morning the smoke does not let up. It is their last day on the river, and everyone is ready for this vacation turned nightmare to end. The lower canyon, the most scenic part of the trip, is hidden from view by smoke.

When Cache Bar and the take-out come in sight, there is relief in getting off the river but still no escape from the smoke. They find their car covered in ash. A pilot vehicle leads them to the main highway through a scorched landscape; rocks loosened by the inferno roll down from the hills above. They stop in Salmon, Idaho, for food. The town is like a military encampment, swarming with young soldiers brought in to fight the fire. The locals say the smoke has been enveloping the town like this for forty-five days.

They drive for a hundred miles before getting their first breath of clean air, just east of Stanley, Idaho.

· · · — — — · · ·

Jay reflects back on the river trip they took during one of the most intense fire seasons the West had seen in decades.

"My wife thinks it was the worst trip ever. I didn't feel right for about three months and wondered if I hadn't done permanent damage to my lungs. Yet I was intrigued by the whole thing; there was an element to the experience that was so difficult and surreal in those conditions."

To this day he can open up his rafting dry bags and smell the smoke from that trip down the Salmon River.

He turns thirty-eight today. He absolutely
refuses to die, alone, in the woods, on his
birthday.

CHAPTER 16

FIVE LOST DAYS

In the heavily forested foothills above the town of Packwood,
Washington, just south of Mount Rainier, six hunters have
teamed up. A six-point bull elk has been seen bedding down just
off the top of Hall Ridge, where the old-growth forest ends and the
overgrown clear-cut begins. Three beat the brush from above.
Three wait below, rifles at the ready.

The excitement starts when not one but three elk are driven
from their hiding places. The three men below take aim at two
four-point bulls. The wily six-point turns back into the old growth,
coming into the sights of a brush beater. Four rifles crack in the
mountain air. The three men below miss their marks. Just as the
brush beater squeezes the trigger, he slips in the snow. The bullet
goes high. As fast as they appeared, the elk melt back into the
forest.

When the men come together on the logging road below, there
are only five. They wait, scanning the hillside above with binoculars. The sixth man, Bill, at six-foot-one and 260 pounds, clad in
blaze-orange coveralls, shouldn't be hard to spot against the backdrop of dark green forest dusted with snow.

Time passes and he doesn't show. They yell up toward the
ridge top, calling his name. They fire their rifles into the air and

pause to listen for an answer. They hear nothing in return but the wind stirring in the trees.

Bill had led the other two brush beaters around to the south side of Hall Ridge. He showed them where to start into the forest, about one hundred yards apart. The last they saw of him, he was heading down the spur road to begin his part of the drive. That was an hour or two ago.

As the afternoon progresses, the five men search the hillside for signs of the lost hunter. Other hunters with an all-terrain vehicle are enlisted to ride the spur road back around the ridge to search where Bill was last seen. Everyone is yelling his name, firing off rifles. No one hears any call in return.

With darkness seeping down through the gray November sky, Bill's hunting partners, Wilbur and George, drive down off Hall Ridge, through a winding maze of logging roads, to the town of Packwood and the closest phone.

When the Lewis County Sheriff's deputy arrives in Packwood late Thursday, all he can do is record the facts. Bill was last seen at 11 A.M. heading off down the spur road. About three and a half hours have passed since the other two brush beaters came out of the woods. Nothing has been heard or seen of Bill since.

His partners describe him as a white male, thirty-seven years old, with dark hair; they give his height and weight, and describe his clothing. His rifle is a bolt-action .303-caliber British Enfield. Yes, he had survival gear but left it in the truck because he had made the short traverse across this terrain before and didn't feel he would need it.

Their biggest concern is Bill's medical history. He had a heart attack several years ago and, more recently, back surgery to repair a damaged disk.

As it turns out, Hall Ridge has a reputation for losing hunters. A subtle variation on the mostly flat-topped, heavily forested ridge tends to lead woods walkers in the wrong direction. The natural assumption of most hunters beating the brush across the ridge is to keep heading downhill, because the road has to be down there somewhere.

On Hall Ridge this is true. Down and to the west there are many logging roads.

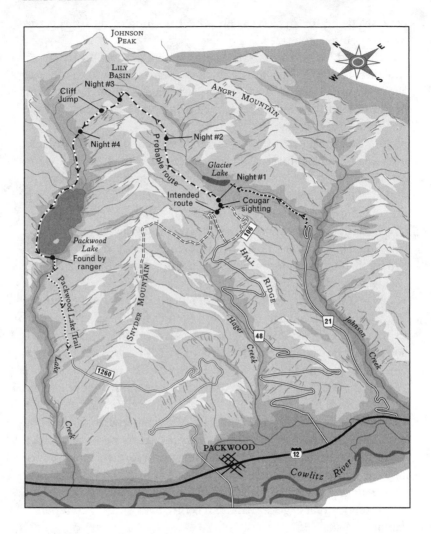

Down and to the east, however, lie many miles of old-growth forest stretching up to the Cascade Crest across a series of high basins with no roads and few trails. In this region, known as the Goat Rocks Wilderness, a hunter could walk for days in search of the logging road that has to be down there somewhere.

Later that evening, when a Lewis County search and rescue deputy arrives on the scene, darkness obscures the mountains. Bill's partners have continued searching the surrounding roads but have found no signs of the lost hunter. The terrain is too rugged to risk searching on foot in the darkness.

The deputy explains how the terrain tends to funnel hunters off to the east and down. Only four days earlier another hunter was lost in this same location. The next day his hunting partners found him, on the wrong side of Hall Ridge. He had been lucky enough to find and follow the Glacier Lake Trail out of the wilderness. The best thing Wilbur and George can do is to walk into Glacier Lake first thing in the morning. If they haven't found Bill by 10 A.M., the deputy says, call 911 and the search and rescue operation will begin.

· · · — — — · · ·

When Bill opens his eyes, his head is throbbing. Darkness is falling. From the color of the sky he guesses that three hours or more have passed from the time he stepped off the spur road. He can remember working his way into the forest. He wasn't far from the road when he caught some movement out of the corner of his eye. He barely had time to turn for a better look. He caught a glimpse of golden brown fur in motion, a cougar coming right at him. Then a waist-high impact, like a blind-side body check, tossing him down the slope, his head smacking hard against something, then blackness.

Now awake and aware, he looks around, cautiously scanning the nearby brush and deadfall trees. No sign of a cougar.

He slowly moves his arms, then his legs.

He discovers his coveralls are shredded down the back from his waist to his legs. Underneath, his denim pants are mostly intact.

Nothing else seems damaged, but his head throbs something fierce. He raises his hands to his skull, feeling for a bump.

Then he realizes his rifle is missing. He frantically searches the forest floor in the near darkness until his fingers brush across the wooden stock and cool steel barrel. The familiar feel of the rifle in his hands has a calming effect.

He checks his pockets and finds his Zippo lighter and seven spare rounds of ammunition. He can't find his compass, waterproof match case, or the three candy bars he brought along just in case.

He yells for help, hoping someone is near. The forest is silent— no return call, no echo, no sound.

He fires his rifle, pausing to listen. Again no response can be heard in the ever-darkening forest.

No problem, he says. *I've been through these woods before. Straight ahead will take me to Packwood Lake. Downhill to my right is Lily Basin. Downhill to my left is the logging road where the truck is parked. If I miss the road in the dark, which is unlikely, I will eventually walk into the back of the Packwood Mill way down in the valley below.*

Confident about his location, he strides off through the forest, angling left for the logging road.

He doesn't make it far when darkness begins to black out the forest. In the deep woods, nighttime darkness can be so complete you cannot see your hand in front of your face. Remembering lessons from his Boy Scout days, Bill decides to find shelter rather than risk stumbling blind through the night. He breaks off a few fir limbs for insulation from the ankle-deep snow, stuffs them into a hollow under a fallen tree, and climbs in for the night.

• • • — — — • • •

On Friday morning Wilbur and George hike the two-mile trail to Glacier Lake, sweltering in their heavy hunting clothes while rain pours from the sky. All along the trail and at the lake they yell out Bill's name and fire off their rifles occasionally. Sound travels well in the high basin, rolling south to Angry Mountain, east into the fringes of Lily Basin, and north up the steep, rocky cliffs that rise directly above the trail to Hall Ridge. When they listen for a return call, all they hear is the sound of rain falling through the trees.

That afternoon the first volunteers head into the field. In the parlance of search and rescue, this is the hasty search phase. Twenty-four experienced searchers with local knowledge of the terrain begin from where Bill was last seen and comb through the area as fast as possible. With luck they will find him quickly before the weather or injuries take their toll.

• • • — — — • • •

Friday is a hazy, dreamlike day for Bill, as if he isn't quite in his body.

He leaves his shelter in the morning. The rain drips down through the forest canopy, soaking everything. He makes his way through the woods, sometimes walking, sometimes climbing, going up, going down, the whole time thinking that he should be coming to a road somewhere along here.

He is not alone. At times he carries on lucid conversations with one of his hunting partners, even though he knows that Wilbur isn't there. At other times he converses with his teenage daughter and son as they join him in the deep woods. The smell of coffee seems to be in the air as well, brewing somewhere off through the trees, wafting in on the wind.

The hours pass in a confusing blur. With evening approaching and no roads or trails in sight, he finds another fallen tree to shelter under for the night. Before the light fades completely, he reaches for his wallet and pulls out the photograph of his daughter and son, ages seventeen and fifteen.

I cannot die, because of these kids; I have to look after these kids.

· · · — — — · · ·

The hasty search across Hall Ridge continues through the rain and wind of Friday night into the early hours of Saturday with no success.

More volunteers arrive Saturday morning.

Now, sixty-eight people have joined the effort as the search expands into the areas surrounding the ridge. Searchers in vehicles check the trailheads and patrol the roads to contain the search area. Other teams are sent out on foot and horseback along the trails that fan out into the wilderness to the east.

One of the searchers is sent out to traverse the route that most lost hunters follow, off the ridge and down through the forest toward Glacier Lake. He calls Bill's name as he makes the trek. About three miles into the basin, a voice finally answers his call. With the wind swirling around, it is difficult to track the location through the dense forest. As the searcher closes in on the voice, the words become clear across the distance. It's Bill, calling for help.

The lost man's voice carries far in the silence of the mountains. The searcher follows the sound for another two and a half miles, high above Glacier Lake, into the upper reaches of Lily Basin, before he finds the missing man—the only problem being that there are two men. They're sitting under a tree at their hunting camp, sipping an adult beverage, getting a little tipsy, and having a good time answering back. They thought someone was messing around and the least they could do was play along.

· · · — — — · · ·

Bill wakes at the dawn of Saturday with a new determination. He turns thirty-eight today and absolutely refuses to die, alone, in the woods, on his birthday.

Yet his mind is still playing tricks on him. What seems to be the sound of a truck, or maybe a car, leads him off through the trees for the better part of the morning.

Then, in a rare moment of clarity, he decides to climb up, out of the forest, in search of a vantage point. Perhaps he can sight a landmark and figure out where he is.

It is a long, steep, and exhausting climb to escape from the basin—pushing through brush soaked by rainfall, feet sliding in loose soil and moss, pulling his weary body up over fallen trees. Eventually he breaks into a clearing with a view of the surrounding countryside.

Hungry, sleep-deprived, wet and cold, he struggles to match the terrain to foggy memories. Not long ago one of his hunting partners had shown him a topographic relief map of the area. The pieces of the puzzle slowly fall into place, and the landscape gradually begins to look familiar. It is not long before Bill can see that he has been walking in exactly the wrong direction for the past two days.

From what he can recall, if he climbs to the summit of the ridge he is now on, Packwood Lake should be on the other side. If he can get to Packwood Lake, he can find a trail that will lead out of the wilderness.

Once again the day has passed and daylight is fading. He finds two trees that have fallen together to form a crude lean-to and crawls under the overhanging branches. Every stitch of his clothing is soaked from two days of wandering through the dense, rain-drenched forest. He pulls off his boots and wrings out his socks and boot liners to help warm his feet. Still, he shivers as night falls.

The thought of a fire for light and warmth won't leave his mind. His lighter has proved worthless. In the incessant dampness it won't strike a flame.

Then, a ray of hope. Maybe he can start a fire using the gunpowder from one of his two remaining bullets. The spark from his lighter might ignite the gunpowder, which just might get a fire going.

He gathers the driest kindling he can find and builds a little pyramid in front of his shelter. Prying a bullet from its casing, he carefully sprinkles the small black grains on the kindling. Then he sprinkles the remainder of the gunpowder around the striker of his lighter. Leaning close in over the kindling, he carefully thumbs the striker wheel. Nothing happens. Try as he might, he can't get a spark. Moisture has penetrated the flint.

Defeated, he climbs under the fallen trees for his third night in the woods. The dark, damp, cold hours pass slowly. Groggy from exhaustion, yet unable to sleep, wild sounds and thoughts race through Bill's semiconscious mind.

Wait a minute. Did I just hear a logging truck go by? Am I that close to a road and I just didn't see it?

Then a faint light becomes visible in the darkness. *Is that a house? There is no way I could be near a house.*

He gets up to investigate, only to find fungus on a nearby log glowing with phosphorescence.

The image of that cougar coming for him is burned into his memory. Today he passed a couple of carcasses, just bones really, scattered across the forest floor. A deer or elk had been killed and eaten. Maybe the cat has followed him and lurks out there in the darkness, waiting to attack.

Late in the night the rain turns to snow. Desperate for warmth, he pulls his arms out of his sleeves, slides them in next to his body, and zips his coveralls up like a makeshift sleeping bag.

· · · — — — · · ·

Saturday's search covers the high trails around Hall Ridge as well as the low routes into the surrounding basins. The rocky cliffs on the north and south sides of Hall Ridge are too dangerous for ground teams to traverse, but these areas are checked by voice from above and below. Despite the rainy, overcast weather, the searchers are positive that if the lost hunter could call for help, they would have found him.

At the close of operations Saturday night the search becomes an exercise in deductive reasoning. Search leaders consider possible scenarios: Bill is down and unconscious and has been so from the very beginning; or Bill is in one of the two cliff areas and the searchers could not hear him; or Bill has left the area and has not told anyone.

Considering what they know of his medical history of heart attack and back problems, the most likely scenario is that Bill is down and unresponsive.

Sunday morning more volunteers arrive. Close to one hundred people gather for the grim task of grid searching: They will walk, almost shoulder to shoulder, across Hall Ridge. The purpose of this effort is to find a body, hidden somewhere out of sight, under a log or down in a hole.

· · · — — — · · ·

Bill wakes to several inches of fresh snow on Sunday morning. Sticking to his plan, he continues climbing. By the time he reaches the top, he is struggling through fresh snow up to his waist. Just as he remembered from his hunting partner's map, Packwood Lake appears in the basin far below.

Taking a visual bearing on the lake, Bill heads down off the ridge, pushing through deep snow and dense forest. Not far off the top, a band of cliffs cuts off his descent. Looking right, then left, he can see no easy way down.

He turns to retrace his steps and climb back up. For every step up, he slides back two. The snow is too deep, the slope too steep. He tries again and again, floundering in the snow, but can make no progress.

Exhausted and alone, Bill is trapped high above Packwood Lake. As far as he can figure there are only two options: freeze to death up here, where no one will ever find him, or take a chance and jump.

He takes a second look over the edge. The drop doesn't look to be more than twenty or thirty feet to the slope below. Years ago in the Army he once watched a group of Rangers jump out of a plane five hundred feet above the ground. Five of the men's parachutes failed to open completely. They walked away with only broken bones. If they can survive a fall of several hundred feet, then this little leap should be easy.

He shuffles back and forth along the edge, looking for a spot with a clear fall line. Then he packs snow around his legs, thinking this might help absorb the impact. Holding his rifle tight to his chest, Bill takes a moment to get his nerve up, and then slides off the edge.

A few moments of free fall, eyes shut, then he hits hard, rolling and rolling, snow flying, the world spinning. His body eventually comes to rest in a rumpled heap below the cliff.

His chest hurts from where the rifle smacked his ribs on impact. He wiggles his toes, flexes his arms, checking for pain. Everything seems to work.

He stands up carefully, dusts off the snow, and shakes off the impact. Remembering his bearings to the lake below, he places his back to the cliff face and sets off downslope through the trees.

The remainder of the day is an obstacle course of exhaustion. Cliffs and steep ravines block his way, offering only the occasional rivulet of water from which to quench his thirst. Twice he stumbles on rocky ledges, catching himself just before careening headlong over the edge.

Finally down from the heights, he enters the old-growth forest to find a maze of deadfall giants. His strength fades as he is forced to crawl under or walk the full length of the massive trunks to find a way around. Three days in wet denim pants has chafed the skin from the inside of his thighs. His feet are wet, blistered, and raw from scrambling across the rough terrain. Fiery pain radiates up from his feet and legs with each step.

As the fourth day comes to an end, Bill drags himself into another shelter, next to a stream, somewhere near the bottom of the basin.

Late that night a powerful storm sweeps down from the mountains. Rain pours into his sleeping space. The old-growth firs slash wildly back and forth. In pitch-black darkness the ground shudders with heavy impacts as if big trees are falling nearby. Wet, cold, and paralyzed with fear, Bill stares wide-eyed into the darkness.

· · · — — — · · ·

The grid search on Sunday is an exercise in futility. All that is found is a sheath knife. Family members cannot identify it as belonging to the lost hunter. The teams are pulled out of the field Sunday night, soaked to the skin and chilled from the heavy rain.

A break in the weather is forecast for Monday morning. The search will be continued one more day. If the clouds lift, helicopters will be used to visually check the two inaccessible cliff areas. With a second storm due to arrive Tuesday, and the snow level dropping well below the elevation of Hall Ridge, it may be the last opportunity.

· · · — — — · · ·

As first light filters down through the trees on Monday, Bill crawls from his shelter to the bank of the creek. He lies on the damp ground to drink, savoring the cool liquid. It takes all the strength he has to push himself up off the ground into an upright position. Standing there, deep in the forest, shaking from cold, his legs and feet burning, his mother's voice comes to him from way back in his childhood.

You are not a quitter. Whatever you do, never give up.

Another night out will kill him. He has to find help today.

He shuffles off through the woods, following the flow of water downstream toward Packwood Lake. Taking no chances of losing the creek, he hugs the banks through dense brush.

The forest turns to swamp, the mud so thick it sucks his boots off. He has to stop and dig down in the mud to pull them out.

Logjams block his way. Bill crosses the creek on fallen trees or just by jumping. He falls in the water several times, never stopping. There is no energy to spare now. He pushes on, feet sloshing in boots filled with water.

Eventually Bill emerges from the forest to find himself at a campsite along the eastern shore of Packwood Lake. He is too tired to celebrate.

While fighting through the forest and swamp this morning Bill worked up a plan. On the far end of the lake he knows there is a dam that controls the water supply to the town of Packwood. If he can make his way to the dam, he might be able to mess with the system. Someone will have to come and check out the problem.

But the dam is still a mile and a half away and his body is numb from exhaustion. As he looks about the campsite, something on the ground catches his attention. Stooping over to pick it up, his eyes open wide. It's a can of wintergreen-flavor mint chew, unopened! He pops the lid and crams the sugary mint leaves in his mouth.

The sweet treat gives him enough energy to keep moving down the lakeshore trail.

Halfway to the dam, an aircraft sound fills the basin. Bill snaps to attention. Across the lake to the west a helicopter is flying low along the high rocky ridgeline. He hustles down to the lakeshore as fast as his damaged feet and legs can carry him.

Out in the open, he waves his arms and screams frantically, trying to attract the flight crew's attention.

When the helicopter disappears behind the far side of the ridge, Bill falls into a sudden silence. He turns back to the trail, willing his feet to move one step at a time toward the dam. He listens intently, hoping for the helicopter to return, occasionally looking back up to the high ridge. The only sound is the scuffing of his boots with each weary step.

Reaching the far end of the lake, Bill finds a Forest Service cabin boarded up for winter. As he stands before the cabin, the sound of an approaching motor filters through the trees.

· · · — — — · · ·

The Forest Service wilderness ranger had been waiting until the end of elk hunting season to head up into Packwood Basin. He had been assigned to help retrieve air-monitoring equipment for the EPA before winter set in. Just a one-day trip, and today happens to be the first day he can head into the woods without worrying about being mistaken for a game animal.

He rambles up the access road, pulling a trailer with his all-terrain vehicle. As he nears the end of the rutted route to Packwood Lake, he can hear someone screaming for help. He shuts off his machine and runs toward the voice. A man waves urgently to him from near the Forest Service cabin.

When Bill meets his first human being in several days, the words just avalanche out.

"Oh my God I am so glad to see you. I have been lost for the last five days, I know I have hypothermia, I'm dehydrated, I have trench foot, my legs are killing me, I need help."

The ranger had heard a search was on. There were helicopters flying search patterns this morning, but that was up on the ridge, miles away. He hands Bill what little food and water he has with him.

While Bill wolfs down the snacks, the ranger radios to the Forest Service office in Packwood to let them know he has found the lost hunter. Communications are a little difficult, with the Forest Service and the searchers on different frequencies. Messages are relayed back and forth.

A voice broadcasts from the ranger's radio: "They want to know if the lost hunter is named Bill White."

The ranger looks at the dirty, disheveled man before him.

"Are you Bill White?"

"Yes," Bill answers, a little puzzled.

"Yes, I have Bill White," the ranger repeats into the radio.

Again there is a pause as the message is relayed, and then the voice crackles back. The searchers are taking no chances this time about having the right man.

"The sheriff's department wants 100 percent positive ID, repeat 100 percent positive ID, that you have Bill White standing next to you."

The ranger turns to look at Bill.

Bill, who has been listening, pauses between bites to wonder how many people who look like him are lost out here. Then he remembers his wallet. He fishes it out of his pocket, pulls out his driver's license, and hands it to the ranger.

· · · — — — · · ·

When Bill arrives by ambulance at Morton General Hospital, he is greeted in the emergency room by the head nurse.

"We are happy to see you!"

He is a little taken aback. "Well, I'm happy to see you as well."

"No, we are really happy to see you because the sheriff's department called us today and said to expect a body. He said, "We have a lost hunter; he has been lost for five days. He will either be in a body bag when he comes to you, or in the time it takes to stabilize him for a medevac flight to Seattle, he will die.' You don't know how happy we are to see you."

The days of walking in wet denim pants abraded the skin between Bill's legs so badly that he is treated like a burn patient. His feet swell more than two shoe sizes larger than normal, from trench foot. It will be a month before he can walk normally.

To this day Bill doesn't know why the cougar attacked him. Much of what he can remember of those five confused days in the hills above Packwood remains incomplete and troubling.

"There is a void in my life that I can't answer for."

He rides completely blind in a white storm of swirling snow, but somehow he manages to stay on the board.

CHAPTER 17

THE AVALANCHE RIDER

When it comes to building a career as a backcountry snowboarder, the game is to get on film doing something crazy, get noticed, get sponsored, and who knows what could happen next? Maybe an all-expenses-paid lifestyle that has you carving turns for cold, hard cash. It's a gamble that has a certain appeal.

Make no mistake: Backcountry snowboarding is not a sport for the reckless. Nel, his brother C.L., Chris, and Annie are experienced and prepared. Most of them have attended the classes put on by the Gallatin National Forest Avalanche Center. They always carry avalanche transceivers and other rescue equipment. Last night they put a call in to the Avalanche Center even though no snow had fallen for several days. The report gave them the green light, with the avalanche danger at only "moderate on all recently wind-loaded slopes steeper than 35 degrees."

On this Thursday morning in March they are making their way by snowmobile through a maze of logging roads in the Gallatin National Forest north of Bozeman, Montana. Today's destination: their favorite backcountry locale on the eastern side of the Bridger Mountains. The official mission: to capture extreme snowboarding footage for a couple of winter-sports movie production companies. Jeff is along with his 16mm camera to film the day's action.

By 9 A.M. they have climbed to a high plateau above tree line. The plateau drops off into a deep cirque with a frozen lake in the bottom. Across the cirque, the main escarpment of the Bridger Range rises high into the kind of blue sky that makes people dream of living in Montana.

As they turn off their snow machines, the mountain quiet settles around them and they look across to the runs they plan to snowboard today. What they see is perfect for the task at hand—one thousand feet of near-vertical terrain that looks insane on film. The runs are shaped like an hourglass: small bowls at the top leading down to narrow, snow-lined gullies that fan out at the bottom into wide-open slopes. Cliffs and body-busting rocks are evenly distributed. The rides will be more like controlled falls, requiring precise moves and fast reflexes.

They have been here many times before. The lines are steep but definitely possible, even fun. Today they are just excited to make the first tracks in snow that will carve as smooth as cream-cheese frosting.

A strategy session settles who will ski which run in which order. Then they quickly gather their equipment, snowboard off the bench down to the frozen lake, and begin their climb up to the main escarpment.

It doesn't take long before they are spread out on top at the entry points of their chosen runs. Chris will go first, then Nel, and third will be Annie. C.L. is in place on top with his 35mm camera to catch still images of their efforts.

· · · — — — · · ·

All eyes are on Chris as he drops off the edge, leans into a couple of tight turns, then aims straight for the pinch-point and the narrow gully of snow leading downward. The entry is precise and he hits it dead on, accelerating at free-fall speeds, a white wisp of ice crystals whipping up behind.

Then he is through the narrows, past the cliff band, and carving big S curves on the wide-open slopes a thousand feet below. He skids to a stop and the radio chatter is filled with excitement, all about the great conditions, great snow, awesome run.

As they wait for the sun to come out from behind a cloud, Nel takes a moment to focus, tracing the route in his mind, visualizing his moves. He has run the chute he stands above before, but low snow depths this year have left the center section, about fifty feet of rock cliff, exposed. Today he will drop in, carve hard right across and out for a short run in Chris's line, then continue across into a third chute for the run down through untracked snow to where Chris waits below.

With an okay from the cameraman, Nel gets his calm going, takes a breath, and leaps into the chute.

Annie has found a perfect place to watch his run. From an outcropping that juts out just to the left side of the chute, she can see all the way down a thousand feet to the bottom.

As Nel leans forward into his first turn, Annie glances back up to the top of the chute to see a mark in the snow that wasn't there a moment ago.

Is that a snowboard track at the top? Did someone just cut across the top when Nel dropped in?

As Nel carves hard for the exit point, the turn feels mushy, and suddenly the exit point whips past him heading uphill.

As Annie struggles to make sense of what she sees, the mark becomes a fracture line and a windblown slab of snow forty-five feet wide begins a silent slide off the ridge top and into the chute.

Nel leaps around into a heel-side turn wondering how he could have missed his exit point. Suddenly his situation is frightfully clear as he looks upslope to see the fracture line opening wide. He's riding a slab avalanche. Thinking fast, he tells himself, *No problem, I've been down this run before. I know the fall line. I know how long it is. If everything goes well, I'll just ride this out.*

As Annie watches from above, the slab, with Nel in the middle, accelerates with incredible speed and rams into the pinch-point. A cloud of white erupts into the clear air and he disappears from view.

Inside the cloud, Nel's goggles are torn off by the blast. Vaporized ice crystals explode into his mouth and nose, wrapping him in a suffocating fog. Snow penetrates deep into every opening in his clothing, instantly chilling him. He rides completely blind in a white storm of swirling snow. Somehow he manages to stay upright.

As the first rocks tear at his board, Nel can feel the jarring blows like fast, hard punches reverberating up through his spine. All he can do is try to hang on and maintain control.

I can deal with this, he tells himself, and then a rock outcropping hidden in the swirling snow catches his hip. The massive blow catapults him into the air.

He free-falls through a claustrophobic confusion, heavy snow pressing in around him, ice crystals choking him, a roaring in his ears. Time seems to slow down.

Racing through his mind is a mental map of the run. In the past, as he exited the chute, he had to carve hard to miss a rib of rock that wraps across the fall line. All he can imagine now is that he is flying through the air, with no helmet, toward a deadly head-first impact with this rib of rock. Somehow, as he falls through the air, he executes a complete diving roll. At the base of the cliff band, Nel lands in a sitting position, still on his board, in a deep cushion of snow.

The main body of the avalanche follows, hammering him from behind. He fights to regain control but he just can't stand up. Again he is tumbled down the fall line, pushed and pummeled by a flood of snow.

· · · —— —— —— · · ·

Nel was in the middle of his first turn when, from below, Chris saw the slab break loose high above. He watches, frozen in horror, as Nel is forced down the chute, riding the slab into and over the rock cliffs. The cloud of white explodes as the slab breaks up at the pinch-point, and Nel is gone.

Only then does Chris realize the avalanche is heading straight for him. He scrambles across the slope to escape. Turning to look back, he can barely discern a figure tumbling down the mountainside through a cloud of snow and ice.

With no idea how much snow may be piling down upon him, Nel uses the last of his strength fighting to carve out of the avalanche path and away from the bone-crushing rock rib at the base of the slope.

Finally an edge catches and the snowboard jerks him out of the roiling avalanche and into open air. Nel bounces down the slope, his body dragging behind his board. He comes to a stop at Chris's feet, coughing ice out of his lungs, rubbing snow from his eyes. His snowboard is broken in half, hinged in the middle by the thin plastic top sheet.

Chris orders Nel to lie still as he gets him out of his snowboard bindings. Fearing the worst, he stabilizes his neck, praying that his spine isn't fractured. A quick inspection reveals no obvious injuries or bleeding.

Nel can feel that he is badly hurt. The base of his back took the impact. Pain wracks his body. Muscle spasms jerk through one hip, shaking his legs. He might be bleeding internally.

Chris uses their two snowboards to improvise a platform on the mountain slope. He wraps his coat around them for insulation from the snow. Gingerly moving Nel onto the platform, he tries to make him as comfortable as possible.

Moments later Annie and C.L. arrive, having snowboarded down the route they climbed up. After watching Nel's body tumble a thousand feet through snow and rock, they are stunned to find him alive and talking.

The celebration is short. Even with the three of them, their ability to haul Nel out of the deep cirque, up to the snowmobiles, and down several miles of bumpy trail is questionable at best. A helicopter is the only way to get him out of here.

They call Jeff on the radio, where he waits on the plateau above. Shortly after making contact they hear one of the snowmobiles fire up and head out.

Within a few minutes they all decide that Chris should go for help as well, just in case Jeff has a problem with his snowmobile. C.L. and Annie will stay with Nel.

Before he leaves, Chris turns to Nel one more time.

"I'm worried about your back. Do not move."

With that, he makes his way across the lake and runs up the slope, climbing to the bench to disappear from view over the edge. Annie, C.L., and Nel hear a second snowmobile start and the high whine of its engine retreat into the distance, toward where their cars are parked along the highway seven miles back through the woods.

· · · — — — · · ·

As time passes, Nel isn't warming up, even with Annie lying next to him and sharing body heat. He just can't get comfortable lying down. There is no position that relieves the pain in his back.

Nel recalls the weather forecast. A winter storm is supposed to roll in sometime this evening. Clouds are beginning to obscure the blue sky. Things will get bad if they can't get out soon. Nel wants Annie and C.L. to hand him his ski poles.

Against their protests, he struggles to his feet. Standing seems to relieve some of the pain. Now, with a little blood circulating, he starts to warm up. Annie and C.L. support him with their shoulders, doing their best to hold him vertical.

Nel shakes off their grip and shuffles around under his own power. His body is really stiff. He can move, but only very slowly.

"Let's just walk out of here," he says.

Annie and C.L. won't have any of it. Even if he could get up to the snowmobiles, how could he handle seven miles of hard riding on the rough track out? They persuade Nel to settle down and wait for rescue. Jeff and Chris know what they are doing. They should be back any time now.

· · · — — — · · ·

Two hours pass with Nel alternating between bouts of trying to lie down and trying to walk. Ominous clouds have gathered. The wind is picking up.

No one brings up the subject, but they all know enough about mountain travel and the limits of helicopter flight. None of the three wants to think about spending the night outdoors. They had packed for a warm afternoon, not a bivouac in a winter storm.

Finally, their radio crackles to life.

Chris is close by. With him is Scott, a first-responder from the Gallatin County Search and Rescue Team.

A Life Flight helicopter is on its way from Butte, Montana, running just ahead of the storm. If the helicopter can't get to Nel within the hour, everyone is in for a long night.

In a short while they spot Chris and Scott descending into the cirque. The two men arrive and quickly take charge of the accident scene.

Scott has come equipped for what was described to him as a potentially serious back injury. He inspects Nel and finds a large protrusion midway up his spine, but the patient seems to be holding up under his injuries. Nel remains standing, so packaging him for evacuation goes quickly. They wrap him in blankets and then envelop him in a full-body vacuum suit. The suit is inflated and Nel is completely immobilized to protect his spine.

Within minutes the helicopter swoops down out of the gray sky into the frozen cirque. A small snow dome just steps away makes for a perfect landing spot. It takes only moments to load Nel in, and the helicopter is off.

Forty-five minutes later, falling snow obscures the landscape as Chris, C.L., Annie, Scott, and the rest of the rescue party ride snowmobiles back to the trailhead.

· · · — — — · · ·

The hospital in Bozeman is only minutes away by helicopter. After a thorough examination including X rays, Nel is shown the diagnostic film. Years of looking at his chiropractor father's work have educated him in this science. The front side of his first lumbar vertebra has been compressed 20 percent, and a front-to-back hairline fracture is clearly visible. It appears stable, the doctor says, but if the right precautions aren't taken it could slip and damage the spinal cord.

"Whoa!" Nel exclaims. "I was walking around."

The iliac crest on his left hipbone is chipped as well. The first impact probably caused the damage. Why the fractured vertebrae didn't slip and cut his spinal cord when the avalanche tumbled him the rest of the way down the slope is a mystery.

He is a very lucky man.

· · · — — — · · ·

Nel had to pull out of a snowboard trip to Alaska he had planned, but after about two months of recuperation, including six weeks in a back brace, he was surfing in Costa Rica with no noticeable after-effects.

A year later he was better than ever. Chronic back pain had plagued him from a childhood accident, but after his time in the back brace, the pain was gone. When snow conditions are favorable, Nel promises to return and complete the run that should have killed him.

All the days of fighting off fear and panic spill out in one moment as she begins to cry, shout, and wave, all at the same time.

CHAPTER 18

BAD BREAK

The Selway-Bitterroot Wilderness sits high in a forgotten corner of Idaho's panhandle, well over a million acres of rugged landscape draping across the crest of the Bitterroot Mountains, along the state's western boundary with Montana. There are few places in the lower forty-eight that are less forgiving. These are the mountains that were almost the end of the Lewis and Clark expedition as it crossed to the Pacific Coast in 1805. Time has not mellowed their nature.

In the summer it is a hot, dry, bug-ridden and lonesome place of dense forest and raw granite peaks that appeals only to seasoned backcountry explorers. Shelley, a former wilderness ranger for the Forest Service, falls into this category. Life has taught her to be independent, and she prefers it this way. A multiday trip with her two dogs—longtime companion Kilgore, a Heinz 57 terrier, and her latest hiking partner, eight-month-old Trekker, a golden retriever—is nothing out of the ordinary.

On a previous trip a Forest Service fire lookout had raved to her about the stunning landscape around Diablo Mountain and Duck Lake, south of the Lochsa River near the Elk Summit Guard Station. Always ready to check out new territory, she made a note of the locale. That is why, on this balmy Wednesday in August, she is walking the high ridge of Diablo Mountain in the western section of the Selway-Bitterroot Wilderness.

To the east she can see the crest of the Bitterroot Range, to the south Goat Heaven Peaks. Here and there, off in the distance, columns of smoke from the many forest fires burning this summer billow into the sky.

On a western scale, the fires are burning small areas, mostly in remote locations, but media reports have scared off a good number of summer visitors, emptying the wilderness even more than usual. Of course this only increases the potential for success in a prime criterion by which backcountry trips are judged. Now Shelley has an even better chance of not seeing a soul the whole time out.

Yesterday's five-mile hike in from the trailhead had been the typical Selway-Bitterroot experience: biting flies, sweltering heat, not enough water. Now, after a good night's rest, Shelley and the boys, Kilgore and Trekker, step off the end of the Diablo Mountain trail. For the next five days they will be making their own path through the wilderness.

Shelley keeps a close eye on her companions as they work their way east along the shoulder of the mountain. Just steps away, the north face of Diablo drops eight hundred feet straight down into the basin that holds Duck Lake, their destination for the day. She knows the history of the mountain. People have died up here when they lost their footing too close to the edge. There are few second chances in this wilderness.

Eventually they come to a saddle that seems to offer a safe route down to the lake. Always cautious, Shelley gauges the incline and looks for potential obstacles. She can see solid footing and plenty of vegetation to grab on to, so she lets Trekker and Kilgore lead on.

They take their time in the descent, sidehilling when the route becomes too steep. The lake glistens in the valley below, getting closer with every stride.

With the worst of the terrain behind, Shelley steps out on a slab of slightly inclined granite. Her foot slips. A loud crack, like a rifle shot, rings in her ears.

She lands hard on her left side, staring in complete disbelief. Her right foot hangs at an odd angle, as if no longer properly attached. A strange bulge pushes out from the inside of her calf, just above the foot.

Then the pain radiates up her leg like an electric shock.

Oh, God! No, not here, not now!

She struggles to stay calm, the throbbing like static in her mind.

Think, she says to herself. *Breathe. You can't go into shock. Keep it together.*

She struggles out of her backpack, then pulls it close; adrenaline makes her movements fast and frantic. Out comes the first-aid kit, then her hands rifle through her pack, searching for something to splint her leg. The fire grill! She yanks on it, swearing when it won't pull free. Another yank and it's out. Pull it out of its cover; toss the two sticks of kindling aside.

Wait, I can use the sticks as well.

When she turns back to her foot, the bones seem to have realigned themselves. The pain is now just a dull ache. She eases the boot off and carefully pulls her heavy wool sock up as far as possible. Using gauze and a roll of stretch-wrap—heavy-duty bandage material she normally uses on her horses—she carefully wraps her lower leg. The grate is placed on the inside of her calf. The kindling sticks, wrapped in foam from her sleeping pad, go on the outside of her calf. A second layer of stretch-wrap secures the splint.

Thoughts stream through her mind a mile a minute. *I never trusted the shallow lugs of my boots. Why didn't I get better soles? Why do I always overload my pack? Why is this happening?*

Her boot is worthless now. She pulls out a river sandal and slips it on, securing its top strap so that it serves to anchor the splint.

With the leg taken care of, her thirst is suddenly raging. Last night's summit camp was dry. With no water in her pack she has to get down to the lake. The terrain is steep and rugged, with rock ledges and brush. Fighting panic, she half crab-walks, half scoots on her rear while dragging her pack behind. Kilgore and Trekker pace nearby, never straying far.

The pack is too heavy. Her thirst adds to rising anxiety. She can't stay here on the mountainside. She has to get to the water.

Digging a couple of plastic bags out of her pack, she assembles a few supplies: a water bottle, the first-aid kit, some food, extra clothes, and a sleeping bag.

Leaving the pack behind, she starts for the lake again, throwing the bags downhill, then crab-walking/scooting over the rocks and through the brush to reach the bundles and throw them forward again. What seemed so close on foot is now impossibly distant. The journey quickly breaks down into a series of small goals. Get to that next rock. Get to that little bit of shade.

The heat of an August day beats down. Flies buzz around. Kilgore and Trekker stay nearby, tongues lolling. The dirt and grit grinds into her palms as she scoots along, sweat rolling down into her face. Tossing the bags, scooting, tossing, scooting. She takes a break only when her shoulders scream for a rest.

Four hours of scooting down the mountainside, easing off rock ledges, and pushing through brush pass before Shelley and the boys break out of the forest and onto the lakeshore.

Grabbing her water bottle, she leaves her bags and drags herself the last few yards into the lake. Lying in the shallows, she gulps down great swallows of water. The soothing coolness holds panic and worry at bay for a few peaceful moments.

Rehydrated, she drags herself out of the lake. The heather and grass where her bags lie will make as good a bed as any. Trekker's dog pack comes off and becomes a prop for her damaged leg. Sitting back for a moment's rest she exhales relief, happy to be still after the marathon scoot down the mountain.

Then her mind starts in. It's Wednesday. She told her neighbor she would return on Sunday. No one will even begin to wonder what has happened to her until late Sunday or maybe even Monday. That's more than four days from now!

Her wilderness ranger philosophy takes over. *I got myself into this place, I am going to get myself out.*

Looking at her map she plots a route west, down Duck Creek to a trail that climbs over a low pass and back to where her truck is parked at the Elk Summit Guard Station. It looks to be a six- to eight-mile crawl, with no trail for the first two or three miles. Given today's experience, that would probably take three days or longer. Better to get started right away than to wait.

A second voice chimes in, still unbelieving and scared. *How did this happen? What if you fall again on the way out? What if you get stuck out here and die? Better to stay put and wait for help.*

The day passes slowly. Indecision fuels the debate raging in her head: *Stay or go? What should I do? Am I going to die? I am not done living. What about the boys? This is a pretty place to die. I will not die here!*

Evening arrives. Fear has erased any hunger, but she forces herself to eat a few crackers, a slice of cheese and salami. The left-overs go to the boys, along with their standard fare. As she watches them wolf the food there is a little jolt of anxiety, and calculations start again. *How long will our food last?*

It is when darkness falls that she realizes she left her flashlight up on the mountain with her pack. Anxiety rushes in once more. What else did she leave up there that might mean the difference between survival and surrender? Shuffling her plastic bags around, she pulls out the sleeping bag, uses the extra clothing as a makeshift mattress, swallows an ibuprofen, and tries to make herself comfortable. The boys snooze in the heather by her side.

Throughout the night, every time she wakes, the whine of mosquitoes is a constant reminder that this is not just a bad dream.

· · — — — · ·

Thursday dawns. Shelley wakes to find a mass of bug bites where her neck had been exposed as she slept.

She drags herself down to the water and fills her bottle. By the time she makes it back to her sleeping bag, she is exhausted.

Still unable to decide whether to stay or go, she fills the day with a list of chores.

She has worn through the seat of her shorts scooting down the mountain. She adapts her denim pants to the task by splitting the hem so the splint on her right leg can slip through.

She scrounges around for something that will work for a crutch. It's a battle, wedging a deadfall branch between two trees, then finding enough leverage, with only one good foot, to break it to length. This done, she quickly discovers one isn't enough. The battle begins to create a second crutch.

Other small tasks keep her mind distracted. By the time the heat of the day has cranked up, she is exhausted. Creating a shelter was on the list of chores, but she has no motivation left.

The go-or-stay debate remains just below the surface, grating on her nerves. On top of that, reality has set in. With one little misstep, she has devolved from independent backcountry explorer to wilderness bag lady, shuffling around with all she has in the world stuffed into two plastic sacks.

Her appetite fails to arrive for dinner. She tries to eat but is just not hungry. The boys eagerly take her leftover salami and cheese again.

Night falls. As she tries to sleep, lightning flashes out of the darkness. A thunderclap rolls around the basin. Big drops of rain begin to splatter on her sleeping bag. Struggling out of the bag, she curses herself for not building a shelter. The only thing to do now is make a break for the trees before the shower turns into a downpour.

Before settling in for the night, she stripped off her clothes in the heat. Now, almost naked, she frantically grabs what she can find and shoves it into her bags. With sticks, brush, and rocks jabbing her, she shuffles blindly through the dark to a small grove of evergreens, hoping to shelter under their branches.

The thundershower passes quickly and Shelley returns to her camp by the lake. She was lucky this time. The equipment abandoned up on the hill could make a big difference in her fight to survive. The backpack must be retrieved.

With a renewed sense of purpose comes a calming strength. She falls asleep easily, knowing exactly what tomorrow's task will be.

· · · — — — · · ·

Friday dawns and Shelley is up early to take advantage of the cool morning temperatures. The boys are eager to get going. Trekker is wearing his empty dog pack to help with the retrieval. Shelley fills her water bottle, ties it into a sweatshirt, and then wraps the sweatshirt around her waist.

She scoots along in her crab walk for a while, with thoughts of the four hours it took to come down the mountain prominent in her mind. Then, while moving around an obstacle, she discovers that she can crawl without pain. It's a quantum leap in mobility, like going from walking to running. Hope comes rushing in for the first time in days.

Two hours later she is back up on Diablo Peak near the site of the accident. The panic from breaking her leg didn't leave the clearest picture of the location in her mind. Everything starts to look the same on this mountainside of broken rocks and thick brush.

Pulling herself up over rock ledges, pushing with her good leg, crawling through dirt and dry foliage, she climbs higher and higher, knowing that she must be close to the backpack. Fear is never far away. One small pack on the slopes of a big mountain. Supplies that could mean the difference between life and death. It was two days ago. She crawls around a bush, and finally the back's familiar shape appears.

Calling Trekker over, she fills his bags to lighten her load and then lets him go. Slipping the lightened pack on her back, she begins the long crawl back down.

Backpacks weren't designed for crawling. The frame bangs against her head. She rigs a harness with parachute cord from the side pocket and starts dragging the pack downhill.

Two more hours pass before they arrive back at camp. The bag lady has been banished. They are living in style now, fully equipped with a bed, cooking pot, more food, and a rain fly. Shelley celebrates by cooking dinner for herself and her two faithful companions. Once again the boys get the larger share.

· · · — — — · · ·

Saturday morning she wakes to smoke in the air. As a ranger she has experienced forest fires firsthand. From what she can see, the flames are still distant, several drainages away. If fire does approach, it will be easy enough to scramble out on one of the rocky peninsulas jutting into the lake.

The smoke may be a good thing. With fire in the area, spotter planes and helicopters will be flying. A passing aircraft might see her encampment on the lakeshore.

Yesterday's pack retrieval was the seed for an evolving survival strategy. Each day must be used for some small task. Today, now that she has all her cooking gear and food, it will be to gather firewood.

With resolve taking the place of fear and panic, she considers her options. The lack of campsites or any trace of trail indicates that very few people visit Duck Lake. Someone may come in over the weekend to fish. If no one shows over the weekend, there is enough food to wait another four days. If by Thursday morning rescue doesn't seem imminent, there is no choice but to start the multiday escape crawl down Duck Creek.

Throughout Saturday afternoon she calls out for help on the odd chance that someone is nearby. The echoes of her voice roll around the lake basin, coming back as the only answer to her calls.

Creeping thoughts of hopelessness are fought off with visions of being back home just a few hours away in Grangeville, Idaho, of treatment at the hospital, and of the gatherings she will have at her house throughout the rest of the summer. The characters from the paperback novel stashed in her pack are adopted as family to keep her company in this high, lonesome wilderness.

. . . — — — . . .

Sunday morning she wakes to a cow moose dipping for water plants out in the lake.

The fire must be closer because air traffic appears. As the early hours pass, a helicopter flies along the tree line about a mile away across the lake. Several planes pass over as well. Whenever she hears the sound of approaching aircraft, Shelley starts waving her shiny Mylar space blanket, hoping a glint or flash will catch the pilot's eye. None of the aircraft sweep around for a closer look.

She does not let the overhead distractions interrupt the day's project. Gathering her fishing gear, she scoots down to the lakeshore and floats out onto one of the rock promontories. A few hours of casting into the lake produces three beautiful rainbow trout to add to the evening meal. She serves this bounty with couscous. The boys are not nearly as excited about the fish as she is.

The light fades from the sky on Sunday along with Shelley's hopes of weekend visitors.

. . . — — — . . .

Pat and Bill live and work in Michigan, but when it comes to back-packing they both like to head west.

When the time came to choose the next location for their annual backpacking adventure, another of Pat's interests helped to make the choice. He has read just about every Louis L' Amour book he can get his hands on. The Selway-Bitterroot had been the scene of one of these popular westerns. Pat decides it's time to see the place for himself. Bill comes along as a hiking partner, his mind swimming with visions of rainbow trout waiting in undiscovered fishing holes.

Their plane lands in Missoula, Montana, on a Saturday in August. They rent a car and drive west. A forest fire holds them up, pilot cars leading one lane of traffic through dense smoke. Across the border into Idaho, they follow the Lochsa River on Highway 12 through the settlement of Powell. Their first night is spent at a lodge on the river.

The next morning, after a last breakfast in civilization, they leave the pavement and drive south for half an hour down a dirt road. Densely forested mountains rise high and rugged above them. At the trailhead adjacent to Elk Summit Guard Station only one other vehicle, a small pickup truck, is parked. They walk into the ranger station to sign in and inform the ranger of their plans.

Normally they would stick to trails, but Bill's inquiry with the local fish and game department indicated that Duck Lake was a prime fishing spot in the area they plan to explore. They ask the ranger for the best route down from the end of the trail at the summit of Diablo Mountain.

With heavy frame packs loaded for a week in the wilderness, they begin the climb up Diablo Mountain. It's a long, hot day of walking. They had planned to replenish their water supplies at a spring shown on the map, but they couldn't find a trace of water. At the summit, both are thirsty. With empty water bottles in their packs, they can see the surface of Duck Lake in the basin below, shimmering like an aquamarine mirage in the midst of a blistering hot forest.

After taking in the view, they shoulder their packs and begin the descent, diligently sticking to the ridge top and descending to the east, as the ranger instructed. It is not long before they are deep in the forest. Exhaustion and thirst bring them to a halt for the day at the first source of water they find, a gathering of small, muddy ponds at the base of the eastern flank of Diablo Mountain.

. . . ⸺ ⸺ ⸺ . . .

Shelley wakes on Monday morning. Five days have passed since the accident. Somebody might be looking for her by now, but not being one to follow a strict plan, she didn't tell anyone exactly where she would be hiking. It may take them a while to find her pickup at the trailhead. She is looking at three more long, solitary days of waiting until her departure deadline of Thursday morning.

Her project for the day, a signal fire, is put off. If searchers are looking, they may be closer by tomorrow. Around midmorning she crawls under her rain fly to rest and read.

. . . ⸺ ⸺ ⸺ . . .

Monday morning Pat and Bill break camp and take a compass reading off their map. Duck Lake is due west of their current position. They head out, picking their way through untracked forest.

It's not long before the gemlike blue waters of Duck Lake appear through the trees. They hesitate on the forest edge, surveying the scene before them. They can see what looks like a blue tent back under the evergreens across the lake.

From up on the mountain there was no sign of anyone staying at the lake. Disappointment is first in their minds. They haven't come this far to stay in a campground.

The two men decide to keep walking, way down toward the west end of the lake and out of sight. There is no reason to disturb this other group's privacy. Tomorrow morning the two of them will move on to more remote locales.

As they turn to leave, Bill decides he should at least take a picture. The rugged face of Diablo Mountain juts into the sky, right there across the lake. The water in the foreground is an unbelievable color of blue-green. He steps out of the trees and onto the shore for a clear shot.

. . . — — — . . .

Just as Shelley is getting settled in the shade for another long day of waiting and reading, Kilgore starts barking. A moment passes and then she remembers that Kilgore doesn't bark at anything but people. Scooting frantically out into the open, she spots two people with backpacks on the other side of the lake.

All the days of fighting off fear and panic spill out in one moment as she begins to cry, shout, and wave, all at the same time, at the two figures standing on the far lakeshore.

. . . — — — . . .

As Bill snaps his picture of Diablo Mountain, a dog begins to bark from the campsite across the lake. Before long a human voice joins the cacophony. It's hard to understand the words, but it sounds like a cry for help.

Fifteen minutes pass as they work their way around the lakeshore. Shelley is crying with relief as Kilgore and Trekker growl and bark, keeping Pat and Bill at a distance. She tries to calm the dogs, but it is not until the men pull beef jerky out of their packs as a peace offering that the dogs relent, take the treats, and let the men approach.

They are surprised to find Shelley out here by herself in the wilderness.

Shelley has never been so happy to see two people in all her life. Her story spills out as the men listen, look over her splinted leg, and decide what to do next.

Pat has a cell phone, but reception is nonexistent this far out. Their two-way radios are equally useless.

Pat quickly puts a day pack together with a few essentials: food, water, a sleeping bag. He takes a map, compass, and GPS unit for navigation. He needs all the daylight he can get to find his way out across unfamiliar terrain.

Backtracking over the mountain is out of the question. The distance is too far and there are too many opportunities to lose the way. He will travel cross-country following the same route along Duck Creek that Shelley had planned for her crawl. According to the map, in about two or three miles he can intercept a trail that will lead back to Elk Summit Guard Station.

Not quite half an hour has passed at the lake when Pat leaves Bill to tend to Shelley and heads west down the lakeshore and out of sight.

With a new lease on life, Shelley is deliriously happy. Another human being is present and she can't stop laughing and babbling away after so many lonely days.

The afternoon passes, and with the approach of evening Bill begins to prepare dinner. He tells Shelley that it took them five hours to get in yesterday, so Pat is probably just making it to the guard station about now.

"Don't worry, tomorrow morning someone will come in with horses or whatever to get you out. I wouldn't expect anything tonight."

With the words still hanging in the air, the sound of rotor blades comes to them from a distance. Within minutes a helicopter swoops over the mountain and pulls into a hover over their heads.

Bill moves quickly to pull his tent out of the only clearing nearby. The helicopter eases down, the skids coming to rest in heather. A man jumps out, and the helicopter takes off, flying back over the mountain.

Nick, an emergency medical technician with the helicopter rescue crew out of Orofino, Idaho, gives Shelley a quick evaluation as he explains what is going to happen. The helicopter will be returning quickly with a Forest Service ranger who has volunteered to hike out with her dogs.

As she moves to speak, he stops her. With the heat and late afternoon winds, the pilot doesn't want to take any chances with extra weight.

"Don't worry," Nick says, "the ranger is a dog person."

The helicopter lands a second time, and as they load Shelley, Kilgore frantically tries to climb up the skids. She pleads with the pilot. Trekker will be fine, but she has rarely been separated from Kilgore. The pilot agrees to give it a try. Kilgore is lifted up to Shelley's lap. Nick is next, climbing into the third seat.

As the helicopter rises above Duck Lake, Bill and the Forest Service ranger are holding onto Trekker in the downdraft of the rotors. Shelley waves as the chopper makes a wide turn over the water. There is one last look at the rocky summit of Diablo Mountain in the late afternoon sun, then the helicopter heads west out of the emptiness of the Selway-Bitterroot Wilderness.

· · · ▬ ▬ ▬ · · ·

Back at the hospital in Grangeville the doctors find a break in both the upper fibula and lower tibia of Shelley's right leg. After surgery on Tuesday, she is home on Wednesday.

Friends and relatives help shuttle Trekker, backpacking gear, and her truck back home to Grangeville.

What has stayed with her is the disbelief.

"I have the story and sometimes little bits and pieces will come back to me, but I still have a hard time believing it actually happened. I do, however, have the rods and pins in my leg to prove it."

The snow beyond the crevasse feels solid, and it certainly looks safe. Rick yells back to John that he is going ahead.

CHAPTER 19

PRISON OF ICE

Mount Rainier swallows climbers. They stumble on steep ice, wander off-route in whiteout conditions, or just step on the wrong patch of snow and disappear. When they are found, if ever, it may be days, weeks, months, or even years later in one of thousands of crevasses, dead from injuries or exposure, whichever comes first after falling deep into the frigid heart of a glacier.

This mountain, centerpiece of Mount Rainier National Park, dominates the horizon south of Seattle, Washington. There are few places on earth that can compare. Only two hours of driving and a few hours of climbing separate the comfort and convenience of a modern city in a temperate climate from conditions that can rival the high, icy, windswept peaks of the Himalayas.

Rangers at Mount Rainier serve many functions: hiking through the backcountry; pulling parking-lot duty at the Paradise visitor center; patrolling the climbing routes from Camp Muir at the 10,000-foot level. After staring up at the massive dome of ice and rock all week, it's not uncommon for rangers to team up on their time off and spend a couple of days climbing to the 14,411-foot summit.

Rick and John are young seasonal rangers primed for climbing from several months of walking the trails and high routes of the park. In late July, with two days off, they make plans for a summit climb via Fuhrer Finger. This steep, narrow couloir of mixed rock and ice leads to the top along the western flank of the upper Nisqually Glacier.

On a Wednesday evening, after finishing their shifts, they traverse from the ranger station at Camp Muir across the 9,500-foot level of the Nisqually Glacier. Camp that night is at the base of the route on a small snowfield.

They wake Thursday morning at a reasonable hour. No need to hurry. Their plans have them bivouacking on the summit tonight. Tomorrow, Friday, they will return to Camp Muir via the main climbers' route down the Ingraham Glacier. Saturday morning they need to be back in uniform and patrolling the park, but that is the last thing on their minds as they break camp.

At 7 A.M., with crampons on their boots and ice axes in hand, they tie into their rope and the climb begins. The day evolves into a long grind upward, carrying full packs, putting one foot in front of the other. The men weave around the many crevasses in their path. Spirits are high with the weather clear and the air warm, even far up on the mountain. All of the Southern Cascades lie at their feet, with Mount St. Helens and Mount Adams standing out to the south. The chance to camp on the summit in weather this fine drives them on.

At about two in the afternoon they reach the 13,800-foot level and the slope angle eases off. The last obstacle of the climb lies directly in their path. With a width of fifteen feet, the crevasse is too large to jump. Looking over the edge, they cannot see the bottom. This great gap in the glacier's surface runs at least a hundred feet in either direction. Rick leads off to the west, paralleling the crevasse, to find a way around. John follows behind and they both walk along the edge, separated by seventy-five feet of rope.

Eventually the two walls of the crevasse pinch together and the gap closes up. Rick continues farther—ten, twenty, thirty feet beyond—to where a climbing wand planted in the snow marks a previous group's path. Relatively fresh footprints lead across and up toward the saddle between Point Success and the summit.

Rick pokes at the surface with his ice axe. The snow feels solid, and it certainly looks safe with the footprints leading across. He yells back to John that he is going ahead, and he takes a step, then another. The snow around him suddenly gives way, breaking up in all directions, and he falls down through snow and ice.

John has only a moment to react as the snow cover over the crevasse collapses and his climbing partner plunges below the surface. John drops to the snow, jamming ice axe and crampons into the icy surface, fighting to arrest Rick's fall.

The friction of the rope against the side of the crevasse slows Rick's plunge. He pendulums in a long arc, swinging down and back, falling the full length of the seventy-five feet of rope as it whips taut and yanks John off the surface. In an instant their pleasant climb in the sun transforms into a surreal tumble through light and dark as they both free-fall into the abyss. Rick is first to hit bottom, slamming into snow, his head ringing, his mind dazed. The world comes slowly back into focus. The first thing he can see is blood on the snow.

"Oh no."

He doesn't move. Slowly he begins flexing fingers, toes, arms, legs, checking for pain or, worse, paralysis. Everything seems to work. As his mind begins to clear he touches a hand to his face. His fingers find the ragged skin and warm blood of a small cut across the top of his nose where his glacier glasses were torn off in the fall.

He gazes around his impact zone. The afternoon light reflects down from a hundred feet above. The crevasse walls are twenty feet apart. Snow has built up between the walls, forming a relatively flat floor. The space is like a cave open to the sky. His partner is nowhere in sight.

"John, John, where are you? Are you okay?"

A voice answers from a distance. Rick stands up to follow the sound.

"John, can you get up? Can you move?"

"I think so," the voice answers.

As Rick walks toward the voice he is relieved to see John struggle to his feet about thirty feet away and walk up a slight incline toward him.

"I've got a lot of pain in my hips." John winces when he comes near.

Rick goes into action. Shock is a concern. John needs to be stabilized and kept warm. First he gathers their backpacks and has John sit down. Then he levels out a space on the floor of the crevasse and sets up their tent. John climbs inside and wraps himself in his sleeping bag. Once in the bag, John says he hurts badly. His hips have stiffened up. Rick makes him as comfortable as possible.

The pocket containing their only stove was torn off of John's pack in the fall, and Rick can't find it in the crevasse. Worse yet, both ice axes are missing. Even with the axes, climbing one hundred feet of near-vertical ice to reach the surface would be very risky; without them it is near impossible. They do have dehydrated food for several days, a little water, and all their other cold-weather gear.

They did file a trip plan, so their fellow rangers will know what route they were following. But it's only Thursday afternoon. They aren't due for work until Saturday morning.

Meltwater drips into the crevasse from far above. Rick places their two cook pots under a couple of trickles, hoping to supplement their meager supply of drinking water.

There is nothing much else to do but wait. John pulls out a deck of cards and they play round after round of gin rummy inside the tent as the day passes. Dinner is uncooked freeze-dried food eaten directly from the bag. It's crunchy, takes a lot of chewing, is somewhat lacking in flavor—but at least they have something to eat.

$\cdot \ \cdot \ \cdot \ \text{———} \ \text{———} \ \text{———} \ \cdot \ \cdot \ \cdot$

With no way out, the two men sleep until the sun is high enough on Friday morning to start melting the ice again. John is doing okay except that the pain in his hips makes sleep difficult. Rick keeps himself busy using the tent as a water collection system. He creases it just right so the drips roll down into one of the cooking pots.

He's restless, unable to just wait for rescue. It could be four or five days before they are found. There has to be something he can do.

A second search of the crevasse floor fails to reveal either of the ice axes. Getting creative, he grabs the second pot and a metal spoon. He walks up and down the uneven floor of the crevasse, judging the angle of the walls and the distance to the surface. Picking a section that is not quite vertical, he scrapes at the wall with the pot to carve out a step.

Using the handle of the spoon like a dagger, he stabs it into the ice, then kicks his crampon spikes into the step and pulls himself up with the spoon handle. He scoops another step, jabs the spoon in above his head, jams crampons into the second step, and pulls himself up a little higher. The technique is primitive, but it seems to work.

Over the next hour, Rick scoops, stabs, and kicks his way slowly up toward the surface.

Eighty-five feet off the bottom, the crevasse walls transition from near vertical to a treacherous overhang. Further progress without proper ice tools and ropes would be foolish if not impossible. Rick scoops out a small alcove where he can crouch and look out one end of the crevasse.

No climbing parties are visible on the thin sliver of mountainside he can see. Yelling seems futile, but he calls for help a few times. No one answers.

A couple of hours go by while he sits on his perch, hoping for a climbing party to pass within sight. No one appears.

He climbs back down, the spoon jabbed in the snow to anchor his upper body. The cook pot is in the other hand while he balances carefully on the ice wall, kicking his crampons solidly into each step.

There are gin rummy breaks throughout the day. John plays solitaire or reads a book while Rick makes additional climbs up to the perch for a look-see. They have an occasional freeze-dried snack. The water supply is still meager, coming a drip at a time.

They burn the rubber padding that protects their packs from the sharp points of their crampons, in the hope of creating a sooty black signal cloud. But the smoke thins out on its way up and disperses quickly in the light breeze on the surface.

Maybe if they put a message in a stuff bag and tie it to their rope, Rick might be able to sling it up on the surface from his perch. Any passing climbers would be sure to see the red bag in the snow.

Rick crouches in the little alcove high on the crevasse wall, whipping the rope back and forth. He tries every angle. There is just not enough room for a good swing. The overhang deflects the bag every time.

Another plan forms that evening. If no one shows up on Saturday, tomorrow, then on Sunday Rick will begin excavating a tunnel, with spoon and pot, from the perch up through the overhang to the surface. It might take a day or two, depending on how hard the snow is.

Someone will come looking, they reassure themselves. It's just a matter of time. Once again dinner is uncooked freeze-dried food eaten from the bag.

· · · — — — · · ·

When neither Rick nor John show up for work Saturday morning, it doesn't take long for the news to spread throughout the park staff. Two of their own are overdue from a climb of the mountain. Park employees who were climbing in the same area at the same time are tracked down and questioned.

No one saw them on the summit. No one saw them climbing down to Camp Muir. No one has seen anything until the phone rings at Longmire Ranger Station and Dick picks up the receiver. The search coordinator, Bob, wants to know if Dick and his climbing partner Pat saw anything when they ascended the Fuhrer Finger route to the summit over Thursday and Friday.

"Did you see Rick or John up there?"

"I haven't seen them."

"Well, they were climbing that route and they haven't come back."

Dick's heart skips a beat. A sudden sense of dread comes over him.

"I know where they are," he answers.

Early Friday morning Dick and Pat left their camp at the 12,000-foot level on Fuhrer Finger and started the steep climb to the summit. As the slope angle eased off, close to the top of the Nisqually Glacier, they were breathing hard through the thin air, with the straps of their heavy packs digging into their shoulders. They circled around the west end of a huge crevasse. Dick just happened to look back.

Several hundred feet away, right on the edge of the crevasse, an ice axe was sticking out of the snow. He pointed it out, calling back to Pat.

"Look, there's an ice axe over there."

It looked as if it had been there for years. Dick has done a lot of climbing on Rainier. He has seen junk all over the mountain—

pieces of rope, carabiners, lost crampons. He didn't think anything of it, just another piece of junk.

The weather was perfect: clear, warm, little wind. They were making good time on one of their days off, not thinking about work or much of anything.

He and Pat had walked by this crevasse with an ice axe jammed into the snow, right on the edge, and never imagined that there could be somebody in trouble. The thought that he might have left a fellow ranger to die tears him apart.

It is not until 4:30 in the afternoon that a helicopter can be located. A Hughes 500 contracted to the Forest Service out of Packwood arrives at Paradise to begin ferrying rangers up to Point Success. It is a grim group that gathers. Body recoveries up on the mountain are all too common. When it is a stranger, it's one thing. All of these men know the victims, making this mission especially difficult.

The pilot needs to get a feel for how the aircraft will handle at high altitude under load, so the search coordinator is the first to be taken up. High up on the snow-covered summit, as the chopper circles for landing, Bob leans out and looks down. His eyes scan the surface of the mountain. For just a millisecond he can see deep into a crevasse. The scene sends a jolt through his body.

Way down at the bottom of a crevasse he can see a tent. Rick is standing next to it in his red down jacket.

Then the helicopter is past and the scene gone.

In a flash Bob intuits what happened. They both survived the fall. John is hurt. Rick is okay.

· · · — — — · · ·

Fifty-seven hours after their fall, Rick and John are hoisted out of the crevasse, courtesy of seven climbing rangers and a Maasdam-rope-pulling device. The rescue team moves both men and all the equipment back up the mountain and closer to the landing zone. By now darkness has fallen. Rick and John end up camping at the top of Mount Rainier after all, although not as they had originally planned. It is a tired yet elated group that gathers in tents on the summit that night.

In the morning the group is flown off the mountain by helicopter. John is taken to Good Samaritan Hospital in Puyallup and diagnosed with a broken pelvis.

Rick walks away from the accident. His superiors persuade him to go home and take a few days off.

When Rick arrives at his parents' house, they ask him how his summer job at the mountain has been going. The conversation goes something like this:

"It's nice to have you home. How are you doing?"

"Oh, fine, fine."

"Are you enjoying your ranger job?"

"Oh yeah, yeah, I enjoy it."

"Anything interesting happening up at the park?"

"Nothing much really. Just ranger work, you know, tourists and stuff, except that, uh, oh, well, the last couple of days I was in the bottom of a crevasse."

The next day an article appears in the newspaper, detailing the accident. Rick's parents receive more information than they might ever have wanted to know.

After a few days in the hospital, John returns to the park to recuperate.

A week later, Rick feels the need to shake off any jitters left over from the accident. He joins another climbing party of park employees and completes a summit ascent by way of the Kautz route, just to the west of Fuhrer Finger.

He dreams of catching rabbits to make shoes for his freezing feet. Bunny slippers would be oh so warm.

CHAPTER 20

EASY WAY DOWN FOR BEGINNERS

On a wintry Thursday in January the high school in Pullman, Washington, is closed by snowfall. With the day off from classes, and fresh powder snow in the mountains, Andy, Jamiel, and Elliot jump at the chance to drive three hours over icy roads for an afternoon of skiing at Silver Mountain in the Bitterroot Range of Northern Idaho.

After a couple of warm-up runs the boys stand together at the high point of the ski area on the summit of Kellogg Peak. Clouds lie low and heavy on the mountain. Light, downy snowflakes fill the air. A hundred yards in all directions the trees fade to ghostly shadows obscured by fog.

Having already performed several spectacular face plants in the deep powder snow, Andy, skiing for only the second time in his life, is debating whether the sport should actually be described as fun. On the other hand, Jamiel and Elliot are ready to ski down a steep hillside of rounded snowy bumps—a mogul run. To Andy this sounds like a guaranteed trip to the emergency room. He needs the beginner route off the peak.

"Just follow the signs down," one of his friends tells him. "We'll meet you at the bottom."

A short distance below the summit, Andy spots the first sign. "Easy Way Down for Beginners," it reads, with an arrow pointing off down the mountain. Merging onto the track, he carves careful turns in the deep powder, searching for the route through a landscape obscured in falling snow and clouds.

As he concentrates on technique, his form smooths out and he begins linking turns. For the first time this day, skiing becomes fun as he works his way down a long, steep slope of untracked powder.

· · · — — — · · ·

Jamiel and Elliot spend the rest of the afternoon watching for Andy. Each time they complete a run they expect to see him waiting in line for the chairlift or inside the midmountain lodge. They scan the slopes from the chairlift on their rides up. With all the terrain at Silver Mountain, it's easy to become separated, especially if Andy is sticking to the beginner runs or has decided to ski a different section of the area.

When the lifts shut down at 4:30 P.M., Jamiel and Elliot wait for Andy to show up at the base. They search the lodge, check the parking lot.

He has to be here somewhere, they tell themselves, as concern begins to rise. They look everywhere, but there is no sign of their friend. They report his disappearance to the ski area.

A long night of searching by the ski patrol over two mountains' worth of ski runs comes up with nothing.

At 6 A.M. Friday, dozens of search and rescue volunteers gather at Silver Mountain. After interviewing Jamiel and Elliot and evaluating Andy's experience, the search team's best guess is that he skied off a groomed run and fell into one of the deep snow pits that have formed beneath trees all over the ski area. He could be injured and unable to move, or just trapped in one of these tree wells. They will concentrate their search on terrain within the ski area itself.

Overnight, temperatures hovered at 10 to 15 degrees Fahrenheit. Snow continues to fall. Weather reports call for a winter storm to arrive at any time.

The Civil Air Patrol will try to fly a search pattern today, but the weather has grounded all helicopters. If Andy is going to be found in time, it will have to be by searchers on the ground.

Dean, a volunteer ski patroller and a longtime local, is assigned to work with one of the dog handlers. Dean spends a lot of his spare time skiing the backcountry and hunting in these hills. He knows the area better than most.

Starting at the summit of Kellogg Peak, near the point where Andy was last seen, Dean and the dog handler circle their way around the top. Their route weaves through groves of trees, with the dog leading the way. Special attention is given to the tree wells, with no luck. Just down off the summit, along the southern boundary of the ski area, the dog acts up, snuffling in the snow, excited.

The dog is called back, only to return to the same spot, searching for something.

Dean and the trainer look over the slope. The snow is wind-blown and no tracks are visible. The handler doesn't think the conditions would offer a legitimate scent anyway. It's probably just a rabbit or something.

The dog is pulled back a second time and straightens out. Over the next couple of hours Dean and the dog handler clear the southern and eastern boundaries of the ski area, turning up nothing.

Around 10:30 A.M. they are back at rescue headquarters.

. . . — — — . . .

Dean can't get those early actions of the dog out of his mind. A traverse across the out-of-bounds terrain parallel to that southern boundary is the only thing that will put him at ease. Any track will be obvious in the deep, undisturbed snow down below the wind-blown ridge. With volunteers searching in-bounds all over the mountain, Dean partners with a volunteer named Gary and they head back up to the summit of Kellogg Peak.

Dean's mountaineering skis are ideal for out-of-bounds travel, with bindings that allow free-heel, cross-country-style striding and climbing but that lock the heel in place for skiing downhill. Gary has standard downhill ski equipment, heels always secured, but he is able to keep up as they ski south along a ridge leading off

217

the top of Kellogg Peak and out of the ski area boundaries. At a point about halfway down the mountain, they begin the east-to-west traverse. Out of the wind, the drifts are deep and undisturbed, the skiing smooth.

Midway across the southern side of the mountain, the two men come across a path plowed deep through new snow. It's hard to tell what caused it. An elk may have been running downslope, plowing the trail. They walk up and down for several minutes, searching for a clear sign in the chopped-up snow. Finally, there it is, a ski boot print headed straight downhill.

They try to radio search and rescue headquarters to request more help, but they can't get through. Either the battery is dead or the signal is too weak to reach the other side of the mountain. A debate ensues.

It would take a long time to backtrack for help, and the kid may be somewhere close. With the frigid temperatures, he needs to be found as soon as possible. The better part of the day still remains, and they may be able to get to him and get him out before dark.

The decision is made. They follow the boot prints down into the basin, thrashing through brush and deep snow. The tracks lead up onto an abandoned logging road and then back into the ravine. They find several places where the kid broke through and fell into the creek. In a grove of trees they find a bed of boughs. Looks like he must have spent the night here. They yell his name again and again, their voices muffled by the snow-covered landscape and deep quiet of the remote basin.

From the bed of boughs the trail leads downstream. They follow until the tracks dead-end where the ravine walls become too steep to continue. The footprints mill around, ranging here and there. With the light failing, they just can't decipher which way the kid went.

Dean has his pack with survival gear, and he's prepared to spend the night. If the lost skier made those tracks today, he must be nearby and probably still alive. If the two men stay in the area and get a fire going, the light might catch his attention when darkness falls.

Gary is exhausted after slogging along all day in downhill boots and skis. He's wet from sweat, tired, and cooling off quickly in the subfreezing temperatures. Gary can't spend the night, and

Dean is the only one who knows the route down the backside of the mountain.

Reluctantly, Dean leads the way out. The two men climb back up the hill a short distance to find the route. Before leaving they sit up on the slope for a long while, yelling, screaming, calling, hoping to hear a response. There is no sound save the silence that has haunted them all day.

With darkness falling fast, they turn and start the long slog out. The next several hours are spent struggling through deep drifts and dense forest in skin-biting cold.

By the time they get out to a road and back to the ski area, it's eight o'clock. Both men are exhausted, soaking wet and chilled.

At the ski area, television reporters mob Dean and Gary. They have no comment. After finding the tracks but not finding Andy, they agreed to report only to the search coordinator and to let him decide what information should be released. They don't want to raise the hopes of Andy's family only to have things turn out badly later.

The search and rescue crews have spent all day Friday combing the inbounds terrain at Silver Mountain, trudging through the deep snow, checking tree wells, and concentrating on places where skiers have been lost in the past. Not a clue has been found.

The crews are beat. Night has fallen and a bitter cold seems to sift down with the darkness. A snowstorm is hammering the rest of the Pacific Northwest, grounding aircraft all across the region. It has yet to hit Silver Mountain, but threatens to arrive at any moment. The searchers' lives are at risk at this point. There is little hope the lost skier will be found alive.

Dean and Gary walk into search headquarters just as the coordinator and the ski area manager are coming out to announce that the search is being suspended due to nightfall and the coming storm.

. . .   ──   ──   ──   . . .

Shawn has been following the story of the lost skier at Silver Mountain since he came home from work Thursday and caught the evening news. Tonight, Friday, he turns on the TV to find the skier still missing and the search teams being pulled from the field for the night.

The description of how the high school boy was dressed flashes through his mind: a mix of wool and cotton, nylon jacket and ski pants. Fine for an afternoon of skiing, but pure death for multiday survival in subfreezing temperatures. That kid is out there somewhere. With a winter storm approaching, his time is running out.

Shawn starts working the phone lines until he is routed to the search coordinator at Silver Mountain. He volunteers to search that night. He just needs a little time to recruit a few of his fellow survival-school instructors, get permission from his commander at Fairchild Air Force Base, and make the hour-and-a-half drive east from Spokane, Washington, to join the effort.

· · · — — — · · ·

Dean lies awake that night at home in bed. All his equipment is drying over the woodstove. He can't get that lost kid out of his mind.

It was miserably wet and cold during the day he just spent floundering in deep snow, back in that lonesome drainage, trying to trace those footprints. He had to be so close.

One night out in those conditions would be brutal. A second night, with temperatures dipping down to 9 or 10 degrees . . . well, he can hardly imagine what it must be like.

· · · — — — · · ·

Hours before first light, Shawn and his three survival-school buddies, Sean, Todd, and Colin, pull into the parking lot at the base of Silver Mountain. On the drive from Spokane they have been talking strategy. More than likely they are looking for a body. Anyone, including the media gathered at the ski area, can listen in on the radio traffic. To handle the situation with some discretion, they have worked out a radio code that will allow them to notify search and rescue headquarters when, where, and in what condition they find "the package." The boy's parents deserve this much.

In the predawn darkness, as they unload their equipment at the ski area parking lot, a woman approaches and taps Shawn on the shoulder.

"Excuse me, are you the Air Force boys?"

Shawn turns to her. "Yes ma'am, we are."

She looks him right in the eyes and pleads, "Please, please find my son."

Stunned, scrambling for the right words, he looks right back. "I will find your son."

As she turns to leave, Shawn resolves to stay out on the mountain until, one way or another, he finds that boy.

Up at the midmountain lodge, introductions are short and sweet. The search and rescue leaders give a quick briefing, covering the areas that have been searched. They report that footprints were spotted yesterday off the back of the mountain. Shawn wants to concentrate in that area.

Dean has arrived early as well and is there to lead the group down into the drainage.

The sky is beginning to lighten as they ride the chairlift to the summit of Kellogg Peak.

Up on top the five men split into two teams. Each team will zigzag down separate ridges that contain the area where the footprints were found. They will call back and forth as they work into the basin.

Half an hour into the search, Shawn spots a trail in the snow. It has to be fresh. Falling snow and wind haven't filled in the tracks. As he digs down to determine whether the tracks are human or animal, the radio crackles to life.

Dean has led the other team to the base of the slope. They have a definite trail along the stream.

Shawn and Sean hustle down to join the other team. The track by the stream shows an obvious series of right-foot boot prints. But on the left are a puzzling series of what look like small holes in the snow with no boot tracks. The searchers fan out where the tracks mill around, yelling back and forth to each other.

It's not long before one of them hesitates. "Hey, do you guys hear that?"

They stop and listen. Faintly, off in the distance, they hear a call for help.

. . . — — — . . .

Back on Thursday afternoon, Andy had carved his way down off the mountain heights until the ski run ended in a thicket of trees. It seemed odd to find a thicket in the middle of a ski run. He paused for a moment, gazing around. Untracked forest stretched for as far as he could see. It occurs to him that he hasn't encountered any other skiers for a long time. A queasy feeling stirs in the pit of his stomach as he tries to recognize anything about the landscape.

Where was I going? Andy thinks. *And how was I supposed to get there?* At this point the best strategy seems to be to return the way he has come. There will be no climbing back up with his downhill skis on. Leaving them is drastic, but they are no good to him now, and all Andy wants at this point is to get back to someplace familiar.

He pops his ski boots from their bindings and turns to follow his tracks back up the mountain, trying to ascend a slope that seems almost vertical. Without the support of his skis, he sinks up to his neck in the snow, sometimes wallowing in over his head. Climbing through the deep snowdrifts is like half swimming and half drowning, against a strong tide.

He sees a nearby ravine that offers a more gradual slope up to the ridgeline. Using his ski poles for balance, he stumbles down and over toward this route.

In the ravine a glaze of ice coats everything. His plastic ski boots are like out-of-control roller skates on the slick surface. Panic begins to rise in his chest. He's trapped down here, there is no way out, and now that he has stopped skiing, the bone-chilling cold is seeping through his clothes.

Fighting for calm, he remembers a lesson from Boy Scout camp. There has to be a stream down in the bottom of the basin somewhere. He will follow it out to the nearest road.

An hour or two passes as Andy makes very little progress fighting through deep snow and tangled brush. With daylight waning he picks a grove of small trees for a shelter and shakes the heavy snow off them.

He is thankful that he remembered to slip his knife into his pocket this morning. He pulls it out and uses the blade to trim boughs off nearby fir trees. The evergreen boughs are arranged as a bed, providing insulation from the snow. Andy settles down under the trees and pulls more boughs over his body as a blanket.

As Thursday night falls, the temperature drops. His clothes become stiff as they freeze. Shivering in total darkness, surrounded by a vast, empty forest, he abandons all hope. There is no question in his mind. He is going to die.

Digging through his pockets, he finds a scrap of paper and a pencil and goes to work scratching out a message:

"Whoever finds me I am a man, or should I say male. My name is Andrew Zeller. To my parents Jeff and Eileen Zeller who live in Pullman, Washington, I love you. I am sorry for all the trouble I have put you through. For that I am truly sorry. You have been the best parents in the world. Tell my little brother Jake that I love him too. Andy."

The cold begins blurring his thinking. Maybe he should just end it now, finish himself off before ice slowly fills his veins.

Somewhere deep in his mind, amid the black thoughts, a seed of hope sprouts. Like a switch turning darkness to light, he makes the decision to fight back.

I will not will myself to die, I will not be the cause of my death.

Andy hauls his cold, tired body off the ground. At school he has been performing in musicals—acting, singing, dancing—so he starts his feet to tapping. He works through the time step and the soft shoe, a one-man show in a frozen forest amphitheater within the winter silence of the Bitterroot Mountains. He gives encore after encore until his body warms to the exercise. Thoughts of death fade. Eventually Andy settles back into his bough bed under the trees, this time with a will to live. As the long, shivering, dark hours pass, he considers the difference a fire would have made. This might have been a cakewalk if not for losing his lighter in the snow after crashing on the first run down the mountain. Then he used his last match to light a cigarette on the chairlift back to the summit.

His pack of cigarettes sits uselessly in his pocket with no source of flame. He pulls out the pack and looks closely at the camel on the label, the desert in the background, palm trees, pyramids, the blazing sun. *Oh man, give me some of that desert heat right now.*

His thoughts shift yet again. *What if nobody has noticed that I am missing? What if Jamiel and Elliot think that I met some girl and just took off with her, and that there is no reason to say anything to anybody?*

Every so often the sound of an airplane filters through the trees. Each time this happens, he wakes out of a half sleep, confident it is a search plane looking for him. But each time, he discovers just another jetliner passing far above, flying east from Spokane.

He imagines the passengers sitting in the warmth of the cabin, eating, drinking, relaxing, completely ignoring the fact that he, Andy Zeller, is outdoors in subfreezing temperatures, with no food, no blanket, no pillow from the flight attendant. The manufactured anger helps keep him warm.

· · · — — — · · ·

On Friday morning when light begins filtering down through the flurries, Andy shakes several inches of snow off his makeshift bedcovers.

After yesterday's experience any plan for walking out seems futile. The best strategy is to get out of this wooded creek bottom. If anybody is searching, he should be out in the open where he can be seen.

He remembers a clearing on the slope above. Maybe he can climb up there and make an X in the snow. Stepping out from under the trees, he sinks up to his neck in the deep snow.

Andy lost one of his ski poles when he took a tumble coming down the slope yesterday. It disappeared into the snow and could not be found. With his remaining ski pole, he begins cutting stair steps up the slope through the deep drifts. The pole is jammed in and swung back and forth; then, with his hands, he slides a block of snow out of the way, jams the toes of his ski boots into the snow a little higher, and repeats the process.

Hours pass in this effort. As he works, he continuously fights off panicky thoughts.

Is this the right way?

Am I burning energy I might need later?

Will my sweat freeze and kill me when I stop?

Eventually the terrain levels out and progress is easier. The snow is only up to his knees as he lifts a leg up for each step.

Finally reaching the edge of the clearing, he sinks in up to his armpits. Struggling to pull himself out, the buckles on his left ski boot catch on something. When he heaves his leg out of the hole, the boot stays below. His foot, clothed in only a damp wool sock, is exposed to the freezing air.

In desperation he digs deep into the snow and pulls the boot out. Crawling to the edge of the clearing, he leans against a tree for balance, fighting desperately to shove his freezing foot back into the boot.

Suddenly a small plane flies directly overhead, so low he can read the numbers on the wings through the overhanging branches.

The plane quickly disappears into the clouds and falling snow.

He pauses, stunned, unbelieving, straining to listen, hoping to hear it turn around, as the sound fades away into a heartbreaking silence.

At least I know people are looking, he says to console himself. *If they are in the air, they have to be on the ground.*

The boot is covered in ice. His hands are numb and useless, the exposed foot too swollen and painful to jam back in. He abandons the boot under the trees and crawls out into the clearing, hoping the plane will make another pass. He's exhausted from fighting to keep his body warm and stave off hypothermia.

This is where he will stay. A bough bed won't keep him warm enough out here in the open. Another vague Scouting memory gives him the idea to excavate into the snow. Unable to stand because of sharp pain in his exposed foot, he digs into the slope from a prostrate position. He struggles to shove the snow out of the way.

Eventually he digs down to ground level. Andy then starts pulling out frozen rocks, trying to make the shelter deeper. The final result is a shallow sort of snow cave—a poor one, but the best he can do.

He tries to care for his exposed foot. With a knife he trims off the bottom half of his cotton T-shirt, then slices into the lining of his ski coat to pull out insulation. Taking off his sock, Andy wraps the foot with the insulation, then with the T-shirt scrap.

Before leaving Thursday morning, he had grabbed a pair of surgical gloves from a box left on the table by his mother, an emergency room nurse. He thought they might keep his hands dry if his ski gloves became wet. He now pulls one of the rubber gloves over his wrapped foot and slides his half-frozen wool sock back on to finish the job.

All he can do now is sit back in his shelter and wait. Exhausted, he slips in and out of sleep.

As daylight begins to fade on his second day in the woods, the view from his snow cave becomes sublime: long shadows, frosted trees, snowfall. Across the valley, mountain peaks light up with alpenglow.

Andy knows that with the night the temperatures will drop again. He doesn't hold out much hope of saving his feet, but he won't give up his hands. He pulls off his frozen gloves, shoves them under his rear for added insulation, and buries his fingers in his armpits.

I wasn't the fastest runner anyway, he thinks to himself as he curls up in his cramped shelter.

Sleep is fitful as Friday night passes. Andy fades in and out of wakefulness, through a long series of debates with all the gods he can recall, pleading for help.

At one point, pondering hunger, he finds a strange sympathy for the nineteenth-century Donner party. He can now understand the desperation of a wagon train of pioneers, trapped by winter snows in the Sierras, and why they may have eaten human flesh to survive.

For a while he dreams of catching rabbits to make shoes for his freezing feet. Bunny slippers would be oh so warm.

· · · — — — · · ·

As the sky lightens Saturday morning, Andy rouses from his night of semiconscious ramblings. He makes the motions to stand, but his body doesn't respond. His arms are sluggish, hard to move. His body is tapped out from the effort to stay alive. The only extremity still answering the call seems to be his head.

With great difficulty he drags himself out of his shelter and rolls up to a sitting position on the lip of the cave. The snow has let up a bit. He enjoys the fine view again. *Life is good,* he finds himself thinking. *At this point it's a joy just being alive.*

The exhaustion and lack of sleep must be making him punchy. He sees strange colors; hears whistles, clicks, and weird songs coming from everywhere and nowhere.

He listens to the songs and sounds, enjoying the strange chorus until somewhere deep in his brain a pattern begins to emerge. Slowly, out of the fog of his mind, he realizes that someone is calling out from nearby.

* * * ▬ ▬ ▬ * * *

Shawn scans the hillside with the binoculars as the other four men listen closely, trying to zero in on the source of the cry. Several hundred yards upslope and only about a hundred yards from their route down, Shawn focuses in on a figure sitting in the snow, yelling for help.

Dean is the first to reach him. As the rest of the group struggles up to the little snow cave, Andy tells them he heard their voices but he thought they were angels.

* * * ▬ ▬ ▬ * * *

Andy's parents have been waiting at a hotel near the base of the ski area since early Friday. His mother, unable to sleep, has spent the night walking the streets around the base of the ski area, praying for her son to be found. His father has never felt more helpless. Neither of them wants to believe Andy is dead, but they haven't been given much hope.

On Saturday morning his father cannot sit any longer. There has been little he could do to help their son. After last night's suspension of the search he is afraid the effort will be canceled altogether. He has to talk with the search and rescue supervisors.

He rides the gondola up to the midmountain search and rescue headquarters. When he finds the people in charge, he beseeches them, "Please, please continue searching for my son."

They assure him they are doing their best.

With a heavy heart he leaves and walks back to wait for the return ride down.

Only moments after Mr. Zeller's impassioned plea, the broadcast channels crackle to life and a message comes across the radio. The "package" has been located and is in good condition. The headquarters erupts in celebratory hooting and hollering. Somebody runs to find Andy's father, but he has already caught the downward-bound gondola.

The ride off the mountain is the longest of his life for Andy's father. Looking out the window, he sees so much snow. Visibility is poor and it is so cold. His son has been out in that for two nights.

Nearing the base of the ski area, he can see people running back and forth. Something has happened. The doors open and he bursts out to the news that his son has been found, alive.

· · · ▬ ▬ ▬ · · ·

Back in the basin behind Kellogg Peak, the five men assess Andy's condition. He is immobile but relatively lucid, cold yet conscious. The foot without the boot appears badly frozen. They will have to carry him out.

They cut him out of clothes frozen stiff as tin, peeling the layers away from his body, then quickly dressing him in dry garments. The frozen foot will be left as is; best to keep it on ice until reaching the hospital.

Andy is given trail mix and a cup of steaming coffee. Halfway through his second cup, as the hot fluid begins to warm him from the inside out, Andy starts shaking uncontrollably. Coffee is splashing out of his mug. It's a good sign. His body is fighting back up from advanced hypothermia, shivering to get warm. Blood is now circulating back into the extremities.

The rescuers wrap Andy in a quilted poncho liner and slip him into a down sleeping bag. Then he is wrapped again, and finally tied into a rubberized poncho.

Escaping uphill with Andy is out of the question, impossible with the steep incline and deep snow. They will follow Dean's route from yesterday and pull Andy downhill to the closest logging road.

With one person out front breaking trail and the other four each grabbing a poncho corner, they tap into Andy's choir background and command him to sing as they begin dragging him

through the forest. This is no time for the "package" to relax and let hypothermia come back.

· · · — — — · · ·

Hours later, soaked through with sweat, the five rescuers are still wallowing through waist- to chest-deep snow in the depths of the forest. They are only about halfway out and Andy has run out of songs. As the rescuers huddle, grim-faced and exhausted, around a small fire, they ask him to tell all the jokes he knows.

Andy pauses for a moment.

"I can only remember one joke. How do you get a clown to stop smiling?"

They look across the fire at each other, then back at Andy. "We don't know."

"You hit him in the face with an axe."

Tired, hungry, and dehydrated in bleak surroundings, they think it is the funniest thing they have heard in a long time. They get back to dragging Andy, chuckling at the joke for the rest of the afternoon.

Six hours and about three miles from where the evacuation started, they break out onto a road to find two snowmobiles waiting. Andy is put on the first snowmobile and hauled out to a waiting ambulance just as the light of day begins to fade.

· · · — — — · · ·

At the hospital in Kellogg, Idaho, Andy is quickly stabilized. His legs below the knees, especially the foot without the boot, are badly frostbitten.

The emergency room doctor places Andy's hand in the thawing tub so that he can feel the water temperature.

"I want you to know that this water is lukewarm, because when I put your foot in, it will feel like it is boiling hot."

As one foot is eased into the water, even through morphine the pain is stunning. It is all he can do to keep from passing out as his feet are slowly defrosted.

Andy's mother's medical background doesn't give her room for anything but reality. She knows that when an extremity is

frostbitten, there is no treatment. The limb will amputate itself as it dies, or demarcates, as the orthopedic surgeon back at the hospital where she works in Pullman tells her over the phone. It can take up to six months. "Frozen in January, amputate in June" is the catchphrase.

· · · — — — · · ·

By the next day, Sunday, there is nothing more the hospital staff can do. Andy is checked out to go home on Monday morning.

Sunday afternoon an older gentleman arrives in Andy's room and introduces himself as Dr. Cramer. He has studied hyperbaric medicine in Houston, the use of oxygen under high pressure in treatment of certain conditions, including frostbite. Just last October he transferred up to Kellogg because he wanted to ski. The twenty-bed hospital was eager to have him on staff, so much so that they agreed to his request for two hyperbaric chambers so he could continue his research. He thinks he can help save Andy's legs.

Over the next ten days Andy goes through twice-daily treatments in the oxygen-saturated atmosphere of the only hyperbaric chambers between Salt Lake City and Seattle.

Watching through the window of the chamber, Andy's mother can see the dead gray flesh of his legs pink up with each treatment, the oxygenated blood reinfusing and repairing the damaged flesh.

After ten days no additional improvement can be seen. Andy is sent home to continue a regimen of water therapy to stimulate circulation in his legs.

Six weeks later Andy's father is getting ready for work when Andy's twelve-year-old brother, Jake, comes screaming into the bathroom.

"Dad, Dad, Andy's foot, Andy's foot."

Fearing the worst, his family gathers at his side. The blackened, dead flesh that was one of Andy's big toes has popped off. Beneath the ugly mass, a fresh, completely whole, wonderfully pink and alive toe peeks out.

Over time, all of Andy's toes reappear and he eventually recovers full use of his feet. His legs will be forever sensitive to cold, however. Pain is with him constantly.

"I have gotten to the point where I treasure the pain," he now says, "because I can wake up every morning, step out of bed, and remember: 'Oh, yeah, I get to live today.'

"It is with every step that I am reminded to never give up."

ABOUT THE AUTHOR

Brett Nunn has spent decades wandering the landscape of the Pacific Northwest. Before he was old enough to drive, he was hiking the mountains of Washington State and canoeing the remote lakes of British Columbia.

With an eye toward a career spent outdoors, Brett earned a geology degree from the University of Washington. After thorough reflection, however, he decided that the printed word seemed the best way to pursue all his varied interests. So he returned to the University of Washington and found inspiration among his many fine writing instructors. His first writing efforts were as a columnist for a Seattle newspaper and as a regular contributor to an outdoor sports monthly. This is his first book.

Brett has never failed to return to where he feels most at home, the great outdoors. Weekend climbing, hiking, and mountain biking trips to Washington's Cascade and Olympic mountain ranges have been intermixed with overseas travel to the islands of the South Pacific, the national parks of New Zealand, the Australian Outback, the wild rivers and cloud forests of Costa Rica, the tropical islands of Thailand, and the legendary mountains of Nepal.

Brett and his wife, Becky, live in Port Townsend, Washington.